Those
Glamour

Glorious
Years

by Margaret J. Bailey

The Citadel Press

Secaucus, N.J.

DESIGN BY LESTER GLASSNER

First edition

Copyright © 1982 by Margaret J. Bailey
All rights reserved
Published by Citadel Press
A division of Lyle Stuart Inc.
120 Enterprise Ave., Secaucus, N.J. 07094

In Canada: Musson Book Company
A division of General Publishing Co. Limited
Don Mills, Ontario

Manufactured in the United States of America by
Halliday Lithograph, West Hanover, Mass.

Library of Congress Cataloging in Publication Data

Bailey, Margaret J.
  Those glorious glamour years.

  1. Costume design—California—Hollywood—
History. . Costume designers—California—
Hollywood. 3. Moving-picture actors and ac-
tresses—California—Hollywood. I. Title.
TT507.B33 792'.026'0979493 81-15510
ISBN 0-8065-0784-5 AACR2
  384 p.

Acknowledgments

First and foremost to Alfred D. Bailey, who took many valuable hours and days away from his own writing to help and encourage me, whose infinite patience is matched only by his generosity and personal unselfishness, and who provided a much needed wall against which to bounce ideas or take out frustrations.

Special thanks to three sources of information and stills:
  Eddie Brandt's Saturday Matinee (thanks, Eddie and Mike)
  The Academy of Motion Picture Arts and Sciences
    (especially the workers in the Margaret Herrick Library)
  Mr. Gunnard Nelson

Many thanks to the people who granted interviews and helped me glimpse into a fantasy world of the past:

Ms. Gwen Wakeling	Ms. Edith Head
Mr. Walter Plunkett	Mr. Howard Shoup
Mr. Joseph S. Simms of the Adrian	Mr. Cary Grant
Collection in Wyncote, Pennsylvania	Mr. George Cukor
Ms. Sheila O'Brien	Ms. Renee Conlay

Sincere thanks to the collectors who shared their treasures with me and the commercial sources of stills:

Larry Edmunds Bookshop	The Hollywood Revue
Mr. Myron Braum	Mr. Paul Ballard
Quality First	Chapman Stills

Earnest thanks to the many people who helped and encouraged me in this endeavor, especially:

Mr. Arnold Hano	Mr. Jesse Hohglin
Mr. Gene Ringgold	Mr. Joe Finnigan
Mr. Robert Cushman	Mr. Norman Kaphan
Mr. Larry Carr	Mr. James Earie

Thanks to the studios that created the dreams and provided the settings for a fantasyland:

MGM	RKO
Paramount	United Artists
Warner Brothers	Universal
20th Century-Fox	Columbia

And thanks to the magazines that provided much of the color for background stories, especially:

Photoplay	*Modern Screen*
Motion Picture Studio Insider	*Motion Picture*

Although the photographers in this book are not credited by name, their tremendous attention to detail, magnificent composition, and sheer professionalism were primary factors in conveying the glamour and beauty of the star and her costumes in the Thirties. Their contribution to the fantasy must be acknowledged.

And last but not least, acknowledgment must go to the stars themselves, those lovely ladies who spent hours to achieve the physical perfection we so enjoy when viewing these fashion stills. These women had not only the physical attributes necessary to display the costumes properly, but also the inner qualities that sparked a design and caused it to shimmer.

M.J.B.

Contents

Chapter One
INTRODUCTION   7

Chapter Two
EVENING GLAMOUR   18

Chapter Three
DAYTIME GLAMOUR   120

Chapter Four
GLAMOUR AT HOME   203

Chapter Five
GLAMOUR AT PLAY   245

Chapter Six
EPIC GLAMOUR   260

Chapter Seven
WEDDING GLAMOUR   374

Brief Biographies   381

Chapter One

Introduction

Of all the words associated with Hollywood, the one most often used to conjure its unique image is the magic term "glamour." Hollywood glamour is a complex quality composed of many parts contributed by many people—most of whom are never seen on the screen or even mentioned in the credits. Glamour encompasses fantastic sets, expert lighting, perfect make-up, a beautiful coiffure, and much, much more. This book is written to display the talents of an important unit in the army of dedicated people who created and maintained glamour, the Hollywood cinema costume designer.

We will focus on the Golden Era of cinema glamour, the Thirties, when films glorified the traditional American dream of success and riches in the face of world depression. Reality then mingled easily with fantasy, and the screen presented us with romanticized and idealized images of ourselves. In the Thirties glamour was the core adjective to any feminine star's aura. The studios took the time and money to find and polish "star quality." No effort was spared to reinforce that indefinable attraction found in a Garbo, a Dietrich, a Crawford, a Hepburn. The Thirties shimmered with Hollywood at its grandest, a dream reinforced by costumes and gowns that even today epitomize sophisticated beauty and timeless fascination. It is this classic memory of Hollywood and glamour that must be preserved, for it will never come again.

The American cinema industry grew and prospered by providing the people with the entertainment and emotional release they demanded. Most definitely the studios were in business to make money—lots of it—but in the beginning they were willing to dispense the effort necessary to achieve quality and excellence too. Never again will such an enormous task force of skilled workers be sustained to reach the magnificent heights envisioned by a handful of gifted designers. "Going Hollywood" then as now denotes a fantastic quality, a slight overdramaticism, an artificiality bordering at times on the bizarre. In the Thirties it also meant style and ultimate good taste. Hollywood was a never-never land where the fine line separating illusion and reality was joyously blurred, where even the stars believed the magic images manufactured for them by studio PR departments.

In the Thirties the public demanded that their greatest fantasies be fulfilled for twenty-five cents a night. Favorite idols always looked fantastic on the screen. As Walter Plunkett, one of Hollywood's most talented costume designers, observed:

> It was just as important to look ridiculously gorgeous as it was to make a beautiful false-front house and have it look wonderful. It was gorgeous. It was expensive. It was phony. You went to see a dream and you had a glorious time because it was exciting, but it was never reality.

Marlene Dietrich for publicity for Paramount, 1932. Designer: Banton

Pictures in the Thirties usually evolved around rich, stylish people, and the movies naturally glorified their clothes. The cinema designer had to create a fashionable screen image but not necessarily fashion. Creating fashion and designing costumes for the screen are two vastly different crafts. According to Edith Head, America's best-known designer, Hollywood was never a fashion center because it did not manufacture clothes to be bought. To her and other designers, a fashion center designs clothes for the public, has shows, and manufactures clothes for stores to buy to sell to faceless people of all sizes and shapes. Patou, Vionnet, Chanel, Lanvin, and Mainbocher were fashion designers. New York and Paris were fashion centers in the Thirties; Los Angeles has achieved that status today. Cinema fashions are more correctly called cinema costumes. They are costumes worn by specific actors and actresses playing a specific role in a movie, nothing more. Occasionally costumes have influenced fashion, but they did not make Hollywood a fashion center.

George Cukor, who directed several Thirties classics and is a renowned director still today, has said:

> Hollywood wardrobes are created *all to serve the picture—not to make fashion* [his emphasis]. They must fulfill two requirements: 1) they must serve the dramatic purpose of the script by helping to make the character believable and not distract from the scene, and 2) they must be photogenically the best for the actress. All these clothes should be a dramatic element in the play, and that is the different between costume and fashion.

Hollywood designers were expected to do more than just design clothes, as their Parisian counterparts did. Again, Miss Head on the role of the cinema designer:

> I do not consider a motion picture costume designer necessarily a fashion creator because we do what the script tells us to. If we do a period piece, then we re-create fashion that was done before, and if we have a character role, we do character clothes. It is only by the accident of a script that calls for fashion and an actress that can wear fashion that some of the beautiful clothes will emerge. I don't consider myself a designer in the sense of a fashion designer. I am a motion picture costume designer.

Hollywood designers avoided creating fashion and followed the basic dictates from Paris and New York in skirt lengths, silhouettes, and so on. However, the glamour and charisma of its stars, the drama of some costume requirements sparked mini-styles in hats, sleeves, or materials. Only a few thousand ladies saw the fashion shows in Paris and New York and read *Vogue;* millions of women around the world flocked to the movies to see Norma Shearer's latest display of evening or day wear. This led to genteel animosity between Hollywood and the fashion capitals. Paris sniffed at Hollywood's vulgarity for impinging on its lofty domain, but when cinema designers such as Adrian and Howard Greer opened respectable couturier salons, Paris and New York loudly applauded their genius.

Cinema designers created fashionable images, not fashion. They also surmounted a complex system of limitations imposed by moviemaking. We now examine a few of these routine problems.

The usual procedure followed by a studio for costume designing began once a script had evolved. The costume designer would read the script and determine what exactly was needed, by whom, what time of day, what year, what type of scene (dramatic or not), any obvious camera angles, and so on. Again Plunkett:

> You never knew if the dress were just going to be photographed from the waist up, and it sometimes killed you because you had done something that needed the full-length shot, and the cameraman and director ignored it. This is why I adored working with Cukor, Minnelli, and especially Selznick. These people appreciated clothes, and you gave them something and sometimes said, "Try to get in a full view of the back of the dress because the train is important," or try to do this or that with it. Very often, after reading the script, you knew she was going to be sitting behind a desk, so you could just hang a skirt so she could walk onto the set and then put all your emphasis on the top.

The costume could also be used to climax a dramatic scene. Take the white evening dress worn by Loretta Young in *Four Men and a Prayer*. The scene, near the end of the movie, shows Miss Young pleading for her father's help. Throughout the dramatic portion, Young is always full front to the camera in her very modest white gown. At the very conclusion of the scene, when the climax has been reached and her father's support secured, Young, with a smiling, quick 180° spin, turns to leave with her beaus and reveals a completely stunning bare back—an exciting effect created by Young's quick movement and Royer's backless engineering.

The designer, then, familiar with the script and character, next considered the actress herself, her physical limitations or assets, perhaps her image. Studio designers realized that they had to meld the two, the actress and the character, and make her look her best while still suitable for the dramatic purpose of the scene. They made designs and clothes for individual people and knew the shortcomings and virtues of those people and the quirks of the camera. Because of the unique problems presented by set lighting, for example, most of the top designers such as Adrian and Head had variable set lighting in their workrooms and fitting rooms. They had to know how a costume would look on the set and on film because sometimes two panels of the same material would photograph differently. Adrian developed a light and special lens to show the grade of colors he was using to prevent any problems in the finished costume.

Lead actresses seldom wore off-the-rack clothing. Even most couturier gowns looked terrible on the screen because they were not made to be photogenic. When Parisian designers made a dress, they made the whole ensemble and did not consider how it would look in black and white or on tricky color film. Orry-Kelly, the lead designer at Warner Brothers during the Thirties, was an acknowledged genius at knowing exactly what was photogenic and how much detail was suitable for a scene and camera angle. In contrast, couture clothing might not be dramatic enough, or it might look exaggerated, or it simply would not suit the star or role. Fashion designers designed for a faceless woman in a vague situation. Adrian once remarked to George Cukor that he preferred that regular models wear his fashions for a *Vogue* layout because actresses had such strong personalities they would usually overwhelm the clothes.

Actresses also varied in their agreeability to a design or designer. Generally, the more important the actress, the more attention and pampering she received. As Cukor said, however:

> Nobody goes against each other. If the star were very unhappy with the dress, [the amount of change] depended on how much the star knew. If the star were a dummy and had no taste, then naturally you'd have to impose it on her. If they had a natural sense of chic and they were intelligent about it and did not destroy the illusion, the director went with them.

Constance Bennett was known for her own sense of style and good taste. Some stars like Garbo, Shearer, and Lombard left themselves completely in the hands of the masters. A few, such as Katharine Hepburn and Bette Davis, discussed their costumes in the third person and were concerned only about the character's needs and what the character would actually wear.

Another responsibility of the cinema designer was continuity, or insuring that the actress's appearance followed a logical sequence in the completed movie. A mud-splattered dress worn in a retake must be identically splattered as the original worn days earlier. Bows, pins, and accessories had to remain together. If an outfit were worn throughout the movie, appropriate wear signs had to be added to show a logical progression, even if the last scenes were shot first—a common practice. Some studios weighed their stars every day. A five-pound increase or loss during filming could spell heartache for a designer trying to maintain continuity on the screen.

Before, during, or after a style had been created the cinema designer also contended with other studio personnel with sensitivities that had to be considered. The director, the actress, the set designer, the hairdresser, cameramen, and co-stars all could or did try to recommend and suggest what each thought best for a scene. Occasionally the opposite happened and the designer was ignored. In *Richest Girl in the World,* Mariam Hopkins arrived at the studio on the first day of shooting with her wardrobe brought directly from New York, sight unseen by either the director or the cinema designer. Walter Plunkett enjoyed designing co-star Fay Wray's high-fashion clothes for the movie, but had to meld the two wardrobes for the screen. Fortunately the film was in black and white, so clashes of color were minimized. Meddling eventually drove Plunkett to specialize in period costumes because few people argued with recorded fact. Even the director, the final judge of cinema costume adequacy, usually, but not always, bent to written descriptions in historical books.

Director Cukor, when asked if he worried about fashion in his movies or if he gave complete instructions to the costume designer, replied:

A director doesn't worry, but he concerns himself with every detail of the picture. I never told a designer what to do, I told them what we needed for the scene and they listened, and I listened and respected what they had to say would work.

Walter Plunkett compared three top directors this way:

George Cukor had a great deal to say because he has a strong visual sense of what his film is going to look like, he has great taste, and he pretty much knows what is right and what is wrong for the scene that he is going to do. [He] has much to say. Vincent Minnelli is another to whom the bouquet of flowers on the table is terribly important, the dress is important, the handkerchief she carries is terribly important. John Ford is not gong to tell you what it is, but [he'll say] ''I have in mind a very dark scene and I want something to reflect light so I can get a glow on this person.'' Or ''I have a very light scene and I want stark contrast.'' He would never tell you what the dress would look like, or how to make it. Another director may see his film strictly all in action and all he cares about is, is she able to run, is she able to jump, what is she able to do, and then to hell with it. [He would not] care much what she looked like.

In addition to collaboration with other department heads, the limitations of the script and actress, the desires of the director, and the tricks of the camera, the cinema designer had to consider collaboration with the finance department and budget, the limitations of censorship, the desires of the public, and the tricks of fashion forecasting.

Between 1930 and 1935, only MGM survived the financial crises, reorganization, bankruptcy, or receivership that afflicted all the other major studios. In the dark days of 1932 and 1933, when the full impact of. the Depression finally hit Hollywood, MGM alone continued to show some profit, albeit only a tenth of its previous earnings. Even at MGM executives such as Louis B. Mayer took temporary pay cuts from $10,000 a week to a mere $750 until the turbulence subsided. At the other studios budgets were slashed on every level of production. Wages for extras fell from $3 a day to $1.25. Admission prices were cut. Many of the studios tried to revive the shocking slump in attendance by liberal use of violence and sex. The double feature was adopted to draw customers and sparked most of the studios' prolific production of ''B'' pictures to fill the bill.

MGM followed a philosophy managed by its resident prodigy, Iriving Thalberg, the studio's vice president in charge of production. His dictum was to make money by spending money. Under Thalberg, MGM acquired a reputation for films of polish and technical excellence achieved by attracting the finest talents in the world with the largest paychecks and biggest budgets. The average budget for an MGM feature film in 1932 was $500,000, or about $150,000 more than any other studio. Actual costs varied according to the status of the star—Camille, for example, cost $1.5 million in 1936. The Thalberg touch seemed golden and rarely fallible. He justified lavish expenses of hundreds of thousands of dollars when the expense produced profits in the millions. Further, MGM was properly considered a women's studio because of its many female superstars—Harlow, Crawford, Shearer, and Garbo. Clothes budgets therefore were consistently the most generous in Hollywood and the studio's top designer, Adrian, used every penny. Real diamonds and gems were used in *Camille,* as well as the finest fabrics for Garbo's underskirts, all to help her feel the role and mood of the times. Authentic French laces and velvets were purchased at great expense in France for *Marie Antoinette* to give historical accuracy and opulence. Many designers in other studios received only a fraction of the largess doled out by MGM, but it is a tribute to their genius that they still managed to create the required illusion of elegance for the screen. The fortunes of Paramount, in particular, fell or rose with the profits from single productions, yet the sophistication and elegance Travis Banton achieved in his costumes, the remarkable style and glamour of Paramount stars such as Lombard, West, and Dietrich, never betrayed the financial crisis the studio faced and surmounted.

After 1933 business slowly began to improve; studios were once again making profits by 1935. Even Warner Brothers began loosening its famous pecuniary purse strings and allowed Orry-Kelly and Milo Anderson more leeway in films such as *In Caliente, Anthony Adverse,* and even *Captain Blood.*

During the financial traumas of 1931–33, as the studios frantically sought to bolster sagging profits, Hollywood and its audiences enjoyed a period of wickedness and titillation that seems only mildly shocking today. Nudity was common, particularly for the numerous chorus girls in the many musical spectacles. Sheila O'Brien, organizer and head of the Costume Designers Guild, remembers one of her duties for the film *George White's Scandals of 1934* was to distribute three little flowers and some glue to fifteen girls for their "costume" in a musical number. Although the correct amount of flowers had been made for everyone, all were gone before the eighth girl received hers. The ladies were grabbing extras to cover themselves more modestly. The cast director yelled "You knew this when you took the job!" to the sobbing chorus, and the show went on as designed. All the girls had been completely shaved, and they wore only their small, small flowers. Miss O'Brien commented that at least in burlesque they would have had G-strings. Walter Plunkett's first assignment in the costume department at RKO involved a hundred or so chorus girls in long, sequined skirts and tall headdresses. His job was painting dainty, small flowers on their dainty, bare nipples.

The pendulum swung after the censorship code of 1934 was reinforced and the Hays Office began ruling the studios. A censorship code had actually been on the books since 1930, but studios paid only lip service to its restrictions in the battle for improved profits. The Hays Office was powerful because it finally caught and held the studios' attention with something any mogul could understand—the threat of boycott by millions of Americans who joined the Legion of Decency and other such organizations in 1934. Will Hays, with a salary of $100,000 a year, used friendly persuasion and the seal of approval of the Motion Picture Producers and Distributors of America (MPPDA) for the necessary leverage to gain adherence to production and advertising codes. The MPPDA directly affected theaters supplying thirty percent of gross box office capacity, and without the seal, distribution of a film was severely limited and profit almost unattainable.

The censors of the time were quite extraordinary. Every dress had to be tested for modesty, and all tests were reviewed by a representative from the Hays Office, who also constantly insured compliance on the sets. Films could not show female navels, although male navels were properly modest. No sign of pregnancy was permitted, no garters, and—heaven forbid!—no cleavage. Even the slightest shadow that suggested cleavage was shocking and could suspend production until the offensive costume was reworked to suit the censor. Designers were called to sets to justify necklines, and handkerchiefs and extra ruffles were always in great demand by wardrobe. Logic was not the prime mover in the fight for the country's morals. For example, while cleavage was anathema and perfectly flat, malelike chests were the ideal of the censors, in *The Three Musketeers,* a Forties period film, one of Lana Turner's dresses, cut low to reveal the side contours of her breasts, was permissible so long as the cleavage in the center was covered by a very large jewel.

Most of the directors were aware of the strict requirements of the code, but they left the details of modesty completely to the professional abilities of the designers. It was their job, after all, to know every aspect of their trade and their responsibility to insure smooth processing of all costume designs.

Audiences of the Thirties sought the escape and glamour that Hollywood provided. They went to the movies to see the stars and the costumes and to feel the excitement. Often the beautiful clothes that so thrilled audiences as the latest in fashion had been designed one to two years before they were actually shown. This time lag tested the genius of every Hollywood designer. Studios cranked out many more movies each year in the Thirties than they do today, and most took only a few months from filming to exhibition. Sometimes, however, a sound track would need reworking, or a new scene would be added, or the producer would consider the timing bad for the star or story, and so on. A designer did not have certain knowledge when his clothes would be seen, and that is why most cinema designs are classics that can be worn any time. There were exceptions, of course. Clothing had to be fashionable but not too flashy unless the scene allowed it. Adrian always went fanciful when dramatic effect by the actress was not required and the clothing could take center stage. The design was still restricted by the character and all other limitations, but Adrian was not afraid to test surprising new styles or have a bit of fun with a design. He maintained it would either be fashionable by the time the movie was reviewed or be so unusual that it was exempt from fashion. In *Mannequin,* Joan Crawford appears as a model in a mini–fashion show. Adrian drenched her with elaborate, thick fur to set her apart while modeling afternoon tea gowns and luncheon suits, gave her full skirts when the other models were in slim silhouettes, and encased her in gleaming brocade when the rest were dull and filmy. It was pure ''Hollywood.'' Less bold, but no less stunning designers, such as Banton at Paramount and Orry-Kelly at Warner Brothers, must have been psychic in their abilities to foresee and incorporate future trends in their screen wardrobes. Their styles may have been less sensational, but their effects were exactly calculated to fit the character and remain fashionable while the film played in the world's theaters. Most of these costumes would draw envious glances if worn even today.

There was one final influence sometimes imposed on Hollywood designers. Although cinema designers consciously designed one gown, for one definite person, in one definite role, in one definite scene, the studios were aware of the publicity potential of the costumes and were not adverse to using points in cinema wardrobes to sell more tickets. The designers themselves never seriously tried to set fashion in the same way as Paris, nor did they try to create gimmicks solely for exploitation, but that did not prevent millions of average women from trying to copy a style worn by their favorite star. Nor did it prevent studio publicity departments from forming relationships with manufacturers to produce millions of usually second-rate copies of a hat, or a dress, or whatever to generate free publicity for a film. The Eugénie hat Adrian created for Garbo in *Romance,* a period picture, was copied by more than one manufacturer and sold to thousands of Garbo fans. Each hat was a small advertisement for the movie, and the studio encouraged its sale.

Although it took the personality, charisma, and beauty of stars like Lombard, Dolores Del Rio, Loretta Young, Dietrich, Crawford, and Shearer to set styles copied by millions of women, the styles themselves were generated by a small group of highly creative individuals sprinkled among the studios. Most were born diplomats and tacticians who carefully threaded their designs through the written reqirements of the script, the sometimes unyielding desires of the actress, and the visionary limits of the director. This need for diplomacy, of course, varied according to designer, director, studio, and star. Adrian was considered a god on the MGM lot. Everyone who knew him agrees he was a totally delightful person who used his natural humor, wit, and charm to captivate any director or actress concerned with a design. Adrian was, nevertheless, quite aware of his position as the top designer for the top studio and could be difficult when necessary. One such time occurred during the production of *Romeo and Juliet* when Oliver Messel, a noted authority on sixteenth-century design, was imported from London to do all the costumes. Adrian asserted his right as resident designer during heated and important conferences with MGM production brass. In the end, two costumes were made for each of Norma Shearer's scenes, one designed by Messel, one by Adrian. Shearer wore Adrian's creations. Travis Banton, more introverted than Adrian, was involved in few debates over his designs. His acknowledged skill and reputation, as well as the pure beauty of his gowns, were more than enough to preclude negative discussions. Orry-Kelly, who stirred his champagne with a swizzle stick, could at times be arrogant and call his actresses a salty name or two. He also was a recognized genius, and women would endure much to wear any of his costumes.

Actresses did not keep their dresses. Most costumes were modified and used many times, particularly at the poorer studios such as Fox. Fur pieces were constantly reused. All fur was removed from clothing and either put in cold storage at the studio or, in the case of RKO, returned to the department store or rental company.

Studios often loaned ensembles from their wardrobe departments for premieres and other special publicity events. Sometimes original designs were created for important stars on significant occasions. On direct orders from Selznick, Walter Plunkett fashioned the gowns worn by Vivian Leigh to premieres and award ceremonies for *Gone with the Wind*. The point was to present Miss Leigh in a glamorous image suitable to the stature of the picture and her role.

Although no designer admits to knowing of petty jealousies among the stars of a studio, Howard Shoup learned early in his career at Warner Brothers never to talk about one actress to another during a fitting. If there was any rivalry, the actress being fitted would bristle, interrupt in the middle of a sentence, and complain about the neckline, or sleeve, or whatever she suddenly did not like about the design. However, Shoup and the other designers generally agree that in the old days there was genuine loyalty and devotion between designer and star. The two might fight mercilessly over the style points of a gown, but they remained friends. Shoup adds, however, "Today the relationship is cold. Many of the actresses are here today and gone tomorrow." Indeed, it is almost impossible for a young actress to be adopted by one great designer and elegantly groomed as Carole Lombard was by Travis Banton. Today's starlets are essentially on their own and develop their brief images along more mundane lines, afraid to tackle the glamorous look alone. Help is certainly not forthcoming from the studios or networks. Time is too short; money too tight.

The salaries paid to the designers varied according to persistency, ego, and reputation. None was excessively paid. At his peak Adrian earned about $1,000 a week, a relatively moderate amount for such an important studio figure. His greatest output was between 1931 and 1934, when he designed for almost all MGM pictures, for stars and extras. Later he only designed for the cream of the studio's films, and he himself decided which he would do. Dolly Tree, another talented MGM designer, did most of Myrna Loy's films as well as several Jean Harlow pictures and period pieces. In 1942, after Adrian left MGM and opened his own couture salon, he was replaced by Kalloch and Howard Shoup. Kalloch shortly committed suicide, and Shoup joined the armed forces.

Of course, all the glamorous designs and magnificent dreams would have remained on the drawing boards without the expert talents of an army of skilled seamstresses, sketch artists, beaders, fitters, cutters, and others. It would do no good to have a designer like Edith Head without the artisans necessary to translate her concepts into the incredibly beaded and jeweled gowns worn by Mae West in *She Done Him Wrong*. Yet these great and important people received no recognition, and some were paid less than the janitors at the same studios. Sheila O'Brien's starting salary at Paramount as a seamstress was $16.50 a week. An experienced seamstress earned $21.60 for a forty-hour week and could earn "golden time" for special projects (time and a half for work over forty hours). When faced with the need for long hours during particularly frantic periods, studios often temporarily "promoted" their seamstresses to the title of cutter and fitter. Cutters and fitters earned a flat $40.50 for a six-day workweek and were not entitled to overtime. Of course, it was the Depression, and most people were thankful to have a job that paid anything. Edith Head's starting salary as a sketch artist at Paramount was approximately $30 for a six-day week.

RKO had a very limited costume budget and worked on a shoestring most of the time. Plunkett's early Thirties staff consisted of one cutter-fitter and five table ladies. Table ladies were in charge of groups of seamstresses who took patterns from the cutter-fitter and developed them into the final product. The seamstresses were hired by the week or by the day and were summoned only when there was work. The table ladies would also be discharged if there was a slump in duties. Cutters and fitters were the last to go. Even at MGM during the darkest days, cutters and fitters would alternate and take two weeks off to rotate the work schedules.

The hours worked by the wardrobe department could be gruesome. Unexpected crises would always arise, requiring round-the-clock hours. Plunkett remembers the shooting schedule for *Rio Rita*:

> There was only one Technicolor camera; it had to be used by one company in the daytime and by *Rio Rita* at night. So I slept in my office—with what little sleep I got, went home, took a quick shower, changed clothes, and came back. I just stayed for days in my office.

Why did Banton, Plunkett, O'Brien, Head, Kalloch, Orry-Kelly, Wakeling, and Adrian stay as long as they did? Consider the environment in which they toiled: a make-believe world populated by only the most beautiful and most talented people imaginable. Their jobs were to give substance to fantasy and dreams. Not only did these designers and workers create glamour, they also were seduced by it like millions of others throughout the world.

This book will focus exclusively on feminine costume designs for two basic reasons. The most obvious one is that feminine costume design created the world of glamour that was part of so many star images of the Thirties. The clothing of the leading ladies had impact, greater dramatic effect, and, as was true in the world of fashion, attracted more attention than the relatively straightforward styles of the male stars. Another, less well known fact is that male stars were their own cinema designers and provided their own contemporary wardrobes, thus eliminating the need for a costume designer except to coordinate colors with the wardrobe of the leading lady.

Throughout his career as one of Hollywood's handsomest and most sophisticated stars, Cary Grant had all his modern clothes cut and fashioned by master tailors around the world. For *To Catch a Thief* he used an exclusive ready-made shop in southern France because the character he played would have used a ready-made shop in southern France. He provided the studio with eight copies of the suit and twelve copies of the tie he wore in *North by Northwest*. A bolt of the same suit material was reserved in his tailor's shop should those eight be destroyed during filming. Because the studio did not provide the wardrobe, should all copies of a tie, for example, be unusable, expensive production could be halted until another was made. A delay for this reason never occurred during any of Grant's movies.

Once shooting had begun, the studio assumed full responsibility for the care and cleaning of Grant's clothes, but it provided no compensation or rental fees to Mr. Grant except when a suit was completely ruined. Needless to say, Grant has amassed an extensive personal wardrobe, and his friends and associates of the same size are probably as well dressed as he. It was Grant who decided the cut, color, fit, and details of his cinema wardrobes. The studios and directors recognized his impeccable good taste and intelligence, and there was little or no difficulty in coordinating with the regular cinema wardrobe for the female lead. As Edith Head commented, ''Cary Grant, had he not been a superb actor, would have been a superb designer. He is extraordinarily talented in interpreting fashion to the needs of acting.''

Grant strongly maintains, in contrast to the ladies' clothes, that his screen wardrobes were correctly fashion and not costume. He wore costumes only for period pictures, and uniforms, and those were provided and designed by the studio. This method of a man's providing his own clothing for a screen role was the rule, not the exception. All screen actors in the Thirties, such as Spencer Tracy and Adolphe Menjou, another screen sophisticate, used their own tailors or favorite stores. Therefore, on the grounds that men's clothing was much simpler and had much less variety in comparison with the women's and that studio designers played a small role if any in their screen wardrobes, this book will conveniently ignore the men, in true chauvinistic style, and concentrate on the elegant accouterments of the lovely ladies.

Movie stars were their own showcases, and they could not risk an inferior first impression; their clothes were as important to them as to their observers. This book attempts to preserve a handful of the thousands of costumes created by cinema designers in the Thirties. It shows only a glimpse of an incredible period of fashion in America, a period epitomizing old elegance. Many stars are not represented, some major ones only sparsely. It is impossible to show all the stars in all their roles or publicity shots wearing all the styles that were important then. It is impossible in part because many of the most priceless still photographs no longer exist or are unavailable. Private collectors who share the joy of conserving a memory have supplied the majority of photographs in this book; so have two excellent commercial sources in Hollywood. If the studios had only recognized the treasure they had in their archives of stills, the fans of today could revel more easily in the beauty and glamour of yesterday. As stated before, it was glamour the likes of which will never again be seen. Hollywood in the Thirties was a true fantasyland, never to be equaled.

Marlene Dietrich in Angel *by Paramount, 1937. Designer: Banton*

Chapter Two
Evening Glamour

The Thirties truly epitomized "glamour" in the best and truest sense, and among the most glamorous gowns were those designed for evening wear. Paris had always projected a love of dressing up for each and every occasion, but it took Hollywood's magic to truly inspire evening glamour for men and women of the middle class. Women were not bound by girdles and corsets, bustles, hoops, or even bras. Their bodies were not artificially molded or pinched as at the turn of the century, nor were their figures hidden as in the Twenties. Fashionable women could now revel in soft fabrics such as soufflé and chiffons and luxuriate in dresses covered by hand-sewn beads and sequins. Because the Thirties was a time of economic depression for the world, masses of women yearned for a release from their daily poverty, a lift, even for a few moments, into dreams of riches and extravagance. Hollywood readily provided that release, and evening fashions showed such extravagance. Women could vicariously thrill with Marlene Dietrich when she wore a $3,500 dress for a few minutes in *Angel*. This ensemble, shown opposite, which was a solid mass of glittering gold and spangle embroidery strewn with emeralds, rubies, and pearls and bordered with sable, caused no little trauma on the set when producers refused to give it to Dietrich for her private wardrobe. Banton, the designer, once described it as one of the most expensive gowns he ever designed:

> It was simple in lines, of Persian design, and looked like a piece of woven jewelry. A score of embroiderers worked on it two and a half weeks. Which was very fortunate, because sometimes we have to produce such intricately made gowns on short notice, in one day or less.

Although, as stated in chapter one, the cinema fashion costume was designed to serve the needs of the film first, to overcome the limitations of the actress second, and to remain within the requirements of "fashion" only third, the great studio designers were aware of a fourth element, the need to balance all the above and still provide the audience with the magical dreams they demanded.

Because fashionable women truly did dress for dinners, the theater, and parties, evening clothes had the best opportunity to reflect elegance, timeles glamour, and genuine extravagance in the face of dreariest poverty. While the audiences feasted on the evening fashions worn by the female stars, the men dutifully wore their evening "uniforms" and stayed in the background. As Cary Grant so gallantly stated, "The reason a man wore a dinner coat in those times was to show off his lady in a colorful gown in front of him."

It is impossible to display all the fashion forms in evening

Ginger Rogers for publicity at Paramount, 1930. Designer: Banton

clothes in the Thirties or all the special couture peaks in sleeves, necklines, materials, and evening wraps in a few pictures on a few pages. This chapter will show some of the great beauty created for the screen using the latest Paris and New York fashions as a starting point, not the final objective—a reverse philosophy dictated by the requirements of cinema costumes.

The group shot gives a glimpse of the evening styles that predominated in the mid-Thirties. The major fashion hallmarks are neatly displayed: sequins, chiffon, fur, lamè, and satin. That beautiful blonde Fred Astaire is eyeing is Lucille Ball.

In the winter of 1929, an important decision was made in Paris that had costly repercussions in Hollywood. Jean Patou, a well-known French designer, initiated a bold style change by raising the waistline from the hips back to its natural level and dropping the hemline evenly to the floor for evening clothes. Instead of the relatively minor changes that culminate in a new fashion look after several years, this was a significant and surprising departure from current vogue that overnight transformed what was "in" to what was "out" and caught most of Hollywood's motion picture studios, and some New York and Paris fashion designers, unprepared.

In Hollywood, films already "in the can" for release in 1930 had to be reshot if the female star were not to be caught with her hemlines uneven. Current shooting schedules had to be revised while wardrobe departments worked overtime to remodel dress after dress to follow the new vogue. The publicity shot of Kay Francis in velvet and satin shows the very latest fashion as of winter 1929. In contrast, Paramount released the photo of Ginger Rogers for publication on June 10, 1930, under the headline "Fashions from Filmland." The dress was pink satin with cap sleeves and flowers of satin in deep rose and mulberry shades. The style molded a natural waist but was not quite floor-length; it also did not have the uneven hemline seen on Francis.

By the winter of 1930 audiences even in the heartland of the United States were laughing in the theaters when a female star, purporting to be a fashionable character, appeared on the screen with uneven hems and a dropped waist. Cinema costume designers scrambled to insure that films released in 1930 were strictly in line with the new look. The trauma of this experience left a definite impression on studios. Fortunately, the suddenness of this change did not recur until the early war years of the Forties.

The very early Thirties look in evening wear does not fit the sleek, sophisticated Thirties stereotype. The silhouettes, though slim, are not quite as clinging as later evolutions, the figures not quite chic enough; the design techniques a bit too close to the gaudiness of the Twenties. The more refined use of beads and satins and the slim, sexy fashions generally came after 1932–33, when studios were on the financial upswing and designers such as Banton, Orry-Kelly, and Adrian were in their prime. Audiences, too, were reaching a better appreciation of less fantastic fashions—less fantastic, that is, relative to the Twenties. As the Depression continued into the middle and late Thirties, moviegoers idolized the more elegant and glamorous Hollywood evening fashions seen in the rest of this chapter.

Kay Francis for publicity at Paramount, 1930. Designer: Banton

Fred Astaire and Lucille Ball in Follow the Fleet *by RKO, 1936. Designer: Bernard Newman*

Mary Lou Dix in The King Steps Out *by Columbia, 1936. Designer: Dryden*

Gladys George in Straight Is the Way *by MGM, 1934. Designer: Tree*

When Walter Plunkett began to design costumes for a movie, he required two things: the script and a roomful of materials. The script told him what was needed and what he must do, and the materials showed him his limitations:

> I learned a long, long, long time ago you don't first make a sketch and then go hunting for a fabric that will do what you want it to do. You get that piece of fabric and you hold it, you play with it, you throw it around to see how it moves, how it reflects light, then you know how you are gong to use it. It's like building a house, you have to know the materials you are going to use before you design the house. So, getting everything together for the costume, putting the star into the costume, making it becoming to her, all just have to naturally go together and they flow out of you.

Material became as important a fashion item as the actual forms and shapes created by the designers, and Hollywood used only the finest materials available—or only what would photograph as looking the finest. Designing for "B" pictures required consideration of substitute materials such as cotton or cheaper chiffon, but Adrian and Banton used only true silks and satins.

Today, when someone remembers great actresses of the Thirties like Harlow or Lombard, these lovely ladies usually appear in our minds in something satin, bias-cut, and very, very slim. The bias-cut dress was considered extremely daring and created quite a stir when first "invented" by Madelaine Vionnet in Paris in 1929, yet it took Hollywood and its stars to make satin elegance the hallmark of evening fashion. Simplicity and good taste, words you will see continuously throughout this book, were the general rule. Generally, solid-colored satin was used to achieve a sleek and elegant look. Styles were kept basically simple and uncluttered to enhance the beauty and figure of the actress, which had to be near perfect. "Sexy" satin—an adjective coined by *Vogue* in 1933—would forgive few figure faults. Simplicity was also mandatory for strong dramatic scenes when flashy styling could detract from the action or story. Simplicity did not mean that the actress need go unnoticed. Mary Lou Dix's rather plain gown lost little in the way of impact, and it effectively showcased her exquisite figure in this advance publicity still for her first movie at Columbia. Publicity photos that helped create the right image were important parts of any starlet's career.

Nothing need be explained about Harlow's figure or the molded gowns she wore in her early career. Later, when her status as a superstar was secure, she would modify her image into one more sophisticated and subtle, but no less glamorous. Gladys George achieved her classic Thirties look with an ultrasimple, pale blue satin style effectively combined with a blue chiffon scarf.

Jean Harlow in Reckless *by MGM, 1935. Designer: Adrian*

Satin did not have to remain smooth, slim, and shiny. It could be textured (matelassé) to give a three-dimensional effect, or the shine treated to form a waxy or ciré appearance. But a dress is just a sack without imagination and style. The cinema designer had to maintain interesting style while limited by the script in the impressiveness of his creations.

The low, revealing bodice outline was just one stunning but subtle design detail on Ursula Jeans's slinky and daring black ciré satin cinema costume. The actual application of jewelry was restrained but strategic, especially on the cleavage and on the scarlet red feathered fan.

Of all the clothing designed for Carole Lombard, she liked this black satin dress, designed by Travis Banton, the best. It was close-fitting and appears to be twisted and tied about the knees in a large, draped bow, with a twisted halter about the neck and shoulders, held in place by huge, brilliant clips. The three-quarter-length cape of satin, heavily banded in black "simian" (monkey) fur, was to fall outward in "graceful sprays," according to studio publicity.

In 1938, when *Motion Picture Magazine* asked Banton if he always used real materials, he answered:

> Absolutely. You can't cheat the camera. In a close-up, the details of a dress are magnified several times, and any defect in material or workmanship will be shown with painful clarity. I always use the most beautiful materials I can get. For instance, the three leading silk companies in the world are in Lyons, France, and they always send me their latest samples. In France, people are very cinema-conscious. These manufacturers appreciate the prestige of the American screen. I had an amusing experience in London last year. Duplicates of all the clothes I had designed for Carole [Lombard] in *Rhumba* were on exhibit in the windows of one of the most fashionable stores.

Carole Lombard in Love Before Breakfast
by Universal, 1936. Designer: Banton

Ursula Jeans in Cavalcade *by Fox, 1933.
Designer: Luick*

When silk is interwoven with metallic threads of gold or silver, the combination is called lamé, and the effect is usually memorable. If a female character needed to stand out a bit, but not to the extent of bugles and beads, the designer could use lamé. Few actresses fought that idea.

The publicity still of Carole Lombard on the opposite page does not show a designed ensemble. Rather, a bolt of lamé material was simply but expertly draped over her by Travis Banton for a remarkable still photograph. Sometimes a rather plain dress was temporarily swathed in boas or furs for the camera's amusement. Both ideas saved the studio money and made great publicity stills.

Equally dramatic is the dazzlingly extravagant gold lamé formal on Frances Langford. The design featured lamé worked like soft cotton to form golden pleats not only for the shirred shoulders and open fishtail tunic, but also for the lavish train panel in back. A wide self-fabric belt, with a buckle that carried the vertical theme, emphasized the waist. The dress, the pose, the model, everything worked in this still to epitomize the best of Hollywood glamour.

Nina Foley created another unique effect on Loretta Young. The elegant simplicity of this gown gleamed richly with a silver and gold combination. Silver lamé was the basic fabric, accented with a studded belt and collar trim of faceted metal disks of alternating silver and gold. According to studio publicity, Loretta Young was born on Hollywood Avenue in Salt Lake City, Utah, and educated in a convent school in Los Angeles. Young was considered one of the homeliest girls in school, with buckteeth and glasses. It is obvious that she matured to become one of the loveliest stars ever to shine in Hollywood.

Lamé was not confined to silver and gold colors. All the colors of the rainbow were possible. An example is the Venus blue with gold color of the Hubert design on Claire Trevor. Interest centered on the cascading drapery in front, held at the waist with a large diamond brooch. Blended with a molded silhouette, the shoulders were given a youthful touch with simulated bows.

Carole Lombard for publicity at Paramount, 1932. Designer: Banton

Loretta Young for publicity at 20th Century-Fox,
1935. Designer: Nina Foley

Claire Trevor for publicity at Fox, 1934.
Designer: Hubert

Frances Langford for publicity for Collegiate
by Paramount, 1936. Designer: Banton

If lamé easily attracted attention to the central female character, bugle beads and sequins had drawing power that was spectacular.

Of all materials for evening wear, perhaps none so suited the Hollywood image as the beaded or sequined dress. The designer could "go Hollywood" and create a totally striking dress for one woman without the worry of mass-producing it or having two clients appear at the same party wearing it. Each Hollywood dress was unique. The actress for whom the gown was designed had to have a perfect figure to satisfy the cameras, and if the script allowed, the extra extravagance of the dress could add opulence to the movie to please the producer, boost the ego of the actress, and thrill the audiences who came to see exactly that kind of display. Of course the famous beaded cinema dresses of the Thirties were all handmade and possible only because of the cheap yet skilled labor on tap at every studio. Beaders earned sixty-five cents an hour in the mid-Thirties, and it took six to eight weeks (six days a week) to make one solid bugle-beaded dress.

The effect of adding a few sequins to generate interest or of completely beaded and sequined costumes is obvious on these pages.

Ginger Rogers' gleaming and graceful gown was turquoise chiffon made stunning by thousands of hand-crocheted, silver-lined bugle beads. Regular rows of beads formed the collar and belt, bands of beads trimmed both bodice and skirt. The buttons were rhinestones. Dancing in this costume was extremely difficult because of the weight of the beads and the swing of the heavy skirt. In fact, the long skirt was discarded during the musical number and freedom of movement restored with a very short, fully beaded underskirt.

Eleanor Powell's black bugle-beaded dress was created for glamour only, not dancing. The dress weighed twenty to twenty-five pounds.

Paulette Goddard, though not a central figure in *The Women*, garnered sufficient dramatic attention for her face as well as her figure in her precisely designed dress by Adrian. Once again, the impact of a superb publicity still is obvious.

Eleanor Powell in Broadway Melody of 1936 *by MGM, 1935. Designer: Adrian.*

Ginger Rogers in In Person *by RKO, 1935.*
Designer: Bernard Newman

Paulette Goddard in The Women *by MGM, 1939.*
Designer: Adrian

Billie Burke in She Couldn't Take It
by Columbia, 1935. Designer: Kalloch

Experienced seamstresses could work bugle beads and sequins into a band of beads to outline a neck, a dash of sequins to emphasize lace, or a swirl of glitter to mold a figure. These valuable ladies contributed much to cinema glamour. In 1931, "Mother" Coulter was head of MGM wardrobe. She was sixty-five years old then, and her position paid $125 a week. Seamstresses started at $22.50 a week at MGM, and a head cutter earned $60 a week. Coulter had forty women sewing when the department was at full load. Electricians at the same studio received $50 a week, carpenters $51 a week, grips $45 a week, stenographers $22.50 to $125 a week, cameramen $50 a day with overtime, and expert cameramen up to $800 a week with no overtime.

Beads and sequins used as design accents could be subtle or stunning. Garbo's gown shows the use of glitter in a more subtle but still effective manner. The base material was a light crepe, and here the figure is not emphasized, only the famous Garbo face, by placing most of the focus around the neck. This was Garbo's favorite contemporary cinema creation by Adrian, and she allowed over 2,000 photos of it to be taken. This dress has been preserved through the years and is occasionally displayed by the Adrian Collection belonging to Joseph Simms and the Cheltenham Township Senior High School in Wyncote, Pennsylvania.

Gladys Swarthout's wardrobe in *Romance in the Dark* was as exotic as it was glamorous. Playing a very successful opera singer, Swarthout appeard in several Middle East–inspired ensembles including this intriguing chiffon evening gown with a molded metal mesh hem for graceful draping and multicolored beads and sequins for brilliant accent.

Billie Burke's brown tulle dinner dress with gold spangles featured pleated tulle flounces on the skirt and an unusual spangle-trimmed cape. Although the dress was very sophisticated and even had an additional Russian sable cape to complete it, the designer's use of a large bow at the chin, lots of spangles, and a flounced ruffled skirt must have pleased Burke because, as Plunkett remembered:

> You couldn't dress Billie Burke without ruffles. Even if it were a tailored suit you had to put ruffles on it. Her character and the characters she played were always that sort of thing. A pampered little child. I loved her.

Greta Garbo and Lewis Stone in Inspiration
by MGM, 1931. Designer: Adrian

John Boles and Gladys Swarthout in Romance
in the Dark *by Paramount, 1937. Designer:*
Banton

Claudette Colbert, Ray Milland, and Fred MacMurray in The Gilded Lily *by Paramount, 1935. Designer: Banton*

Designers commonly used a base material of chiffon on which to sew the sequins or beads because chiffon was a light material that flowed easily with the weight of the beads and sequins. The overall effect on a fully beaded dress was material that clung like static to the shape of the figure but did not incapacitate the actress for the scene. Bugle-beaded dresses fit like a second skin. Dense bugle beads rivaled the shimmer of satin, and even bias-cut satin did not reveal as much as thousands of beads weighing down on and outlining every square inch of body.

Although beading was first introduced in Paris and used by Hollywood for years, the dress that created a sensation in 1937 was the very famous red bugle-beaded dress designed by Adrian for Joan Crawford. The idea of a slither of scarlet caught everyone's attention, even though the film was in black and white. Bugle beads are made from glass and weigh many times more than sequins, which are gelatin-based. Proper care of a bugle-beaded dress took more thought and planning than a studio might ordinarily give because the expensive and heavy beading actually tore the gown if hung up. Crawford's red dress weighed approximately twenty pounds and had cross strings for support in back, not seen by the audience. Publicity said that Crawford lost three pounds wearing the *thirty-five* pound red beaded creation. This garment was inadvertently preserved when someone at MGM put it in a drawer and forgot it. Most beaded dresses were hung on wire hangers only to have the forces of gravity and age rip them to shreds.

Bugle beads were crocheted onto their base material, and their size and impact varied slightly. Regular bugle beads cost ten times more than sequins and gave an effect that was flashy but with an air of good taste. Straw beads, like those on Claudette Colbert, were finer, smaller, and outlined the figure even better—if that were possible.

Intricate back detailing for Jeanette MacDonald's beaded design included a removable capette and narrow shoulder drapes. A muted pattern around the dress bodice was repeated on the cape neckline and shoulder drape. On the screen, one of the very important functions of clothes was to bridge the gap between the personality of the star and the person she played. The gown could and did affix the character type in the minds of the audience. Before she had spoken a word, the gown on MacDonald endowed her with a special kind of glamour.

Joan Crawford, Robert Young, and Franchot Tone in The Bride Wore Red *by MGM, 1937. Designer: Adrian*

Jeannette MacDonald in Broadway Serenade *by MGM, 1939. Designer: Adrian*

Betty Grable in This Way Please *by Paramount, 1937. Designer: Head*

Alice Faye in Now I'll Tell *by Fox, 1934. Designer: Rita Kaufman*

Beading was fairly common in fashions and on the screen in the Twenties, but in the Thirties, although other designers used his ideas and techniques, Travis Banton's name became synonymous with fully beaded and sequined dresses. The combination of beads and sequins was not just for accent or decoration, they were so dense they became the fabric.

The similar effects of small sequins and larger beads can be seen in these photos.

The rising star of Betty Grable and her charming figure were both enhanced by this elegant beaded gown. The large white accent on her shoulder was net, sprinkled with the same sequins as on the dress. This back view shows the net extending to a low V in the back and ending where the narrow trailing panel and shoulder drape begin.

Alice Faye's ensemble for the screen included a narrow shawl or stole of matching beaded material. Faye's curvaceous figure was twenty years ahead of its time, and Faye was extremely self-conscious about her unfashionably large bust. In the early Thirties flat was beautiful, and many starlets bound themselves with adhesive to project the suitable smooth image. Lilyan Tashman, an early Thirties clotheshorse who unfortunately died in 1934, practically destroyed her breasts by her constant efforts to be stylishly slinky. It is ironic that by the mid-Thirties a normal bust was in vogue, and padding was often necessary to achieve the proper symmetrical look.

Ginger Rogers in Change of Hearts *by Fox,
1934. Designer: Rita Kaufman*

Vera Zorina in publicity for The Goldwyn Follies *by United Artists, 1938. Designer: Omar Kiam*

If bugle beads were exquisite, sequins were dazzling. Nothing equaled the flash and dash of bright sequins, and their use, even muted or as accent only, always riveted attention to the wearer. An added bonus for cost-conscious studios was the fact that sequins were cheaper, lighter, and faster to apply than bugle beads. The effect was not as elegant, but it did look expensive. In the Thirties, despite the difference in impact, sequins were considered just as smart as beads.

Vera Zorina, a true prima ballerina who later became George Balanchine's third wife, modeled this lovely evening gown to publicize her first movie. The black tulle gown had a tightly shirred bodice and enormous skirt with a wide band of intricately designed sequins in reds, greens, yellows, and blues. Although an extremely simple design, flashy jewelry would have ruined the subdued elegance of this sparkling formal.

The impressive style on Ginger Rogers was a plain dark green floor-length woolen skirt combined with a blouse of glittering green sequins. The belt was also green wool. This ensemble would be as completely and enviably fashionable today as it was in 1934.

Ginger Rogers became a top box-office draw as a musical star, but she longed to play meatier roles. She enlisted the aid of director John Ford to persuade RKO of her dramatic abilities. The result was the famous "Lady Ainsley" hoax. Producer Pandro Berman was having a hard time finding the right actress to play Elizabeth in *Mary of Scotland.* John Ford told Berman about Lady Ainsley, the famous English actress, who was in town. She had played Elizabeth hundreds of times on the stage and in fact was a direct descendant. Berman authorized a test and a few days later was electrified by the woman who appeared as Queen Elizabeth (Ginger Rogers), her hair piled high on her head, her face vicious with cruelty and power. She was perfect. "Send for her, she's marvelous," ordered Berman. Ford shrugged his shoulders and told him that Ainsley did not care for motion pictures but preferred the stage. Berman tried for a week to find Ainsley until a newspaper item disclosed it had all been a hoax. Rogers did not get the part of Elizabeth, but she did eventually win an Academy Award for her work in *Kitty Foyle.*

Adolphe Menjou and Katharine Hepburn in
Morning Glory *by RKO, 1933. Designer:
Plunkett*

Howard Shoup once said, "Good taste was the major import in fashion. A design could not be so outstanding that it could kill a scene or make the audience gasp. There had to be a reason to have a spectacular dress." That reason was usually a musical number or a chance to reinforce, with clout, a change in the story. When asked why he designed this stunning dress for Katharine Hepburn in *Morning Glory,* Walter Plunkett replied:

> That was done purposely. She had one dress throughout most of the film, a navy blue crepe, which she wore all the time she was poor and trying to get a job. She became an understudy and went on one night and finally made it being a star. The only thing to do was to go the opposite way she had been and make her very shiny and very glittery. This still was not lighted as carefully as on the film. I am sure that there was a shadow from her neck down and a highlight on her face so that she was not overpowered by the sequins.

The gown itself featured a very high collar extending up the head in back, bared shoulders from a halter-type bodice, and low front décolletage.

Less exciting, but still gloriously beautiful, was the fashionable evening dress on Lili Damita, featuring large gold baguettes of metal mesh tilted diagonally. The belt was held with diamonds, and the accompanying wrap was chinchilla. Damita wore this gown not only for studio publicity, but also to a party in 1936 accompanied by her then husband, Errol Flynn. Sam Goldwyn had discovered her in a Paris café.

Eleanore Whitney wore her splendid costume for a strenuous dance sequence. The dress weighed twenty pounds, Whitney ninety-one. She collapsed in her dressing room from exhaustion after filming the dance.

Lily Damita for publicity for The Frisco Kid
by Warner Brothers, 1935. Designer: Orry-Kelly

Eleanore Whitney in Big Broadcast of 1937
by Paramount, 1936. Designer: Banton

Kay Francis in Mandalay *by Warner Brothers,
1934. Designer: Orry-Kelly*

Dolores Del Rio in Wonder Bar *by Warner
Brothers, 1933. Designer: Orry-Kelly*

The two exquisite gowns on these two pages show Hollywood
glamour at its best.

Dolores Del Rio's gold sequin, satin, and mink ensemble was
unsurpassable in glamorous elegance. Del Rio was always cast as the
exotic beauty and once commented, "When they give you wonderful
clothes, they give you bad parts." She may never have won the
Academy Award, but she was the idol of millions of fans around the
world who envied her ability to wear spectacular gowns such as this.
The dress had a high cowl neckline, cut-out cap sleeves, a low back,
and a skirt with a paneled fish train. The glamorous gold satin and
mink wrap was frosting on the cake.

The epitome of glamour in the early thirties was Kay Francis,
posed here in an ultimate Hollywood evening costume. In 1931 Banton described her this way to *Modern Screen Magazine:*

> Kay Francis to me has a slightly barbaric look that is intrigu-
> ing. With her clear dark skin, gray eyes, and almost black hair
> she can carry off the lavish effect of gold and silver lamé's,
> paillettes, and vivid colors. White satin is exquisite on her. So
> are greens that have a yellow cast, also sumptuous furs and ex-
> otic jewelry.

Francis was considered a matinee idol made a superstar by the
women of America who flocked to the theaters to see her in
beautiful fashions. The men, however, did not consider her very
sexy, understandable in light of the many sudsy roles she played.
Ladies such as Del Rio and Francis were fashion leaders, and it is
obvious that they had the figures, posture, grace, and poise
necessary to maintain the glamorous images projected by these incredible gowns.

Janet Gaynor in Servant's Entrance *by Fox, 1934. Designer: Rene Hubert*

Joan Crawford and Norma Shearer in
The Women *by MGM, 1939. Designer: Adrian*

Color and texture produced predictable impressions on the screen. For example, white bugle beads usually were worn by characters when a very chic, high-class, ladylike appearance was desired. White beads signified formality, a refined and dignified status. The design worn by Janet Gaynor was white silk crepe, not chiffon, covered by white satin bugle beads. The straight, simple lines helped give the petite Gaynor the illusion of more height. The neck was high in front with low décolletage in back; the cape was removable for dancing and otherwise remained in place.

Black sequins, on the other hand, almost always materialized in the wardrobes of cinema night club singers. Black implied a struggle from lower economic strata and the achievement of limited success. The wearer was worldly-wise and had learned from her experiences. A version of Simone Simon's black jet sequin gown was supposedly added to her own personal wardrobe. Designed for an appearance in a night club sequence, the form-fitting dress had a halter of large rhinestones fastened to the bodice in front. Sequined arm-length gloves and a bird-of-paradise feather in her hair completed the attractive ensemble.

Although Travis Banton often proclaimed "Conspicuousness is the unforgivable sin in the art of dressing," sometimes it was required by the script for the screen costume.

Joan Crawford lost her man in *The Women,* but she still triumphed over Shearer for impact on the audience. Her daring bare midriff and shoulders, plus the overpowering gleam of sequins, was in direct contrast with Shearer's demure little dinner gown with its dainty use of sparkle. This contrast heightened the personality differences of the two screen roles and effectively demonstrates the importance of costume in reinforcing the script. Crawford's design was a modernized version of a girl's dancing dress. The brassiere top and very full, circular skirt were done entirely in gold sequins; a wide belt was emerald-jeweled and embroidered in gold. Shearer's dress was white crepe, the only decoration a wide rhinestone-studded and silver-embroidered belt.

Simone Simon in Josette *by 20th Century-Fox, 1938. Designer: Royer*

Katharine Hepburn in Christopher Strong
by RKO, 1933. Designer: Howard Greer

Chiffon is a sheer, lightweight fabric made from silk, nylon, or other materials that conveys the idea of femininity and delicacy. The material can cling closely to the figure, but its sex appeal is subtle rather than blatant. When an actress was to appear softly feminine, slightly vulnerable, and charming, she was shown in lighter shades of chiffon. Katharine Hepburn's white *mousseline de soie* evening dress had fabric daisies to form cape and flounce. Each daisy had a rhinestone center. For a dance scene, Hepburn held the hem of her frock in one hand, and daisies seemed to fall from her arms to the floor.

Styles for chiffon were usually very modest, with simple flowing skirts. Claudette Colbert's gown of white chiffon had a high bodice with the so-called "new, seductively wide" shoulder straps. The skirt was a soft, sweeping bias sheath over a clinging slip of white crepe. The jewels were diamonds and rubies. When Travis Banton first attempted to design a cinema wardrobe for Colbert, their initial fitting sessions quickly dissolved into a dismal series of small tragedies. Colbert made it quite clear she considered chiffon unbecoming and couldn't abide the floating stuff. She also loathed capes in general and felt they looked hideous on her in particular. After viewing a street-dress design sporting a jaunty bow, she declared that bows were among her really important hates. Banton was stunned but refused to surrender. He became uncharacteristically testy and irascible, his appetite vanished, and he suffered from insomnia, but the completed styles for his first Colbert movie, *The Man from Yesterday,* proved so successful that eventually she became one of his most beautiful and well-dressed stars, and also his very good friend.

Although most often reserved for softly feminine looks, chiffon could also be delicately alluring. Chiffon avoided the obviously sexy look of satin and lacked the stunning effect of sequins, but in certain colors or on certain stars it was effectively exciting. Sandra Storme's extremely glamorous publicity still shows the expert application of chiffon to enhance civilized sensuality. Storme was England's top model and was named Miss Perfection of Beauty by six contemporary artists. She was imported to Hollywood for extra publicity for *Artists and Models.* This particular still was promoted extensively in fan magazines and newspapers.

Claudette Colbert in Bluebeard's Eighth Wife
by Paramount, 1938. Designer: Banton

42

Sandra Storme in Artists and Models
by Paramount, 1937. Designer: Banton

Sketch by Kalloch for Women of Glamour
by Columbia, 1937. Designer: Kalloch

Virginia Bruce in Women of Glamour
by Columbia, 1937. Designer: Kalloch

Jeanette MacDonald in Broadway Serenade
by MGM, 1939. Designer: Adrian

A flowing scarf was the usual complement for a chiffon dress and looked particularly beautiful on the screen if the actress was directed to walk about or was to appear on a breezy balcony. It was very important that materials harmonize with the action of the scene. Often, the movement of a fabric was photographed even before the gown was made. If the director wanted the action to stand out, the dress could not be so striking that it competed with the action. If the gown was to stand out, the designer had to insure that the materials photographed to their best advantage. If the dress was to emphasize the action of a scene, it had to flow with it, or the design had to reinforce a movement. The extremely photogenic, floating quality of chiffon, and chiffon scarves in particular, was a favorite device for just this last purpose.

The still of Robert Kalloch, Columbia's brilliant head designer, shows him putting finishing touches on a gown for Virginia Bruce. The material is dove gray soufflé over silver gray heavy satin, with mauve and gray velvet lilies and a long soufflé scarf forming the bodice. Notice how the sketch emphasizes the flow of the scarf. A blue velvet neck ribbon was replaced by a diamond necklace for the picture.

Complex sleeves were an integral part of the complicated draping on Jeanette MacDonald's flowing chiffon evening ensemble. The draped lines were placed to diminish MacDonald's unusual heaviness. The vertical folds of the capelike sleeves not only caught the eye, but also tended to add height and slim the torso. All gold and pearl accents matched.

Merle Oberons's unusual evening dress featured a full-length black chiffon veil which repeated the black cellophane daisies and scattered single-sequin design of the dress. A youthful sequined bow at the slightly ruffled bodice emphasized the low décolletage. The position of the arm bracelet reinforced the ensemble's exotic quality and Oberon's beauty.

*Merle Oberon in publicity for United Artists,
1935. Designer: Omar Kiam*

Dorothy Lamour for publicity for Swing High, Swing Low *by Paramount, 1937. Designer: Banton*

Fay Wray in It Happened in Hollywood *by Columbia, 1937. Designer: Kalloch*

Lace shared many of the delicate qualities of chiffon. It, too, allowed a star to appear soft and fragile, but in an old-fashioned way. The stills of Dorothy Lamour capture perfectly the mood a lovely, well-designed lace dress could create. The white cotton lace dinner gown for spring was very simple, with a high neckline and extremely low back. The only accent was deep red velvet roses on the bodice of the removable bolero.

Lace was used most often for formal dinner occasions, with see-through sleeves or bodices which also exposed the intricacies and workmanship of the lace designs. Fay Wray's black dinner gown of cobweb lace and net had a circular skirt fashioned with alternating gores of net and lace. The deep décolletage was complemented by the slightly puffed sleeves. The lace pattern was most visible in the long sleeves and bodice.

Lace photographed with few problems, except when the exquisite detail of a rich gown was lost to the camera. Gail Patrick's smart evening gown was silver metallic lace over white satin. The style molded the figure with a deep décolletage held by narrow silver chains over the shoulders. The skirt was outlined with a band of sable at the bottom. The matching swagger jacket, with its wide ruffled collar and slightly puffed sleeves, completed the ensemble.

The work of a cinema designer differed radically from that of a fashion designer in New York or Paris. A fashion designer followed a set routine, for example, spending every winter working on a spring collection. A cinema designer, however, never knew from one day to the next what he would be required to produce. It could be an 1890 or 1780 ensemble, clothes for a chic modern comedy, or costumes for a western. This uncertainty kept designers on the jump, and often they had only a few hours' notice to produce an elaborate gown that would normally take several days to make. For the studio designer there were no such words as "can't" and "impossible." During heavy demands, the wardrobe department was like a fire department, constantly geared to meet emergencies. Once, at Paramount, Lubitsch wanted an evening gown for Dietrich to be ready for the cameras the next morning for a big scene in *Angel.* Banton made a few hurried sketches on the back of an envelope, drove to her house at one A.M. for a fitting, and had the dress ready at seven-thirty the next morning. At nine Dietrich wore it on the set for a take.

Gail Patrick in Smart Girl *by Paramount, 1935.*

46

Vivien Leigh for publicity for Gone with the Wind *by MGM and Selznick, 1939. Designer: Plunkett*

Jean Harlow in Personal Property *by MGM, 1937. Designer: Dolly Tree*

One of the most luxurious materials for cinema was velvet. It definitely added bulk to a figure, but the richness of look and feel was easily appreciated by audiences. The finest velvet was from Lyons, France, and the most popular evening color was black.

Velvet looked best with simple designs that used the heaviness of the fabric to outline or create attractive silhouettes. As shown on these pages, the camera could not distinguish small details in a sea of black, so shapes of collars or skirts, a few large jewels, or a minimum of light accents, such as the white fur bodice trim and ermine tails on Vivian Leigh, were the maximum styling points for elegant velvet creations. Black velvet was perfect for highly dramatic scenes or to convey the rich status of a star or role. Dolly Tree's imaginative neckline, unusual sleeve detail, use of white ermine for a band at the skirt bottom, and voluminous skirt definitely let the audiences know that Harlow was not the sleazy sex kitten she so often portrayed in her early career. She had now graduated to playing more socially prominent roles.

Carole Lombard's black Lyons velvet winter ball gown was designed for her personal wardrobe by Travis Banton, which meant she wore it for publicity and the studio paid for it. The square décolletage was featured with unadorned sharpness. The skirt was outlined with stiff taffeta, and the peplums carried the crisp, definite theme. This still was taken using the hand-painted dining room wall of Banton's own home as a backdrop. Lombard was one star who had no extreme taste in clothing. She enjoyed wearing the latest fashions, but preferred to go even a little ahead in time. A cinema designer had to be able to foretell future trends and create costumes that would remain fashionable until the movie had run its course. Fads were fatal flaws on the screen. The velvet dresses on these pages encompass classic lines that in no way date them as Thirties garments.

Banton's elegant velvet creation on Kitty Carlisle combined a slim, long tunic idea with a voluminous underskirt that was heavy and difficult to maneuver but spectacular in effect.

Bing Crosby and Kitty Carlisle in Here Is My Heart *by Paramount, 1934. Designer: Banton*

Joan Blondell in Gold Diggers of 1937 *by Warner Brothers, 1936. Designer: Orry-Kelly*

Madeleine Carroll in The World Moves On *by Fox, 1934. Designer: Lambert*

Fake or real flowers were a favorite accent for velvet. The subtle dignity of Annabella's black velvet formal was enhanced by the flexible jeweled floral spray of diamonds and rubies on the bodice front and matching bracelet and earrings. The dress was designed for her first American picture and sought to convey a refined, glamorous image.

When it came to color, Orry-Kelly definitely favored the neutral shades, nothing sharp or vibrant for the main body of a garment, although he thought bright colors could be introduced in the trimming. His prime favorite was black. Kelly thought black was dramatic if you wanted to be dramatic, sleek, suave, and subtle if you wanted to be that. He also suggested that underdecoration was far, far better than overdecoration, and just the slightest touch of light relief on a black gown was the most effective.

The blackness of Madeleine Carroll's severely cut and classically styled gown was relieved by the sparkle of diamonds. According to publicity, the diamonds and emeralds of her bracelet and necklace were her own and had been handed down for generations as heirlooms by her husband's family. Carroll's regal gown dipped to a low V in back.

Black was the favorite color for evening velvet. The second favorite was red, as on Joan Blondell, and the second most popular accent was a touch of beading. Orry-Kelly nicknamed Blondell "Rosebud" and designed her festive frock with a tight bodice, puffed sleeves, and a low, square neckline bordered with glittering brilliants. Too many beads caused a dress to appear too massive rather than rich, but a small band or two enhanced the lavishness of the material.

Annabella in The Baroness and the Butler *by 20th Century-Fox, 1938. Designer: Wakeling*

Linda Darnell in Hotel For Women *by 20th Century-Fox, 1939. Designer: Wakeling*

Most of the styles so far have been solid colors or contrasting uses of solid colors. Prints, however, played an important role in the fashion cycles of the Thirties, and cinema designers could not ignore them, even if they sometimes played havoc with the camera. A cinema designer of the Thirties worked with black-and-white film, the quality and sensitivity of which was constantly changing. White could glow badly under the tremendous amount of light poured onto the set because of the less dense films of that time. Successful use of true black-and-white prints depended mainly on the skill of the cameraman. Walter Plunkett remembered:

> In some cases patterns would present problems. For instance, if there was sharp white on a black background, the cameraman might cry about it because he would have to gauze it or shadow it to tone it down. But if it was a yellow on dark red, or something of that sort, it would already be muted enough that it wouldn't vibrate or glare.

Even for still photographs, whites were masked and high contrast prints slightly underexposed.

Edith Head modeled her own print dinner dress for studio publicity purposes. The Oriental influence was evident in the diagonally swirled flowers and high, wide wraparound sash.

Designers could include a touch of print on an otherwise plain costume to add just enough interest so as not to bore the audience or the actress, but not enough to distract from the scene. The slightly printed style on Linda Darnell is lovely, but it would not distract from the central action and was especially good for long scenes calling for a variety of moods or movements.

Joan Bennett's summer dinner dress blended plain and printed fabrics. The dress dipped low in front, with the bodice of navy and white print cut high in back but slashed down the center to the waist. The skirt molded the figure, and an extra print panel was added to the skirt, with a circular cut for fullness.

The evening print on Bette Davis was subdued and muted for the screen. The unusual pattern was bolder than normal for a cinema costume, but the solid-color area above the knees permitted close shots of Davis without distraction by the material. Orry-Kelly, the chief designer at Warner Brothers and a master at cinema technique designing, came to Hollywood from Kiama, Australia. Publicity claimed he linked his first and last names with a hyphen at the request of studio officials, who had wanted someone with a French handle to head their designing department.

Edith Head for publicity at Paramount. Designer: Head

Bette Davis in Golden Arrow *by Warner Brothers, 1936. Designer: Orry-Kelly*

Publicity photo of Joan Bennett for The Texans *by Paramount, 1938. Designer: Newman*

Marian Marsh in The Man Who Lived Twice *by Columbia, 1936. Designer: Kalloch*

Rochelle Hudson in She Had to Eat *by 20th Century-Fox, 1937. Designer: Herschel*

Printed taffetas and damask made lovely evening clothes, but they had shine plus a pattern to be considered.

A question often asked of studio designers was, why did they use beautiful colored gowns when the film was black-and-white? Ernest Schrapps, head designer at Hal Roach Studios, told *Motion Picture Magazine* in July 1937, "It is the psychological effect of colors, and actresses must be in top form at all times." Some actresses reacted positively or negatively to the colors they wore, and all would soon be bored with nothing but grays, black, or white.

Marian Marsh's formal evening wear was composed of French blue upholsterer's satin brocaded in shades of mauve, pink, and peach. The back decolletage was a deep oval, in contrast to the high front neckline with a jabot of blue accordion-pleated *mousseline de soie.* The matching jacket had semi–leg-of-mutton sleeves and a flared peplum.

Rochelle Hudson's dance dress of mauve-blue taffeta had huge "wallpaper" roses of deeper blue and pink. The dress featured a deep off-shoulder neckline accented by clips and a necklace of synthetic sapphires and silver. The life of a star could sometimes be less than glamorous. For example, just before the noon lunch break while filming *She Had to Eat,* a scene required Jack Haley and Hudson to be arrested and handcuffed together. After the take no one could find the key to the handcuffs, so Jack and Rochelle went to the studio café and struggled through two one-arm lunches. The key mysteriously reappeared after lunch.

Some materials had their own inherent patterns which had a slight ripple effect on the camera. Garbo's evening ensemble was stiff green brocade shot with silver. Adrian included many sophisticated styling features in this design, such as an unusual beanie hat, a slim double skirt, and linear fur along the coat sleeves, but none of this could distract from the glamour of the lady herself.

Greta Garbo in Susan Lenox *by MGM, 1931.*
Designer: Adrian

Poster for The Bride and the Best Man by MGM later retitled Gay Bride.

It was estimated that in 1938 motion picture studios in Hollywood spent over $6 million for cinema wardrobes. Each dress, each costume was unique and designed for one star or one extra. Today most of the clothing seen on the screen is rented from huge warehouses like the Western Costume Company.

Cinema designers produced thousands of costumes in the course of a year, and sometimes great minds thought in identical channels. When Norma Shearer was reigning queen at MGM, she was the first major non–sex-symbol star to appear in a clinging bias-cut dress without undergarments. The film was *Let Us Be Gay,* and she created a sensation in 1930. After that, Shearer insisted that Adrian, the studio's brilliant designer, work a white satin bias-cut dress into every one of her succeeding pictures. Adrian affectionately called them ''Norma's nightgowns.'' Dolores Del Rio's gown for *In Caliente* (1935) was remarkably similar to one Shearer wore in *Riptide* (1934). Imitation, for lack of a better word, among the designers was rampant and expected. A designer could not afford to ignore a new neckline or sleeve treatment simply because someone else had adopted it. If a hip bow looked good on Joan Crawford, it might also be effective on Carole Lombard. Few clothes were exact duplicates because the designers were more creative than that, but every conceivable style was tried and applied more than once by each designer. When Walter Plunkett was asked about plagiarism, he answered:

> I'm sure we all plagiarized. If you are following a trend, even if you are not doing it, the movement is in the air, and two designers locked in separate cells can come up with almost the same thing because that is the way people do it. I remember one gal, a designer at MGM. I wanted to borrow a fashion magazine from her to see what things were in, and there was almost nothing left in it. They were all cut out. Anything that was any good was clipped for future reference.

When a costume was recycled by a studio, it was usually altered in some way to prevent identification—by the deletion of sleeves, change of accessories, etc. For publicity stills, new actresses often wore costumes designed by the studio but not suitable for a script or rejected by a star, or they wore reworked older outfits found hanging in studio closets. The striking lamé gown on Lombard appeared in the movie and on publicity posters for the film *The Bride and the Best Man.* Unfortunately, the title was changed to *Gay Bride,* and the lobby poster shown here was discarded. It is interesting to note that two years later the same dress reappeared, this time with a belt and its collar unironed, for publicity for *The Great Ziegfeld.*

A publicity photo for Ziegfeld Follies *by MGM, 1936. Designer: Dolly Tree*

Carole Lombard in Gay Bride *by MGM, 1934.
Designer: Dolly Tree*

Dolores Del Rio in In Caliente *by Warner
Brothers, 1935. Designer: Orry-Kelly*

Norma Shearer in Riptide *by MGM, 1934.
Designer: Adrian*

Florence Rice for publicity for Awakening of Jim Burke *by Columbia, 1935.*

Costumes were remade and reused often, but it was unusual to have the same gown appear publicly more than once without some alteration. The publicity blurb for Glenda Farrell's dress stated that this stunning creation of pale blue embroidered in silver beads was especially designed for her role in *A Man's Castle.* She wore the gown for a musical number, and the rich, beaded dress added credibility to her role as a successful singing star. The blurb also stated that Farrell loved the dress so much that a replica was made for her personal wardrobe. If so, it did not deter Columbia from publicizing Lillian Bond in an identical dress. The same busy belt also graced Carole Lombard's waist in Columbia's 1933 offering called *Brief Moment.*

Often a new or rising star wore an ensemble donated for publicity by a department store like I. Magnin or Robinson's. The dresses were unsuitable for the motion picture screen, but adequate for fashion layouts in women's and fan magazines. This arrangement satisfied nearly everyone: the studio used free clothing, the actress appeared in something new, the store was always credited as the source of the clothes and therefore was rewarded with its own publicity, and the cinema designer was allowed to concentrate on more important assignments and stars. Ready-made clothing for stock shots was not limited by a movie camera, a script, a director, or a character, and the public loved fashion shows in print. The higher the status of the star, the less rack clothing she wore. Norma Shearer, once established at MGM, never wore department store clothes for publicity. Adrian designed her fashions on and off the screen.

Little embarrassments sometimes resulted when the same dress was loaned to two studios. In July 1935, Florence Rice modeled a striped dinner dress for newspaper publicity for her latest Columbia picture. The addition of a belt and the positioning of flower accents were the only details to distinguish her frock from one worn by Rita Cansino (later dubbed Rita Hayworth) for her publicity pose for an upcoming Fox picture, also in 1935. Stripes were a popular styling point for daytime ensembles, but they seldom appeared on the screen for evening. This dinner-dance dress was unusual; close or bold stripes tended to confuse the camera during a high-movement scene such as a dance.

Rita Cansino (later Hayworth) for publicity at Fox, 1935.

Glenda Farrell in Man's Castle *by Columbia,
1933. Designer: Kalloc*

Lillian Bond for publicity for Highway Patrol
by Columbia, 1938. Designer: Kalloch

Simone Simon in Josette *by 20th Century-Fox, 1938. Designer: Royer*

Ann Rutherford in The Devil Is Driving *by Columbia, 1937. Designer: Kalloch*

Emerging women or teenagers were also costumed by the studio designers. The actual age of the actress was not as important as the age of the character in the script. Years could be added or subtracted and womanly figures de-emphasized, if necessary. The general silhouettes kept close to the Paris vogue of the times, but chiffon, tulles, and net were pupular materials to denote youth and innocence, and ruffles an important accent.

The images possible in high school and college styles ranged from ultrasweet and homespun to smart yet youthful, like the prom gowns on Toby Wing and Verna Hillie. Wing's costume combined rough white crepe with a black skirt and bordered the bodice cleverly with pleated black crepe. Hillie was in baby pink satin, with satin roses edging the décolletage and a band of roses emphasizing a high waistline.

Ann Rutherford's powder blue gown included puffy tulle sleeves, shoulder bows, and a huge circular skirt to soften the sophistication of the satin. The frock closed down the front with square rhinestone buttons.

Simone Simon's gay dance frock featured green satin leaves edged with sequins on the skirt and shoulder straps. The bodice, also of green satin, was made ballet-style, fitted closely and coming to a deep point in the center. Flowers and leaves decorated the garden-style hat.

Verna Hillie and Toby Wing in Search For Beauty *by Paramount, 1934. Designer: Banton*

Elissa Landi in I Loved You Wednesday *by Fox,*
1933. Designer: Rita Kaufman

*Norma Shearer for publicity at MGM, 1936.
Designer: Adrian*

Up to now this book has concentrated on the pivotal role of materials in focusing interest and establishing a character's status. Beads and sequins garnered attention, velvet established wealth, chiffon denoted charm. Once a material had been chosen and the basic silhouette decided, the cinema designer could frost the cake and add the styling details that made a gown truly unique and exciting. Again, the limitations of the script and character were always considered first, but an imaginative cinema designer in the Thirties—and they were all imaginative—knew many tricks to create a gown befitting a Hollywood star.

It has already been mentioned that ruffles were applied extensively to denote youth, but their range was much wider than that. Costumes that were certain to have full-length shots and lots of movement were ideal for ruffled skirts. There is a certain rhythm, a certain pizzazz given to a scene when a lovely woman who walks well wears a flouncy, ruffled evening dress that can tease and delight innocently or openly.

Movement was also sought for the other gowns on these pages. The flounces on Shearer and Landi were fun to wear, and the swing of the skirts was exciting and provocative. Elissa Landi's "moon shot" dress was *the* evening dress from the movie *I Loved You Wednesday*. Designer Rita Kaufman incorporated pearl-and-brilliant-encrusted chiffon over a cream satin slip; a ruffled chiffon train began on one hip and swirled to the floor. A matching short cape appeared in the movie.

The material for a ruffle was usually light and sheer, like nylon or chiffon, and, it seemed, the smaller the ruffle the better and the more the better. Francis Dee's gown was virtuous white to encourage the idea of youthful innocence, although this image is somewhat lost by Dee's quite womanly pose and look.

Frances Dee in Coming Out Party *by Fox, 1934.
Designer: Rita Kaufman*

Shirley Ross in Devil's Squadron *by Columbia, 1936. Designer: Lange*

Ruffles did not have to be numerous or frothy. Heavier materials were suitable, although the number of ruffles was then severely curtailed and the effect very different. The idea of youth still applied to the canary-colored, embroidered organdy dance frock on Anita Louise. This spring costume featured a one-sided motif that had a stiffened cape of organdy ruffles high on one shoulder while the other was bared to a lei of forget-me-nots. A similar ruffle cut diagonally down the slim upper skirt and released the lower fullness. A royal blue taffeta wrap repeated the ruffle theme around the shoulders with an offsetting collar ruffle. Walter Plunkett described Anita Louise this way:

> Perfectly beautiful girl. Not a very good figure. She had a long, long neck and a long and slim torso, not much curve to it, but a gorgeous face. If you wrapped that body and accented the face you had something magnificent.

Taffeta skirts, large, stiffened bows, and ruffles were a few fashion points that sometimes caused havoc with the soundman on the set. The microphones were extremely sensitive and would actually amplify and record the rustle of skirts and ruffles. Cary Grant recalled that filming for *His Girl Friday* was temporarily halted because the soundman was going wild over a strange noise coming through the mikes. After a thorough search it was discovered that the alpaca lining in Grant's suit was making a 'sch sch'' sound that no one heard consciously except the soundman and his microphones. The suit was immediately relined.

Not frequently used because of a tendency to add too much emphasis to shoulders, the halter-type neckline could be modified for highly imaginative evening wear. Shirley Ross's smart dress was black phosphora satin with a pleated neckline of black net. The low-plunging décolletage in front was saved by a tactically large diamond pin. The wide black ruffles not only framed Ross's face, but also narrowed and followed the bodice out to a deeper dip in back. The relative modesty of the front would catch most fans unprepared for the pleasant shock of the bare back.

Anita Louise in Bachelor of Arts *by Fox, 1934.*
Designer: Lillian

Rosalind Russell in The Bishop Misbehaves
by MGM, 1935. Designer: Dolly Tree

Margaret Sullavan in Next Time We Love
by Universal, 1936. Designer: Vera West

For sheer freedom of movement, pleated evening skirts were comparable to ruffled ones. Ruffles could hide a multitude of posterior sins, as could pleats, but pleats gave a straighter, less broken silhouette. Styles on these two pages show the range of fabrics that could be pleated successfully.

Margaret Sullavan's highly imaginative evening outfit of accordion-pleated pink crepe featured a stunning circular cape and tiered skirt. Flowers were popular Thirties accents, and their combination with jewelry was not unusual. The only fault with this ensemble is the overuse of contrasting accents (fake and real flowers, dull jade beads and sparkling diamond bracelets) which detract from an otherwise chic and glamorous still. Vera West, who designed the gown, commented about this problem of proper jewelry to *Motion Picture Studio Insider* in June 1935:

> In the matter of jewelry, it is a temptation to many women to overload with costume jewelry. On the screen this is dangerous. One piece too many will make a woman look overdressed. It is sometimes difficult to get an actress to forego wearing a favorite piece of jewelry, and frequently she will add it to her costume after reaching the set, but I try to impress upon her that every line in a costume means something and if she disturbs the line she is losing something from her own personality.
>
> Rings rarely photograph well. They do not add to the beauty of the hand and if it is not beautiful, it calls attention to it.

Flowers and glitter also appeared on Rosalind Russell, but the effect was more unified. The glitter of the bracelets complemented the belts, and the flowers highlighted the soft ruffles of the collar. High bodices and covered shoulders for the theater or a formal dinner were common for pleated dresses, as was chiffon fashioned to float in some way around or behind the wearer. The huge bat sleeves and long train made Russell's costume cinematically more interesting.

Dramatic and exotic for Norma Shearer was this exciting pleated evening costume. Here an overabundance of heavy jewelry fit perfectly with the tongue-in-cheek mood of the movie and this particular ensemble. Shearer had a problem with a cast in one of her eyes which was noticeable during heavy dramatic scenes when she was angry or excited. It is doubtful, however, if anyone in the audience would have noticed anything less than perfect about this lady when she was in this dress.

Norma Shearer in Idiot's Delight *by MGM, 1939.*
Designer: Adrian

Humphrey Bogart and Bette Davis in Marked Woman *by Warner Brothers, 1937. Designer: Orry-Kelly*

Fringe, another style technique, could be slightly stunning, or strikingly subtle, as on Bette Davis. Fringe could be tiered and made of crystal bugle beads, or flat crepe, as on Del Rio. In all cases fringe was a detail made for movement, intended to draw the eye of the audience.

The enormous pin on Jean Harlow's dress for *China Seas* is another styling tool used frequently by Adrian. Large pins on an otherwise simple design added a touch of completeness to an imaginative gown. Harlow's pin was fashioned from antique silver; her fringe was silk. For *China Seas,* MGM imported real sampans and junks, and at least half of Los Angeles's Chinatown was brought in for background. All over the lot signs were posted in Chinese so the new extras would not get lost. MGM also constructed the largest ship ever built on a lot at that time, with an 800-foot-long main deck. The ship, correct in all details, was called the ''Kin Lung.''

Dolores Del Rio's intriguing fringe costume demonstrated a traditional Spanish look modified for the screen. The raised neck detail borrowed an African flair, and the braided trim of the dropped shoulders recalled a military influence.

Orry-Kelly's exciting white fringe ensemble on Bette Davis was devoid of distracting jewelry. The short bolero jacket covered a simple, narrow-strapped, bare-shouldered top. Elaborate styling was unnecessary and unwanted when the basic material of the design was already this flashy.

Howard Greer discussed the problems of dramatic designing in his biography, *Designing Male.* He said:

Designing for the silver screen is a highly specialized talent. The dramatic flare necessary on film is often too flamboyant and exaggerated for private wear, and, by the same token, subtleties of color, fabric, and drapery in three-dimensional clothes can be utterly devoid of personality and interest before the camera.

Another major complication arose from the difference between real and movie time. In the real world, a woman appearing at a dinner party could be observed for hours, at all angles, full-length as well as close up. Onlookers would have ample time to notice the color and material and decide if the lines were good or bad. But in pictures, an entire evening of impressions had to be given in a few shots, often in a few seconds on the screen. Many times the complete ensemble was never seen but still had to be implied.

Jean Harlow in China Seas *by MGM, 1935. Designer: Adrian*

Dolores Del Rio in In Caliente *by Warner Brothers, 1935. Designer: Orry-Kelly*

Claire Trevor for publicity for Fox, 1934. Designer: Rene Hubert

Necklines, or the lack of them, were important features in a female screen character's wardrobe. Many scenes called for waist-up camera angles only, so the designers concentrated on neck or sleeve detail. Of course the skirt could not be completely ignored because important personages such as Louella Parsons might visit the set. No studio wanted their top stars publicized as being in a satin top and muslin bottom. Unusual necklines, special sleeves, accented waists, and jewelry all helped an actress gain and hold the interest of the audience in addition to looking fashionable and possibly hiding a physical defect or two from the prying, close-in camera.

A good example of a mundane item developed extraordinarily for effect is Rene Hubert's use of kerchiefs for neck detail on Claire Trevor. Trevor's dress was inspired by the Empress Carlota of Mexico and combined *ivoire* crepe with *noir* taffeta. The gown has a center back décolletage, held in place with suspenders of tiny gardenias, and featured a scarf of crepe knotted casually in front and an open-front bouffant skirt that tied about the normal waist, over a crepe foundation. The result, according to publicity, was "youthful and delightfully quaint."

The cut of Dorothy Lamour's sequined dress demonstrates the enigma of censorship. The narrow center strip covering the cleavage area was sufficient to rate the gown modest according to the Hays Office decency codes, even though an interesting portion of chest is still visible.

More unusual was the elevated off-shoulder idea on Mary Pickford, held by gold and beaded trim matching the bodice design of the dress. Howard Greer, who continued to design for motion pictures even after he opened his own couture salon in Los Angeles, described Mary Pickford to *Modern Screen Magazine* in January 1934 as

> . . . one of my most particular and exacting customers. She takes an almost fanatical care in choosing of models and materials but once she has chosen, she does not change her mind. She is small in stature and knows that a dress which looks well on a girl several inches taller than she will not look well on her unless carried out with proportionate changes. Miss Pickford is almost maddeningly meticulous in her demands for cutting down the width of bands, belts, and ruffles to two-thirds of their measurements on the original models.

Despite this, Pickford was a Greer favorite.

Mary Pickford for publicity at United Artists, 1933. Designer: Adrian

70

Dorothy Lamour in a publicity photo for Jungle
Princess *by Paramount, 1936. Designer: Head*

Necklines could vary from high and demure to intriguingly open. The provocative still of Virginia Bruce shows discreet use of accessories, in this case a cascade of artificial flowers, to camouflage censorable cleavage. Wide, lavish ruffles emphasized the bare, low neckline of this stunning mid-Thirties style. Required movement on screen was simplified by the full lower skirt, but the figure was still accentuated by the molded waist and hips.

Virginia Bruce was one of the true beauties of the Thirties, and Walter Plunkett remembers her this way:

> Oh, that was a beautiful figure. Great style. I was so thrilled when she was cast [in a picture I designed] because I had admired her so for her ability to wear clothes. I was just overwhelmed by her beauty when she came into my office. Her skin was so much more beautiful than it ever looked on the screen. The camera never caught it. There was a translucence that was almost as though there was a backlight. It was almost a glow. Gorgeous complexion, beautiful skin. The camera made her just look like a nice face, never the real exciting beauty that she had.

An open neckline, with low décolletage, added much to a scene, particularly a close-up, but Cary Grant remembers the problems it could cause for the leading man. Because of the intense light on the set and the quality of film then in use, actresses had full make-up not only for their faces, but down to their dress tops, wherever that was. The camera was able to detect the line between make-up and no make-up on the neck or around the face, so uniform body make-up had to be applied to all exposed surfaces. During an embrace with an actress in low décolletage, with body make-up even on her arms, the lapels on Grant's dinner coats would become covered with the stuff, which was extremely difficult to remove. If additional scenes were to be filmed that day, it was necessary to have another suit ready.

Ann Sheridan, the "Ooomph Girl" of the Forties, was a rising star in the late Thirties, and her overall image was enhanced by wearing this lovely satin-and-sequin dress. Although deceptively simple, the bared back and sides were sensational and appropriate style points for the character played by Sheridan in the *Broadway Musketeers.* Howard Shoup, the designer, followed the following credo:

> I feel that a dress is only a background for the girl wearing it. I have never tried to startle or disturb an audience with a gown that would distract attention from a performance. I study a script and the characterization. Then I study the actress and, having arrived at a conception, I made my sketches.

Virginia Bruce in Times Square Lady *by MGM, 1935. Designer: Dolly Tree*

Joan Crawford in Letty Lynton by MGM, 1932.
Designer: Adrian

It is impossible to discuss the impact of sleeve styles on cinema designing without first considering one star and designer: Joan Crawford and Adrian. More has been written about Crawford's shoulders and Adrian's brilliant emphasis of them than almost any other aspect of Thirties cinema styles—with the general exception of beads, sequins, and bias satin. Schiaparelli, a Parisian fashion designer, first introduced the padded-shoulder-and-puffed-sleeve look in 1930, and in fact puffy sleeves were seen thereafter on the screen, but the line remained largely indistinct until Crawford created a fashion sensation in her famous *Letty Lynton* dress.

Adrian looked at a star as a doctor looks at a patient. He would assess the flaws and consider how to conceal or treat them. Actually, that was the job of all cinema designers, but Adrian not only corrected deformities, he sometimes exaggerated them for effect. In no way can Joan Crawford be said to have been deformed, but it was true that according to the ideal silhouette of the early Thirties, Crawford's shoulders were wide in proportion to her hips. Schiaparelli, on the other hand, preferred broad-shouldered, slim-hipped models and led the push along with Mainbocher, another fashion designer, for the padded-shoulder look in the late Thirties and early Forties. By then Crawford had had a significant impact on shoulder fashion trends. The popularity of the padded-shoulder-and-puffy-sleeve look is attributed to Crawford and Adrian.

Adrian extended his imaginative native skill to express, when possible, the exotic and dramatic note in costumes. For example, the slimmest of all velvet wraps was the black velvet coat worn by Crawford. Actually a short jacket which ended at the waist to reveal the plain velvet skirt of the dress, the coat look was possible because of the camera's inability to discern details on black velvet. The jacket did not have wide sleeves but did display the dramatic Adrian touch of burnt ostrich feathers above the elbow and large, square, jewel-studded buttons off-center down the bodice. Only the circular lower skirt exhibited a lavish use of material on an otherwise slim silhouette.

Shiela O'Brien, president of the Costume Designers Guild, and many others believe that Joan Crawford had more fashion impact than any other female star because Adrian did great things with her. O'Brien said:

> [Adrian used] bizarre cuts and different things but they were so right because she was always the poor girl who married the rich guy and got all the beautiful clothes, or the rich girl who married the chauffeur and still got all the clothes.

Joan Crawford in Sadie McKee by MGM, 1934.
Designer: Adrian

Joan Crawford in Letty Lynton *by MGM, 1932.*
Designer: Adrian

Joan Crawford in Chained *by MGM, 1934.*
Designer: Adrian

Wendy Barrie in Feather in Her Hat
by Columbia, 1935. Designer: Murray Mayer

Fay Wray in Murder in Greenwich Village
by Columbia, 1937. Designer: Kalloch

The visual impact of large and puffy shoulders was effective on other stars. Dramatic and eye-catching, the elaborate sleeves on Gloria Stuart provided the bulk of styling points for her screen costume. Organdy and chiffon and high-contrast colors were sufficient to rivet attention with a minimum of fuss. Stuart was a former newspaperwoman from Carmel, California. She worked on a small weekly there for two years just before her screen career.

Tiny strands of Nile green tulle, hand-rolled, formed the extravagant sleeves and skirt on Wendy Barrie's evening frock. Crystal beads with green sequin zigzags composed the remainder of the dress. Publicity claimed Wendy Barrie was given a contract because a director admired the way she handled her knife and fork in a London restaurant.

Fay Wray's gown with striking wing sleeves of black chantilly lace with white soufflé was doubly fascinating because it combined the attractiveness of the large sleeve with the appeal of lace and the contrast of black and white. White poppies with shaded centers partially concealed the V-décolletage and black velvet belt. The only jewelry was two diamond bracelets.

Magnified sleeves, extremes in necklines, enormous puffs, and ruffles all had to be worn by the actress as if they were today's jeans. The screen required that she be perfectly at ease in her costume and lose the awareness of it except to reinforce the character. Kalloch confided to *Motion Picture Studio Insider* in July 1937:

> This trick is habit with a star who, after being fitted to a gown, wears it long enough to become used to walking, sitting, and gesturing in it. This is particularly true of evening gowns, which should be worn with an air of nonchalance in order to have the wearer seem perfectly in keeping with her dress. This is also a particularly good rule for hats, which must be studied to be worn correctly.

Constance Bennett, Cary Grant, and Roland Young in Topper *by MGM, 1937. Designer: Adrian*

The evening dresses on these two pages present a few sleeve designs that produced fashionable results on screen.

The scene still of Constance Bennett in *Topper* particularly demonstrates the effectiveness of a costume detail, in this case the shape of the sleeves, to keynote a scene and emphasize an action while not unduly distracting the audience. The wide batwing lines of the sleeves could not be worn by everyone because of the tendency to add too much bulk to the shoulders and sides. For the elaborate resort hotel that was a key set for the movie *Topper*, Hal Roach's new sound stage was used. The set was 180 feet by 120 feet, ceilings were forty feet high and required ten miles of satin to drape, and there were more than two hundred feet of ornamental railings made of glass.

Black velvet and white fringe blended to create the stunning theater dress on Mary Brian. The cut-out shoulder idea and long fringe were exciting styling features. Only the hat dates this costume as early Thirties.

Loretta Young's stunning dinner dress was crepe Roma in imperial blue. Draped folds of the material were lavishly used in the long sleeves, high neckine, and overskirt, producing an unusual effect. The wide bracelets of blue and crystal stones were her only adornment. The draping was strategically designed to preserve the slimness of Young's figure while maintaining an image of extravagant elegance. Loretta Young worked hard at being one of Cinemaland's leading clotheshorses, but she also enjoyed a good roll in the mud if necessary. In *Love Is News,* Tyrone Power deliberately dropped her into mud for a scene—real, slimy mud. The scene was shot nine times, and each time Young was dumped into the mud, hauled out, bathed, and beautified for another take.

Loretta Young in Second Honeymoon *by 20th Century-Fox, 1937. Designer: Wakeling*

Mary Brian in Hard to Handle *by Warner Brothers, 1933. Designer: Orry-Kelly*

Norma Shearer and Clark Cable in Idiot's Delight *by MGM, 1939. Designer: Adrian*

A highly sophisticated shoulder/sleeve style was the one-shoulder look. Norma Shearer in *Idiot's Delight* played an ultra-urbane, worldly wise role, and this treatment elegantly conveys that idea with a dash of Greek classicism in drape and trim to enhance the effect. Norma Shearer was one of the studio's most important stars; Adrian made her waist higher and lowered her hemline because Shearer had short legs and ample hips. Estimates of Adrian's salary at MGM range from a high of $75,000 a year reported by Hedda Hopper to $1,000 a week noted by a studio publicity flyer. When he quit MGM after the decline in glamour and budgets, Adrian opened his own couture shop in 1941. His suit prices started at $135.

The one-shoulder look was particularly effective in black satin and on Marguerite Churchill's glamorous gown. Fitted princess lines and diagonal décolletage both front and back were finished by a large wing faced with French nude satin and caught at the shoulder with a jeweled clip. The skirt, with fantail inset in back, had a diagonal treatment in the front which rose to the knee on the left side and was also faced with matching satin.

Bebe Daniels was costumed by Travis Banton for over five years. She was levelheaded, easy to laugh, and had a slim cinema figure. Her mother, Phyllis Daniels, was one of the few maternal influences Banton ever welcomed in his fitting room. Many of Daniels's fittings were complicated by crutches and bandages because she was constantly in a state of convalescence from some accident. In spite of broken bones and lacerations that sent her to the hospital, she continued to refuse to permit doubles to take the tumbles and jumps for her. Bebe Daniels's fitted chiffon gown had a huge "flower" of chiffon accenting the one-shoulder style with a subdued print pattern that also led the eye upward and to her left. The overall impact of this still was a swirl or circular theme led by the dress itself but reinforced with the pose by the photographer. It was the studio still photographer's job to enhance the beauty of his subject, and most photograhers therefore cooperated fully with the designer to show the style points of a costume in the best possible pose and light. This time-consuming attention to detail is at a premium today. Studios curtailed taking and releasing fashion stills in the late Forties, except for particular stars or fashionable movies. Today studio-released stills are unposed, most often candid, and usually out of focus.

Bebe Daniels for publicity for 1st National, 1931. Designer: Luick

Marguerite Churchill for publicity for Legion of Terror *by Columbia, 1936. Designer: Kalloch*

Marion Davies in Five and Ten *by MGM, 1931, Designer: Adrian*

Although designers generally spent the majority of their time concentrating on front detail, the back of a gown could not be ignored, particularly if a star was to exit dramatically with her back to the audience, dance, or confront a foe. Drapes, ruffles, and flounces were extremely effective when the star moved around in a scene, either pacing or dancing; usually the fronts of these gowns were simple so as not to detract from the back detail. Full emphasis to the back of the dress is admirably demonstrated by Adrian's creation for Marion Davies, which, despite the many styling details, appears visually polished and elegant. A job in a Marion Davies movie was considered a plum because time meant nothing and cast and crew salaries continued for weeks. Most Davies movies took months to film, habitually ran over budget, and lost money, but William R. Hearst picked up the entire tab, including Davies's salary of $10,000 a week. Hearst also provided unlimited publicity in his publications, which included Hearst columnist Louella Parsons.

Pins, visible only from the back as on Bette Davis, also engaged the audience's attention and were very smart for evening.

Use of lamé and unusual lines were also fashionable, on screen and off. Rochelle Hudson's dance frock was navy blue taffeta brocaded in gold crossbar designs. Gold lame formed the surplice front and laced into the back bodice, where it ended in a huge, flat bow.

Although the costumes on these pages were not simple, a designer was safest with classic lines. The job of a regular fashion designer was to change fashion and encourage new trends and wardrobes. The cinema costume designer faced the prospect that audiences, even in rural areas, would recognize that a gown was too faddish and dated if the movie's release was delayed. When audiences were more concerned about the character's outmoded clothes rather than the scene, then the prime directive for a cinema designer—to serve the needs of the script by authenticating the character—would be violated. That was one reason why many of the fashions in this chapter, in this book, were classic and could be worn today.

Rochelle Hudson in Walls of Gold *by Fox, 1933.*
Designer: Royer

Constance Bennett in Bought *by Warner Brothers, 1931. Designer: Luick*

An exquisite hallmark of Thirties glamour was the fully backless dress. Although most costumes were designed for front exposure, when the director and the script allowed, a completely bare back became a dramatic highlight.

Nothing conveyed the idea of sophistication in evening wear quite as excitingly or as fashionably as low back décolletage, but the effect was modified to suit the star. Joan Bennett, for example, appears as a charming and lovely woman, hardly a seductress, even though the cut of the back is extremely low. The designer used the mellowing influence of material and Bennett herself to produce an almost innocent look. Note how the dark straps cut through the skirt waist to form an appealing bow.

The backless style has ranged from the first modest attempts using nude souffle in the Twenties to décolletage that plummeted well below the waist on Marilyn Monroe in *Some Like It Hot* in 1959. In the Thirties the boundary line for good taste was just above the waist. Anything below that lost the sophisticated image and simply shocked the audiences. The low V-décolletage was popular for very formal evening wear and spanned the entire decade and all seasons.

The backless look highlighted a beautiful back; protruding bones or other imperfections could not be tolerated. Of course, to every rule there are exceptions. Constance Bennett's spine was misproportioned, but Adrian, instead of camouflaging it, first flaunted it with good effect. Other designers continued the look for Bennett. This backless evening gown was eggshell taffeta, molded by tucking through the hips but with a wide flounce. Moderate bead trimming edged the low back decolletage. Gwen Wakeling remembered that designing for Constance Bennett was always interesting:

> Constance Bennett was extremely chic. She was very well born, good socioeconomic background. She knew clothes and had a lot of character of her own. She was no rubber stamp or piece of putty. She was also very funny. She and Sidney Landfield did not get along very well; she did not think he was a very good director, and she didn't like the way he did scenes. One time we were having a fitting in her dressing room at Goldwyn, when she was with Zanuck. She wore a very pale, silver gray satin evening gown. Sidney came in and I sort of withdrew into the background. I could see the sparks fly. She would do it deliberately, she would scream like a banshee and carry on. And in the middle of a scream she came back into the other room and said "Got to get this dress off me because when I do these things I perspire and I don't want to perspire on the dress." She knew exactly what she was doing—a consummate actress at all times—to get her own way.

It would seem that a splendid bare back needed little emphasis to catch and hold the audience's interest, but when the script allowed a designer freer reign, stunning details would be added to gain exclusive attention for the star. An excellent example is Karen Morley's exquisite formal evening ensemble, which used contrasting colors of black and off-white as well as contrasting materials of flat crepe and bugle beads to create a strikingly classic, simple, and successful gown. The spangled yoke finished a cape effect in back that continued around to the waist. The dress also had an impressive train.

Two less common styles of the Thirties were the scarf-stole accessory and fur-trimmed skirt bottoms.

Dolores Del Rio wore a variety of materials, styles, and effects possible with stoles or shawls, ranging from Greek to Arabic to Mexican Indian. The deep border motif on the gown shown here was adopted from an old Mexican design. The basic dresses were usually white or off-white to contrast with and enhance Del Rio's flawless olive skin, and the bold colors and lines of the shawls created the necessary interest for garnering attention. When asked about Del Rio, Orry-Kelly remarked to *Modern Screen Magazine* in 1935:

> White is Dolores Del Rio's best color. At least 90% of her wardrobe (for *I Live for Love*) is in white and instead of making her look larger as white is prone to do on the screen, it makes her look slimmer and taller. Next to white I like black for her, black velvet especially is becoming either with or without relief of white.

The fur-bottomed skirt was almost the exclusive prerogative of Mae West, although other stars sometimes attempted it. Lavish fur bands took enormous control and effort to dominate and to avoid embarrassing headlong plunges and trips. West liked the style and could handle it. The beaded gown from *Goin' to Town* was especially cumbersome because of the heavy weight of the beading, the fullness of the lower skirt, and the added movement from the fur. Mae West created a style that was unique for the Thirties. The hourglass figure was fashionably unacceptable, but West flaunted and accentuated hers. Lavish fur and jewelry did appear on the screen, but not to the extent West wore them. Her entire wardrobe, on screen and off, exhibited only a nod to Paris and New York dictates, but somehow they always looked right on her. She was a remarkable thorn in fashion's side, but she was Mae West, and it suited her just fine.

Dolores Del Rio in I Live for Love *by Warner Brothers, 1935. Designer: Orry-Kelly*

Loretta Young in Wife, Doctor, Nurse *by 20th Century-Fox, 1937. Designer: Wakeling*

Florence Rice in Vacation from Love *by MGM, 1938. Designer: Adrian*

Although the slim silhouette is the usual stereotype for a Thirties gown, the full or "romantic" look began to be stylish in the mid-Thirties and was the vogue by the late Thirties. Initially reserved for dance frocks, the circular look added great swirl and movement to a scene.

Florence Rice's sky blue *mousseline de soie* gown was made for an evening of dancing, complete with streamers over the left shoulder and a hoop underneath the bouffant skirt. The gown was accordion-pleated and sprinkled with paillettes, the belt wide and interlaced.

The lovely moonlight creation on Loretta Young, from *Wife, Doctor, and Nurse,* had manifold layers of white tulle embroidered in silver bugle beads and tiny mirrors. The bodice was contrived from deep folds of the tulle and had a flexible floral piece of rhinestones marking the center. The skirt was six layers deep.

After long and boring hours on a set, some stars and some film crews formed a cameraderie that lasted for years. While filming *Private Number,* Loretta Young had a ten-dollar bet with director Roy Del Ruth and cameraman Peveral Marley that she could swim underwater for a quarter of a mile. Losing after ten feet, she promised to be a good sport and come across with the money. The next morning director Del Ruth was presented with a canvas bag containing a thousand pennies. Marley received a long legal document, witnessed by twenty crewmen, which he had to sign in receipt of ten brand-new one dollar bills, beautifully framed fanwise under glass.

Virginia Grey modeled the latest in an upswept hair-do and looked fragile and romantic despite the black color of her tulle dress. A wide, sequined, high-waisted belt and scattered large sequins gave subdued sparkle to this charming design.

Virginia Grey in Broadway Serenade *by MGM, 1939. Designer: Adrian*

Ginger Rogers in Shall We Dance? *by RKO, 1937. Designer: Irene*

Ginger Rogers and Fred Astaire in Shall We Dance? *by RKO, 1937. Designer: Greer*

When Walter Plunkett first designed for Ginger Rogers in her dancing roles with Fred Astaire, he was faced with the problem of the fashionable slim look for evening versus the need for freedom of movement during a strenuous dance sequence. The results were lovely creations that not only smoothly molded themselves around Rogers's perfect cinema figure, but billowed, swirled, and flowed during her dynamic numbers with Astaire. Because Plunkett's styles were so effective, other designers, even those in Paris, took notice and continued his ideas.

In designing for Rogers, Plunkett worked with Hermes Pan, Astaire's choreographer. About Pan, Plunkett remembered: "We always collaborated. You go and see the rehearsal, and sometimes during the rehearsal you could see someone doing something and say, 'Wouldn't it be great to have the costume do something at the same time.'" Sometimes—rarely—there were problems. Rogers's sumptuous beaded gown from *Follow the Fleet* looked magnificent on the screen, but it was a real pain to Astaire. The gown featured the famous full, heavy sleeves which swatted Astaire in the face on the first take. Although well over twenty more full dance sequences were filmed, Astaire's understandable caution to avoid the flying weights of the beaded sleeves seemed obvious to him. The first take, complete with swat, was kept in the movie.

Rogers had a perfect figure and was a joy to dress, but she did present one problem for the designer. Again, Plunkett:

> It was wonderful as far as Ginger's figure and her ability to wear clothes were concerned. Ginger was a little inclined to think that no matter how elaborate the dress was, it just wasn't quite elaborate enough, so you had to stick around until it was established on the film to make sure that she hadn't put some flowers or an extra piece of jewelry, or a ribbon in her hair.

The Astaire-Rogers team was an enormous hit in their first movie together, *Flying Down to Rio,* even though they were not the stars. Afterwards their musicals set high standards of sophistication appreciated even today. One criticism often lodged against musicals as a whole is they have too much music, someone is always bursting into song in an incongruous situation. Mark Sandrich, who directed *Shall We Dance,* replied in 1937:

> If I find that a song or a dance does not take the place of an entire sequence in the story, then I discard the song. If that song could be left out of the picture without spoiling part of the story, then I have done my job poorly.

RKO allowed Astaire's imagination relatively free reign, despite the expense. In *Shall We Dance,* Astaire does a dance in a ship's engine room set on steel plates of different thicknesses so they played a tune under his taps like a xylophone. Astaire and Rogers filmed their dances in soft-soled shoes so as not to mar the glossy finishes on most of their dance floors. Later they danced the complete number again to add the tap sounds to the film.

June Lang in International Settlement *by 20th Century-Fox, 1938. Designer: Herschel*

Carole Lombard and Travis Banton in fittings for The Princess Comes Across *by Paramount, 1936. Designer: Banton*

Flared tunics and overskirts were common fashion notes later in the Thirties. The basic skirts could be slim or full as demonstrated by the gowns on these pages. This style required full or at least three-quarter shots to display the tunic adequately, and movement by the actress in her role was optional depending on the fullness of the skirt. Theater or dinner scenes, when the actress was basically stationary, were better for slim-skirted styles.

June Lang's lovely pale pink lace dinner gown had a sweetheart neckline that was popular in the Forties. Lang's "dinner bonnet" was the same lace as the dress, with two shades of violet flowers forming the flat crown.

Full-skirted designs were described as having considerably flaring tunics which echoed the silhouette of the underskirts. These gowns required some movement for optimum impact. Marion Davies's billowing gown of white organdy, with wide set-in bands of eyelet embroidery, had a skirt that trailed in the back to a flaring train. The tunic top mimicked the flaring theme and uneven lines. The shepherdess belt was white taffeta, laced in front.

Myrna Loy's black net-and-velvet-trimmed gown also had the silhouette design of the skirt bottom repeated on the tunic top. Black net hemmed with velvet revealed a slim, plain black crepe innerskirt.

Travis Banton, shown with one of his favorite "models," created this gown of white tulle with full bouffant lines for a crisp summer look. Here the skirt front was full but simple and uneven. The magnificently puffed tunic, which dipped to form the layered back of the gown, took center stage. Banton's preferred look for evening was a bouffant waltz dress of sheer organdy, similar to what Lombard is wearing. A Lombard fitting was no light matter, nor was it done quickly. Lombard paraded for hours in each new outfit before mirrors, wardrobe seamstresses, stockroom girls, beaders, pressers, clerks, stenographers, and typists. New clothes were happy events she wanted to share with everyone. Each dress Teasie (her nickname for Banton) made for her was rapturously described as "DIVINE!"

Myrna Loy in To Mary with Love *by 20th Century-Fox, 1936. Designer: Royer*

Marion Davies in Cain and Mabel *by Warner Brothers, 1936. Designer: Orry-Kelly*

Madeleine Carroll for publicity for Blockade
by United Artists, 1938. Designer: Irene

There were differences in modes between early evening and late, and dinner and cocktail ensembles. During the Thirties, the well-dressed dinner guest always wore a floor-length gown, usually sleeved, preferably with a slim silhouette. Necklines were more chaste than the scantier versions for night-clubbing. Jackets, short and long, bridged the time between cocktails, dinner, and a night on the town. Filmy materials such as chiffon were used with restraint (no woman wants to find part of her shoulder streamers in her soup during a scene), and awkward sleeves with ultrawide cuffs were kept to a minimum. This rule was relaxed if stunning effect was considered more important than practicality and if the wearer was not actually shown trying to eat on-screen. Crepes and woolens were popular, solid colors the favorite. The designs on these pages give a brief glimpse of the variety and similarities exhibited by dinner gowns in general.

Sylvia Sidney's severe evening frock followed an Elizabethan theme to achieve grace and simplicity. Black crepe, softly draped to end in a long train, was highlighted by starched *mousseline* ruches down the back and on the sleeves. Empress Josephine influenced Mariam Hopkins's high-waisted dinner frock, also of rough black crepe. This time shell pink crepe and a cluster of pink roses added color relief. The side-slit skirt was another detail borrowed from the Empress's wardrobe. The stylishness of this still is marred only by the tackiness of the background, a most unusual occurrence in the days of perfected still photography, especially at Paramount.

Madeleine Carroll could wear this cinema evening formal as a guest or as a hostess. Borrowing from housecoat lines, the mock robe clasped at the waist and revealed a simple, slim slip. Corded detailing edged all outlines except the hem. The muted color was a joy to film; the shine was not.

Paramount tested all costumes before filming because the color might not be right for the camera. Raw materials were purchased directly from weavers, but before the sale was made, sample bolts were placed under klieg lights and color-tested. Black-and-white cameras were colorblind, so some reds looked black, pink and light blue photographed white, and brown was tricky.

Miriam Hopkins for publicity at Paramount, 1933. Designer: Banton

Sylvia Sidney in Thirty Day Princess *by Paramount, 1934. Designer: Greer*

Kalloch once said, "Dinner gowns may be as exotic as the individual wearing them." The styles on these pages attest to that. Of course, Marlene Dietrich was in a class unto herself. Hers was not just a glamorous image, but an ultraglamorous aura. Garments outrageous on anyone else were carried routinely by Dietrich. In Edith Head's view, "She dressed to excite attention. Hers was a more sumptuous, more theatrical, more striking look. I mean Dietrich's things were more than fashion—they were superfashion." The satin shawled gown from *Blonde Venus* was a simple little sparkling dinner dress—Dietrich fashion. Although the hat denoted summer, the dress itself, with its heavy beading and perfectly uncomplicated lines, was proper for all seasons and any year. Even more fantastic was the vision of Dietrich in her black satin, bead-and-sable-trimmed ensemble. The pert little satin beret seems out of place amidst the splendor of the rest of the design. Intricate beading glittered not just around the cuffs, but also extended past the elbows. Lavish fur banded two sets of cuffs. Dietrich could sustain the heavy glamour load this outfit conveyed. Few others could. It is difficult to imagine that this cinematic mirage called Dietrich was a down-to-earth lady whose special delight was cooking goulash in her dressing room.

A dark skirt and contrasting top was a well-used style for cocktails and less formal dinner events. Banton's evening ensemble from *Angel* shows his characteristic good taste and classic fashion sense with a basically simple idea (a flared tunic) made elegant but not outlandish by expert engineering and superb workmanship. A slim skirt of midnight blue jersey was topped by a minaret tunic of Persian brocade; the metal cloth reflected bronze, gold, and red tones. It must once again be noted that the gorgeous designs created by masters of costume design were only sketches on paper without the skilled and able execution by a small army of experienced seamstresses and table ladies. Getting Dietrich's tunic to drape and stay just exactly where Banton—and Dietrich—desired, without losing the look and movement of the material, was no simple task. Note the detail of the swooped cuffs over the hands.

Marlene Dietrich and Cary Grant in Blonde Venus *by Paramount, 1932. Designer: Banton*

Marlene Dietrich in Blonde Venus *by Paramount, 1932. Designer: Banton*

Marlene Dietrich in Angel *by Paramount, 1937. Designer: Banton*

Grace Moore in Love Me Forever *by Columbia, 1935. Designer: Kalloch*

Shirley Ross in Thanks for the Memory *by Paramount, 1938. Designer: Head*

A vogue that foreshadowed the Forties' slightly or heavily padded shoulders is shown on Greer Garson. The jacket was the same
silk damask as the dress but outlined the material pattern with
rhinestones to create contrast and interest.

Gold metal cloth and black crepe made the lavish dinner dress
worn by Shirley Ross. The long, slim skirt was ankle-length, with a
slight train in back and topped by a fitted jacket of gold metal cloth
heavily embroidered in gold thread. The jacket was collarless, with a
V neckline fastening down the front, and had a short peplum
trimmed with a wide band of fox. The sleeves were three-quarter
length. A double black fox scarf, matching fox muff, black crepe
sandals, and gold kid gloves completed the outfit. The jewelry was a
wide antique gold bracelet set with garnets and matching earrings.
The thickness of the embroidery added many pounds on screen, yet
despite the obvious expense in time and labor, this ensemble was
seen only briefly in the movie in a mini-fashion show.

Long overjackets were less popular than shorter versions
because the extra length had a tendency to shorten the wearer on
screen and add a bit of bulk. The cocktail dress on Grace Moore, of
black sheer wool with emerald green satin forming the rounded
neckline, had a gleaming "rajah coat" of black and gold paillettes
that matched the buckle on the braided belt.

Gloria Swanson in Music in the Air *by Fox,*
1934. Designer: Hubert

Cocktail dresses as a separate category of apparel reached full acceptance and vogue in the Thirties. The style evolved from fancy afternoon dresses in the late Twenties to more formalized cocktail suits. This fashion was appropriate for evenings beginning with cocktails and happy hours, then an informal dinner usually at a separate location, and possibly a movie to complete the date. A cocktail dress was easy to distinguish from a formal dinner dress by the length of the skirt. In the beginning they were ankle-high, shorter than formals, a bit longer than street wear. Gradually fashionable cocktail suits became the same length as daytime suits but were much more ornate and dressy, with sequins, beads, lamé, and/or fur trim. Cocktail ensembles tended to be closed and modest in contrast to longer formal attire. The hostess of a cocktail party usually chose a full-length dress, not a suit. As time and fashions evolved, even dinner gowns shrank to daytime heights and by the Forties, and wartime, the custom of full-length formals for dinner became less common on the screen.

The jumper-tunic effect on Mona Barrie was stratosphere blue crepe stitched in storm blue (blue-black) thread to match the storm blue velvet vest and sleeves. The mid-Thirties cocktail-length under-skirt was slit to the knees, and the tunic buttoned to its hem in back. A storm blue double-printed felt turban, pearls, and silver fox accessories completed this fashionable ensemble.

Lamé for cinema cocktail dresses and suits was a popular material, when allowed by the script. Rita Hayworth was stunning in gold lame, which designer Kalloch handled like cotton. The style shows the rising hem of the special cocktail outfit. The dress was fashioned in a typical shirtmaker line, with front pleats and a V neckline. Three-quarter sleeves, a gold kid and suede belt, a matching turban with long black fishnet strands reaching to the skirt bottom, and black antelope accessories completed the ensemble. Kalloch designed this outfit to advance Hayworth's glamorous image for her first major movie.

The ensemble on Gloria Swanson is a prime example of a complete cocktail costume—hat, gloves, purse—and the gleaming touches that were characteistic of cocktail suits. Swanson posed in rich wool and lamé sparked with fox, black velvet, and rhinestones. Always a fashion leader, Swanson often wrote articles on cinema costumes in the Twenties and early Thirties. In an interview with *Photoplay Magazine* in 1931, she said:

But above all—actresses are not mannequins displaying gowns. The gowns are to display actresses. A mannequin shows off the gown. A gown, on the screen, shows off the actress. And a gown must show off the specific actress who is wearing it. Gowns which fit their personalities, which fit the action of their pictures; which stand out or retreat according to the demands of that action. And gowns which can do all this despite the loss of the value of color and material.

Rita Hayworth in The Lone Wolf's Daughter
by Columbia, 1938. Designer: Kalloch

Mona Barrie in Mystery Woman *by Fox, 1935.
Designer: Royer*

Carole Lombard *in* Love Before Breakfast
by Universal, 1936. Designer: Banton

Irene Dunne in Theodora Goes Wild *by Columbia, 1936. Designer: Bernard Newman*

Ginger Rogers in Top Hat *by RKO, 1935.
Designer: Bernard Newman*

A cinema designer's work did not stop at creating glamorous evening dresses. Many scripts required him to complete his ensembles with photogenically beautiful, dramatically correct, and fashionably perfect wraps or coats. The possibilities were endless and usually quite luxurious. Among the most lavish materials were ostrich feathers.

Ostrich feathers have been fashionable ever since the first cavewoman spied her first ostrich. Boas of all lengths and colors denote "fun" evening wraps that float and are super eye-catching. Hollywood costume designers employed feathers to manifest happy affluence, to tease, and to be entertaining. An actress could not remain static on the set when decked out in ostrich feathers, and a bounce to her walk was exaggerated by thousands of wispy tendrils that told the audience this was a classy chick.

Travis Banton was once quoted as saying,

> Ostrich plumes are popular, but they must be worn with discretion. If you are going to a garden party or an important tea, they are in place.

Tickling discretion until it was weak, Banton's flamboyant cinema design for Carole Lombard fitted her sophisticated slapstick screen role. As Crawford's figure, image, and roles encouraged Adrian to design highly dramatic, almost bizarre styles for her, Lombard's perfect figure, sporty and gay image, and urbane roles allowed Banton a chance for amusing and imaginative styles that were still within the bounds of fashion and good taste. Lombard's World War I—inspired gown, for example, had an enormously high feathered hat which flagrantly repeated and reinforced the extravagance and humor of the entire ensemble, yet she remained every bit a gorgeous and elegant star.

Ostrich feather wraps were usually capes, as shown on Irene Dunne, because feathers did not lend themselves to sleeves, and even though capes per se were not always fashionable, ostrich capes and boas were never unfashionable. The painting in the still was by Miss Jerry Mulligan, a young Los Angeles artist.

Cinema designers also highlighted musical numbers with plumes, even though the occasional loss of a wisp or two during a turn or dip was distracting to the audience. The blue satin gown with dyed-to-match blue feathers on Ginger Rogers was made for an important dance scene. The semi-full skirt not only permitted movement but was visually thrilling as well. Rogers's feathered dress precluded any wrap which would crush and mar the frothy and wispy theme. In effect, the dress was also the coat.

Gertrude Michael's ensemble featured dyed peacock feathers. The heavily feathered cape was offset by an even more extravagantly plumed skirt, which made walking difficult. Details of the dress front are not visible in this still, but the back dislayed the best view of the billowing, floating motif.

Gertrude Michael for publicity at Paramount, 1934. Designer: Banton

Sally Eilers and Robert Montgomery in Made on Broadway *by MGM, 1933. Designer: Adrian*

Joan Crawford in I Live My Life *by MGM, 1935. Designer: Adrian*

Hollywood designers used a dizzying variety of styles and fabrics to create elegant evening coats in the Thirties. Evening was a time of peak glamour, and the illusion of wealth and lavishness, which the audiences craved, could be maintained without the usual splash of fur by imaginative cuts and rich fabrics.

The few examples on these pages display coats ranging from waist-length, as on Margo, to full-length, as on Constance Bennett. Fabric could be crepe, satin, brocade, velvet, lamé, or any other luxurious material. Sleeves could be full or short; colors light or dark. The diversity was incredible, but all were limited by the requirements of the script and the vision of the director.

Margo's bright royal blue crepe outfit was suitable for long scenes requiring that the action or the male lead have center stage, but the actress not be forgotten or overlooked. The jacket had an uneven line, soft, full sleeves, and an interesting scarf collar. Margo's full name was reported to be Maria Margarita Guadalupe Bastado Castilla Bolado.

Constance Bennett's white Roma crepe evening coat was heavily embroidered in a leaf pattern of gold thread, gold sequins, and gold jeweled discs. Of course the dress beneath was of matching white Roma crepe.

Lavishness sans fur was possible for coats by repeating the rich fabric of the dress, particularly in the case of lamé. Joan Crawford's lamé coat stirred ripples in the audience because of the unusual application of a well-known style. The wrap was an almost exact copy of the popular polo coat. The lapels were exaggerated, but the raglan sleeves, stitched seaming, and sash belt of the original sports coat were faithfully copied in every detail. The oversized collar was extremely effective on a strong presence like Crawford.

Nothing need be said about the incredibly sequined coat on Sally Eilers. For sheer attention-getting it rivaled the most sumptuous of furs. Although the cumulative effect of the brilliant sequins had to be masked and subdued for the camera, the impact remained.

Margo in Winterset *by RKO, 1936.*

Constance Bennett in Service Deluxe *by Universal, 1938. Designer: Irene*

Lynn Bari in Hotel for Women *by 20th Century-Fox, 1939. Designer: Wakeling*

For elegance in evening coats, a timeless favorite has been velvet. As with evening gowns, rich velvet conveys an unmistakable air of affluence and sophistication. Edith Head designed the simple dinner ensemble on Anna May Wong for the holiday season in a movie. The coat was dark green velvet embroidered in gold braid; the Chinese tunic underneath was green rayon satin, and the slip gold lace. The high neckline on the dress showcased frogs of gold braid embroidery encrusted with pearls and green stones. Howard Greer considered Anna May Wong a dressmaker's delight because, according to *Modern Screen Magazine* in February 1934:

> She adores clothes and spends days making up her mind about a thing before she orders it. She plans a coat that will not only match her suit but several dresses as well. She has jackets— often reversible—that can be worn over more than one dinner or evening dress. She keeps to a certain set of color schemes and suits her accessories to several costumes. She has a dozen changes when the average woman would have but four—and it's all because she uses her head and gives real thought to her clothes.

Full-length velvet evening coats seemed to require abundant use of the material, as on Ruth Chatterton, another fashion leader in the early Thirties. Huge voluminous sleeves made this cellophane velvet wrap in a rich garnet shade notable, as did the extralong hem. Garnet clips accentuated the waist, and the neck scarf was garnet silk.

Extravagant, smart, and very, very beautiful is the black velvet evening wrap on Lynn Bari. The remarkably splendid beads, gold thread, and encrusted jewels of the hem and yoke patterns fitted the concept of the cinematic glamour perfectly. The workmanship was, of course, impeccable.

Ruth Chatterton in Lady of Secrets *by Columbia, 1936. Designer: Kalloch*

Anna May Wong in King of Chinatown *by Paramount, 1939. Designer: Head*

Loretta Young in Cafe Metropole *by 20th Century-Fox, 1937. Designer: Royer*

Anita Louise for publicity for Anthony Adverse *by Warner Brothers, 1936. Designer: Milo Anderson*

Loretta Young in Cafe Metropole *by 20th Century-Fox, 1937. Designer: Royer*

Capes were another favorite style of wrap that worked well wth most fabrics. Hoods were effective on the screen for further emphasizing the face of the star, as do the two shown on Anita Louise and Loretta Young. Generally of matching material, capes photographed beautifully in scenes requiring the actress to move across the set. The lovely white lace cape and hood Loretta Young wore floated behind her and made her the envy of every woman in the audience—an effect studios avidly maintained as part of the star quality package. Young's gown was white crepe with a looped and raised skirt. The cape and hood were heavy white *peau d'ange* lace. A multicolored pin and white crepe sandels completed this delicious evening ensemble. Anita Louise's cape of white transparent velvet, lined with white satin, was heavier than lace, but the flow of the cape as Louise walked was regal and compelled attention. Gold trim around the cape's edges and throughout the long tie belt replaced the need for jewelry. The matching velvet dress had a shirred bodice and wide bat sleeves which would have been too bulky and uncomfortable when worn in a regular coat.

Visually capes were dramatic. There is something about an actress clutching a cape that perks up and excites the curiosity of any audience. Unlike a wrap with buttons and sleeves, a star must work to prevent a cape from revealing the secrets beneath it. Capes swirled and flowed, and with fur trim they were exceptionally elegant.

Loretta Young's exquisite and stunning evening wrap of white begheera was draped like a Roman toga and banded with sumptuous white fox. The dress underneath, of heavy white crepe, was also classically designed and draped. Maneuvering this cape for the screen required skill and determination, both of which Young had in abundance. According to Gwen Wakeling, she could manage any article of clothing, no matter the weight, the size, or the swing, as if she were born in it, and the ease with which Young could carry this incredibly glamorous cape belied the hours of practice in and out of doorways and up and down flights of stairs.

Opulence was the hallmark of the Thirties, and cinema designers missed few opportunities to splash a dash or two of fur onto an ensemble. Fur was proper around the clock, even on cinema negligees, but for elegant evening wear it was almost mandatory. In addition to instant identifiction of a character as well-to-do or climbing socially, fur also advanced an image of softness and pampered femininity for the wearer.

The effect of fur trim on a short cape is shown by Jean Harlow. Arms were free to shake hands with other dinner guests or do whatever was required in a scene. A short cape created no pendulum problem as did some wide, fur-trimmed sleeves. The addition of fur most often meant the wrap was to be removed, even if the script did not always provide that opportunity. In *Dinner at Eight,* Harlow, playing a gold digger striving for social prominence, did not remove her fur "cape," which was actually part of the dress and cut to reveal low back décolletage.

A special application of fur trim is modeled by Claudette Colbert: her mist gray chiffon dress was banded with platinum fox on its full skirt. Fox also adorned the cuffs of the silver and gray brocade jacket, which by itself predicted future trends with its close fit and complete closure. Lavish fur one-third the way down the skirt added an enormous amount of width to an already ample skirt, but the delicacy of Colbert's figure was preserved and emphasized by the form-fitting jacket. A full-view shot was imperative for this costume.

Gypsy Rose Lee posed in a beaded and furred evening ensemble that featured a novel muff-purse of white fox to match her short evening jacket. Chiffon studded with rhinestones was draped over a slim satin pencil; a wide band of silver beads formed the attached belt of the dress. Burlesque king Minsky once remarked about Lee, who made her fame as a modest, ladylike stripper, "She drew more pay and took off less than any other of her kind has ever dared."

Barbara Stanwyck's noteworthy evening ensemble was distinguished by unusual and graceful swoops of fur across one shoulder and down one hip. Fur on both shoulders and hips would have been too overpowering for a scene. Note the high and slightly uneven hem in transition from the shorter, irregular lengths of the Twenties. Concerning the budding Stanwyck, Howard Greer confided to *Modern Screen Magazine* in February 1934:

> Almost entirely bored with clothes and goes about in flat heeled shoes and rolled down socks. More than once I have had to fit long formal velvet evening gowns on her and had the shock of looking at the floor to discover, peeping out from under the velvet, dusty sports shoes and white woolen socks.

Since those early days of clothing indifference, Stanwyck has emerged to grace the best-dressed lists all over the world. Her outstanding and continuing sense of glamour and style have never faltered.

*Claudette Colbert, Robert Young, and Melvyn
Douglas in* I Met Him in Paris *by Paramount,
1937. Designer: Banton*

Jean Harlow and Wallace Beery in Dinner at
ght by MGM, 1933. Designer: Adrian

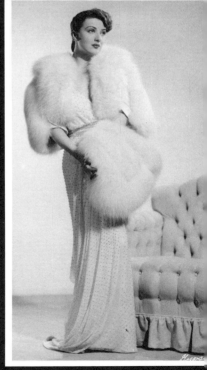

Gypsy Rose Lee in You Can't Have Everythi
by 20th Century-Fox, 1937. Designer: Roye

Constance Bennett and Ben Lyon in Bought *by Warner Brothers, 1931. Designer: Luick*

Adrienne Ames in Woman Wanted *by MGM, 1935. Designer: Dolly Tree*

Irene Dunne in Roberta *by RKO, 1935.*
Designer: Bernard Newman

Fur framing a face was a dramatic plus for any glamour image. The wrap need not be completely fur, just lavish in its collar proportion. It helped of course to have a beautiful face like Constance Bennett's, but how could any audience resist a profile enclosed in mink or sable? The studios abounded with stock girls and chorines, so gorgeous they stopped you in your tracks, who were more attractive than any star but were photographically dull subjects because they didn't have the personality, the inner flame that made a star. The faces in this section had an elusive quality befriended by the cameras and enhanced by unique costume designing.

Fur collars were extremely flattering and provided a very photogenic emphasis of the face. The stunning design on Adrienne Ames used the unusual collars of both dress and wrap to create the main impact on a basically simple ensemble. This dress, with its raised halter neckline, was another "old" costume worn by a chorine in publicity for *The Great Ziegfeld.*

For *Roberta,* Irene Dunne played a chic princess and couturière, so Bernard Newman created many expensive gowns in a fashion tour de force. The gowns cost $250,000; brocaded metal cloth seen in several costumes cost $25 a yard. Dunne's head ornament, shown here, cost $6,000, and the jewels were real. Newman refused to substitute dyed skunk for sable, although that was done frequently. One model in *Roberta's* fashion show wore a full-length wrap of silver fox that cost $19,000. Each costume had its own special shade and gauge of stockings.

The dark fur collar on Constance Bennett contrasted vividly with her light skin and hair and thereby focused attention on her throughout the scene. In a close-up, the frame of fur should have melted any heart. In 1932, when the worst of the Depression assaulted the studios, Constance Bennett was forced to sustain a salary reduction from $350,000 a year to $225,000. Among the other stars, newspapers reported, Ruth Chatterton's earnings dropped from $6,000 to $4,000 a week; Kay Francis's from $2,500 to $1,975 a week, and Loretta Young's from $1,000 to $800 a week.

A goal of the cinema industry during the Thirties was the exploitation of real or imagined beauty for entertainment. Even women at first considered plain bloomed—if they had star quality—under the scrutiny and nurturing of a large studio. The studios in effect were following interesting advice given by Helena Rubinstein, who said in *Cinema Arts Magazine* in July 1937, "Beauty is an art. Practiced in solitude it is worthless. Keep it to yourself and it dies."

Marian Marsh in The Man Who Lived Twice *by Columbia, 1936. Designer: Kalloch*

Jean Harlow in Girl from Missouri *by MGM, 1934. Designer: Adrian*

Una Merkel in Honolulu *by MGM, 1939.*
Designer: Adrian

For the screen, few evening coat designs could match black and white for dramatic highlights. White ermine with dark trim was stunning and polished. In his autobiography, *Designing Male* Howard Greer noted:

> When you strip color and sound and the third dimension from a moving object, you have to make up for the loss with dramatic black and white contrasts and enriched surfaces.

No surface was richer than fur.

A hardly surpassable combination was white ermine and black velvet. Velvet was less bulky than most fur and permitted a slimmer silhouette while effectively complementing and enhancing the lavishness of the fur. Black velvet and white ermine blended with exceptional styling details to create a memorable, smart coat for Jean Harlow. The marvelous ermine half sleeves and high ermine collar and yoke instantly grabbed the audience's attention and favor. Harlow also drew considerable attention when she appeared in her successful role in *Hell's Angels.* Howard Hughes spent $2 million making a silent *Hell's Angels,* then remade it with sound for another $1 million. A different actress was first chosen for the silent version, but Hughes decided to replace her with Harlow and upgrade the role. He coined the phrase ''platinum blonde'' for his new star. Cosmetics irritated Harlow's skin, and she washed her naturally blonde hair every day. She wore slacks and blouses at home and spoke of herself in the third person.

Marian Marsh wore an exquisite ermine cape with ascot scarf fringed with ermine tails to complement her white satin evening gown. The cape was lined with black velvet to provide a striking background and color contrast.

White Russian ermine trimmed with black or brown fur was another evening favorite. The cape on Una Merkel was ermine and kolinsky (Russian weasel) and featured an illusion of square shoulders and a tiny roll collar which could be worn up.

Carole Lombard in The Princess Comes Across *by Paramount, 1936. Designer: Banton*

Joyce Compton in Artists and Models Abroad *by Paramount, 1937.*

Full-length ermine coats were workhorses when it came to creating rich evening images, but mink and fox were also extremely popular. For special occasions and special stars, studio designers often created the styles and had the actual work done by a furrier specialist. Poorer studios most often rented fur coats from a furrier and returned them after use. Few stars complained about wearing these "ready-made" articles.

Little need be said about the cinematic and fashion impact of a full fox wrap. Not as sleek as mink or ermine, the lavish thickness of fox fur happily immersed the wearer in an aura of evening splendor. More common in the Thirties, which is one reason why the fox itself is less common today, the silver fox coat was not quite as elegant as ermine, nor as rich as sable, but it was versatile and heightened almost any character's role in evening scenes.

It must be remembered that ecological thinking in the Thirties was nonexistent, and the slaughter of animals for the sake of fashion was extreme. Fortunately today synthetics can duplicate the prodigal lavishness of almost any fur without the need for this thoughtless butchery.

The most common and adaptable fox coat was modeled by Joyce Compton. Covering day as well as evening wear, this basic style was seen many times on the screen as well as in publicity stills, Despite this, it never lost its ability to project glamour and richness on an ensemble. Joan Bennett's pert, short fox jacket was also flexible for the day and followed the basic tenet that plain was better. The lack of length did not mean it projected richness any less than its longer version.

Strictly tongue-in-cheek Hollywood, Carole Lombard's rather eccentric fur ensemble was wild and delicious, ridiculous and very smart, and it definitely pinpointed Lombard's screen character as a creature apart. Banton enjoyed designing the costumes for this movie because the wardrobe could be all things—charming, extravagant, and a parody of upper-class tastes. Lombard possessed what Banton called "clothes quality." He thought she had the uncanny gift of shrugging herself into any gown, giving it a pat and a twist, and making it devastatingly chic. She moved her body in some mysterious way that made every costume important, whether it was a gingham housedress or a gown of silver.

Joan Bennett in Vogues of 1938 *by United Artists, 1937.*

Katharine Hepburn in Holiday *by Columbia, 1938. Designer: Kalloch*

Accessories could not be overlooked by any cinema designer. The complete ensemble, as a woman would truly wear it, had to be created if the script had her leaving or arriving at a party or evening event. Jewelry was a major requirement for evening and, as shown on Ida Lupino, could encompass not only the usual pins, earrings, bracelets, and necklaces, but hair ornaments, buttons, and belts as well. Scarves applied elegantly, as on Katharine Hepburn, could and did create new fashion mini-trends. This particular cinema costume on Hepburn helped considerably to define her character's role. The scene was a huge formal party to announce Hepburn's cinema sister's engagement to Cary Grant. In a reversal of norm, all the other females at the party were in splashy lamés, beads, and chiffons, with bare styles, and light colors, carrying their soft, flowing handkerchiefs in their bejeweled hands. Hepburn, to emphasize how entirely different she was from this crowd, dressed in plain black and long sleeves, very modest, with her stiffer handkerchief pinned to her left shoulder. The point was obvious. This same gown also showed Hepburn's bare neck, a very rare occurrence. Hepburn considered her neck much too long and unattractive and strongly insisted it be forever covered.

Hats were required to complete any cocktail and most dinner ensembles. If madame were to venture outside her abode for cocktails, she would rather forget her shoes than her hat and gloves. A hat was a fashion necessity, and it was not removed. On these pages are only a couple of the hundreds of possible styles, materials, and moods for evening hats. It was easier for a studio to obtain its hats from department and specialty stores, but occasionally the "right" hat could not be found, or the designer incorporated hat and dress as a single idea. Unlike regular fashion designers, cinema designers were required to design and execute the proper chapeau if deemed necessary by script, director, camera, or star.

In the context of the Thirties, when fashion elegance reigned and ladies dressed beautifully for all times of day or night, an ensemble would be incomplete without the balance of a charming hat. Hats were all shapes and sizes. Claire Trevor's fall hat was paired with a dinner dress called "Reno Rebound." Plum-colored, made of satin and chiffon to match the dress, the hat sported a shallow crown and broad brim.

For Tala Birell's role as a temperamental movie queen, Kalloch designed this stunning evening hat in the manner of an East Indian turban. The basic material was gold and silver net with bands of gold sequins. A fashionable tilt revealed only a glimpse of Birell's blonde hair. Long, dangling earrings augmented the exotic quality of the turban. Robert Kalloch became one of Hollywood's best designers, but his flair for fashion did not make him content. He was described by another designer as a very shy, very sweet person. A very timid person. He was probably happier in his days before he came to Hollywood. Kalloch had great style sense and did gorgeous sketches, but he was so frightened that he could not bear to ride upright in cars. He would lay down in the back seat and put a blanket over his head to be driven to the studio. He was always afraid—afraid of driving in traffic, afraid of everything.

Tala Birell in The Captain Hates the Sea *by Columbia, 1934. Designer: Kalloch*

Ida Lupino in One Rainy Afternoon *by United Artists, 1936. Designer: Omar Kiam*

Claire Trevor in The Mad Game *by Fox, 1933. Designer: Royer, Hat by Dot Gregson*

Chapter Three
Daytime Glamour

Glamour was demanded twenty-four hours a day, and screen roles inevitably required actresses to wear something other than exquisite evening gowns. Day clothing emerged as an important category of apparel for the cinema costume designer. Designing glamorous afternoon ensembles presented particular problems. While the stylist could revel in unbridled fantasy to create stunning evening effects, the day dress or suit had to be somewhat practical—no ostrich feather capes to shed into the midmorning coffee or flowing chiffon to catch in the office machinery. There had to be some semblance of normalcy—no sequined suits for the working-girl role or beaded dresses for the grocery store. Yet even daytime costumes had to be identifiable as part of a beautiful star's wardrobe. Paris and New York clothes did not always meet these requirements. Edith Head explained:

> Our interest was more in making the star attractive than making an attractive dress. That is the difference. In couture it is to make the dress look beautiful and sell. In pictures it was to make the star look the way she should.

And on screen or off, the way she should look was determined by the studio, the roles the actress usually played, and her image. Dietrich's afternoon appearance in public was a far cry from Norma Shearer's style. The images differed as dramatically as did physical capabilities.

Ready-made clothing was used only for publicity purposes on young ingenues still too untested to rate studio designs, on some rising stars appearing in period or costume roles, and occasionally even on a few full-fledged stars like Ginger Rogers (*Modern Screen,* for example, printed a feature story in July 1936 on her trousseau, purchased from New York's finest store). Every movie magazine had at least one and usually two or three features on fashions worn by the stars. Patterns were sometimes offered and homey advice given on how to duplicate a star's glamorous style—on a budget. The fans' desire to see their idols in beautiful clothing was insatiable.

Most of the day clothing seen in publicity releases was created by the studio for an actress in a role. Fashion was not a primary goal; the dictates of the script were uppermost in the minds of all designers. The costume had to establish the character on the screen as quickly as possible, although a little Hollywood embellishment was occasionally added to heighten the star's image. Adrian warned fans in June 1935:

> Don't copy the screen costumes you see exactly, because they are often too "stagey" for the average woman's wear. Our styles for picture purposes are many times the expression of the "mood" of the star in that sequence—and not the expression of the style of the moment—so don't be led astray, and if you copy screen styles, do so in moderation and use the "idea" more than the exact gown or suit that you admire.

This particular article in *Motion Picture Studio Insider* went on to show how Adrian modified one of his Joan Crawford creations into a beautiful adaptation suitable "for the average girl to copy." Studio designers regularly granted interviews to talk about a star, or costume, or movie, or trend. Some, like Adrian, had full-time publicists.

Day clothes had to be rooted in reality because fans identified with this category more than any other. Few women during the Depression had the occasion to wear beaded dresses for evening, but most worked in offices, or went shopping, or attended luncheons. Designers created garments to fit the expectations of the public for that role. On screen a rich woman's shopping ensemble could be swathed in fur, but an average working girl's attire was expected to be more sensible. If the role depicted an executive secretary, the actress would look like an executive secretary, but with a difference. The studio designer might change the blouse a bit so it didn't look completely ready-made or add an interesting style feature to cover or accentuate a physical peculiarity.

The day costumes shown in this chapter demonstrate lavish as well as plain designs. All were dictated by the script, limited by the actress's physical attributes, and directed by her image. The styles from the mid- to late Thirties exhibit a classic timelessness and appear as contemporary today as then. Most so-called fad or fashion features are understated, the transition in trends smooth. The workmanship, materials, and creative imagination are strictly first class. All these qualities are obvious in the still of Ginger Rogers, which also demonstrates the importance of her cinema costume in reinforcing her pretense as the Countess Scharwenka, nee Lizzie Gatz from Indiana, in the movie *Roberta*. Even though she is not a countess, you believe she is a countess because she looks like a countess, a rich, beautiful countess who can afford to be a little daring in the fashion line and wear a polka dot taffeta pom-pom street ensemble. Such a countess would set trends, not follow them.

Day wear, because of its requisite element of realism, was perhaps one of the less glamorized categories of a star's cinema wardrobe, but by no means was it less beautiful or elegant.

Ginger Rogers in Roberta *by RKO, 1935.*
Designer: Newman

Lucille Ball and Manton Moreland in Next Time
I Marry *by RKO, 1938. Designer: Renie*

The ensembles on these two pages forecast the future Forties and echo the past Twenties. Many trends and styles peaked and faded in the interim. This chapter does not attempt to display all vogues seen during the day, but it does present many cinema costumes created for the screen and for publicity.

The two eras of day clothing represented by these outfits show a vast difference not only in outer wear, but in the physical make-up of the models as well. Later years encouraged less obvious make-up, longer and darker hair, blossoming bustlines, and exaggerated shoulders. Skirts became fuller, materials bulkier, and hats broader. Yet some things remained the same. A lady still never went anywhere without the proper chapeau and gloves. The screen designers still enhanced the glamour potential of their stars. The designs still influenced fashion.

Some stars spanned the decades, some would soon be forgotten, and some prepared to vault into the rarefied strata of superstardom. Those actresses whose careers touched the Thirties were a part of Hollywood during its glamorous Golden Era. Unfortunately this Golden Era survived for only a short time. In Howard Shoup's opinion:

> The decline in glamour was due to the decline in the star system. It all goes back to money. Receipts were falling with the advent of radio and the loss of foreign outlets due to the impending war. It became more the style for stars to use their own wardrobes for scenes. Designers' contracts went from seven years, to three years, to one year, to six months, to one picture, to one month—and the designs had to be done and complete in one month.

The stars of the Forties would contend with more reasonable wardrobe budgets, wartime shortages, the desertion of some of Hollywood's finest costume designers, and the deglamorization trend by cost-conscious studios. All this would leave the ladies no less beautiful, but somehow less remarkable and more down-to-earth than their Thirties counterparts.

Thelma Todd in Speak Easily *by MGM, 1932.
Designer: Adrian*

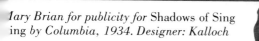

Mary Brian for publicity for Shadows of Sing
ing by Columbia, 1934. Designer: Kalloch

ita Hayworth in publicity at Columbia, 1939.
esigner: Kalloch

Shirley Temple in Curly Top by 20th Century-Fox, 1935. Designer: Rene Hubert

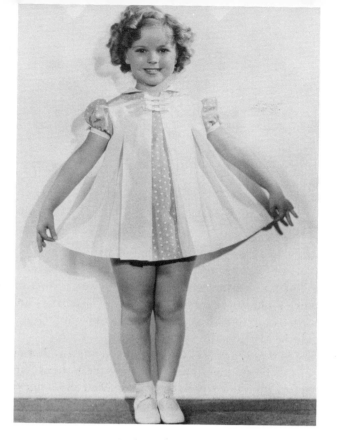

Shirley Temple in Captain January *by 20th Century-Fox, 1936. Designer: Wakeling*

Of all the stars in the vast firmament of Hollywood in the Thirties, few surpassed the fashion impact of a banker's daughter from Santa Monica. Shirley Temple was a phenomenon of her era. The perfect person at the right time and place. She cheered millions of Depression-weary hearts and earned millions of dollars for her studio. Whatever she wore in her movie roles quickly appeared on the backs of multitudes of other little girls. Yet, despite her incredible effect on an entire nation, Shirley Temple remained as sweet and unaffected as her screen roles characterized her, mainly due to the levelheaded guidance of her mother, Gertrude. A grateful studio paid Mrs. Temple $100 a week to teach Shirley her lines, accompany her to the studio sets, and keep watch over a national treasure. Mrs. Temple's six-year-old daughter received $5,000 a week in February 1937. This did not include the scraps of material the wardrobe department saved for Shirley, who regularly used them for doll clothes.

René Hubert designed Shirley's clothes for *Curly Top,* which required eighteen changes, and he noted that every dress made for her cost $35 to $40, or ten times the normal little girl's dress. Shirley was his favorite star, and every costume was given to her when the picture was finished. One classic little girl's dress designed by Hubert was the pink accordion-pleated party-dance frock from *Curly Top.* Dainty maroon velvet ribbons contrasted with the hyacinth pink of the chiffon. The little pumps were white kid, the socks pink.

Shirley's complete and stylish ensemble, topped with a modified black velvet Breton sailor hat, was fashioned from heavy white silk crepe and sheer black velvet. Trimming on the velvet caplet was baby ducklings, hand-embroidered in natural colors. Accessories included the proper white doeskin gloves, white socks, and black patent leather "Mary Janes." Her smart little purse was white suede.

High-waisted and pleated was the polka dot redingote-inspired style for morning wear. A very photogenic outfit, perfect for an on-screen romp with a stork, or dolly, or duck.

Shirley Temple in Curley Top *by 20th Century-Fox, 1935. Designer: Rene Hubert*

Sonja Henie in My Lucky Star *by 20th Century-Fox, 1938. Designer: Royer*

Although dresses and suits were the mainstay of public day wear, blouses and sweaters played an increasingly important role. During the Thirties sweaters were relegated to less formal occasions and were considered sporty rather than sexy. The Forties and Lana Turner would change that. Jean Parker's and Virginia Grey's angoras would be popular for the campus set.

It is a well-known fact that the studio star system dominating Hollywood in the Thirties permitted not only the patient nurturing of future stars of the industry, but also enhanced the longevity of established luminaries. From ingenue to star, the studio insured that an actress maintained the proper image befitting her achieved or desired status. In January 1937, Darryl F. Zanuck told an interviewer for *Motion Picture Studio Insider*:

> The average cost of launching a film star is about one million dollars. To start an actor or an actress on what we hope will be the road to stardom is a definite gamble, for the human element, that unpredictable abstraction, is practically the biggest factor to consider. Contrary to popular belief, stars do not spring up overnight. We select someone we think has the necessary personality, then we place him or her in strategic film roles from time to time and await public reaction. Some players quickly reach success, others never quite attain it. The salaries and expenses go on just the same while "personalities" are being groomed. The cost of make-up, wardrobe, etc., is a considerable item in the whole.

Universal Studios spent between $500 to $800 for each screen test. Three thousand feet of film was shot, all angles. This was cut to a test reel one thousand feet long and run for studio executives. The studios offered a cornucopia of riches and fame to selected actresses, but they also demanded a price not all were willing to pay: total loyalty to the studio and its dictates, and the surrender of privacy to appease the fans.

Lois Mae Green, from Pasadena, posed on a float for a local newspaper advertising swimming for the Olympics. Louis B. Mayer and Irving Thalberg saw the picture, the studio found the girl, a screen test was made, and Green was rechristened Jean Parker. After working at MGM for a year, the studio gave her a party on the set to celebrate her graduation from high school. She was seventeen then.

Sonja Henie's ensemble bridged the sweater-blouse look and was designed to be adaptable for the screen or her private wardrobe. In an effort to please their lucrative new star, 20th Century–Fox allowed Henie the option in her contract to buy her costumes. She usually did.

Virginia Grey in The Hardys Ride High *by MGM, 1939. Designer: Tree*

Jean Parker for publicity for Have a Heart *by MGM, 1934. Designer: Adrian*

Jean Arthur in The Whole Town's Talking
by Columbia, 1935. Designer: Kalloch

Anita Louise in These Glamour Girls *by MGM, 1939. Designer: Adrian*

Patricia Morison in Persons in Hiding *by Paramount, 1939. Designer: Head*

The cinema designers created wardrobes for every type of role, for every conceivable occasion. Blouses, for example, ranged from the rugged and practical to the most eye-catching and sublime.

Jean Arthur's and Anita Louise's ethereal tops implied soft femininity and were photographers' delights. Sheer but still genteel, Louise's long, flowing sleeves floated gracefully with her every movement on screen. Louise's own impeccable beauty made any chance for tawdry misinterpretation utterly impossible. Arthur's blouse did not float, but the transparency of the starched white organdy bouffant sleeves and bodice gathered considerable attention. Featuring ripples of organdy at the cuffs and close neckline, the peasant blouse fastened with a multitude of small, stylish buttons. A simple black crepe skirt completed a demurely appealing ensemble for late day wear or informal dining. A popular star in the Forties, Arthur maintained a routine of drinking a glass of orange juice or other citrus juice every hour while working on the set.

Dressier and flashier, lamé was another frequent cinema and fashion daytime style tool. Daytime lamé blouses carried the impression of serious business, confidence, and a certain amount of wealth. Patricia Morrison's dramatic lamé blouse was devoid of high contrast or eye-catching details and applied flat ruffles and slightly puffed shoulders for necessary interest. Just as reports blossomed of a feud between Hedy Lamarr and Joan Bennett—after the latter dyed her hair and parted it in the middle, ''Lamarr style''—so also did the fan magazines detail the rivalry between Dorothy Lamour, well established by 1938 and noted for her long locks, and newcomer Patricia Morrison. Lamour's hair measured thirty-six inches in length, while Morrison's similarly styled tresses reached thirty-nine inches.

Many people envision the typical Thirties dress to look like the one worn by Jean Harlow. In fact there was no such thing as a "typical" dress. Nevertheless, certain styles are designated as the stereotypes for certain periods to facilitate rapid identification by the public. Thus, for the Thirties, the sleek bias satin dress typically adorns the sexpot, and the plain, drab, uninteresting dress is worn by the down-trodden, Depression-hit woman. In fact the Thirties screen depicted the average woman clothed in a wide variety of styles and materials. For example, for Claudette Colbert's afternoon dress, Banton took a basic dark dress and added an unusually stylized poncho outline in gold glitter. Adrian also employed special draping and beaded trim for Jeanette MacDonald's lovely formal afternoon ensemble. The puffed shoulders and distinctively slashed sleeves provided engaging style details without undue attention.

Betty Douglas, one of the most photographed models at the time and always in demand for screen fashion shows, wore a colorful costume for *Vogues of 1938*. The bright brown wool street dress, with shirred yoke and upper sleeve, had a red band and bow on one sleeve and a green one on the other, with the red and green motif repeated on bands set in the body of the dress. The looped turban and muff were also red and green wool. Wee Willie was the name of Douglas's pet spaniel. Several designers worked on *Vogues*. This ensemble was designed by Omar Kiam. Despite the exotic name, Kiam hailed from Texas and started as a baby-cap designer in a Houston department store. He later worked his way into women's hats and still later headed that department.

Jean Harlow in Beast of the City *by MGM,*
1932. Designer: Adrian

Ginger Rogers in In Person *by RKO, 1935. Designer: Newman*

Wendy Barrie in Breezing Home *by Universal, 1937. Art Director and Designer: John Harkrider*

Dixie Lee Crosby in Love in Bloom *by Paramount, 1935. Designer: Banton*

Pattern design was important for the camera. Dixie Lee Crosby (Bing's first wife) wore a print with a strong design but the boldness was softened with a more subdued background and a stabilizing huge white lace puff around the face. Novel tailoring was the keynote to Ginger Rogers's blue and white print cinema street frock. The dress front was gored from shoulder to hem, with the gores released to pleats below the knees. The effect was repeated for the short puffed sleeves of the dress and three-quarter sleeves of the jacket. A circular flare of blue taffeta buttoned to the bodice, and a navy blue leather belt accented the waist. One year later Jean Parker wore the same dress in RKO's production of *The Farmer in the Dell.*

Walter Plunkett remembered this about prints:

> During periods when prints were in fashion, you used lots and lots of prints. You had to choose them through your experience; you chose them to photograph well. The salesman would come from Bianchini, from Dushon, all these silk houses, to show their lines, and you would pick them over and say, "No, this wouldn't photograph well, but that one will. I want that piece because I know that will photograph well." And the only way you know it will photograph well is through experience.

Prints were very popular for day clothing. Seldom seen at night, prints denoted informal street wear. Adrian discussed prints in general and Ann Harding's dress in particular in June 1935 when he suggested that the predominating color of the print could be emphasized by matching accessories, or, for an even more clever effect, the accessories could be matched to the note of color of the print. For example, Ann Harding's dress was black and white with a dash of red. Red accessories would add considerable snap to the ensemble, while the more conservative could stick with traditional white or black accessories. Adrian also designed a wide-brimmed hat of matching material to emphasize the print even further. John Harkrider, Universal's art director and sometime costume designer, created Wendy Barrie's screen costume using the print dress and matchng hat idea. This spectator sports suit was made of a modernistic print of mustard-colored flowers on a black background with cream accents, combined with plain cream flannel-finish broadcloth for the jacket. Harkrider trimmed the smooth black Baku straw hat with the print material and also applied the print on the jacket revers for a very unified ensemble. The wide brim of the hat was tilted for maximum photogenic potential.

Ann Harding in Biography of a Bachelor Girl *by MGM, 1935. Designer: Adrian*

Cinema designers preferred to avoid highly contrasting and bold stripes because of their possible effect on the camera. But these talented people could break the rules as well as they could make them. Adrian designed a whole fashion wardrobe for Judy Garland to model as publicity for *The Wizard of Oz*. He most of all the designers loved color and dramatic styling flourishes. For Garland he angled the lines of the bodice to diminish the bulk of a growing chest and point the eye to an enchanting face.

Hubert created the modish black and white street ensemble for Billie Burke's role in *Doubting Thomas*. The plain, tailored black wool skirt and black accessories helped to calm a very contrasting pattern. Notice how gray the white appears thanks to masking by the photographer to cut the glare of the white. The hip-length jacket, with scarf, was wool, checked in white on black and vice versa. The little black felt hat was trimmed with the jacket fabric. Irene Dunne's black and white checked style also cooled a bold pattern with a black skirt. The white piping on the overblouse was angora.

Because most actresses stayed with one studio for long periods of time, a continuity of style was possible. The designer learned a star's character traits as well as physical strong and weak points and could therefore create costumes unique to her personablity. That is one reason why certain stars insisted on certain designers regardless of the studio making the motion picture. Walter Plunkett noted:

> The inspiration for the designer was the character and most important the actress herself. The designer would go over her past movies and publicity and try to improve something he considered wrong for her, or continue a good fashion item for her. He would spend two to three weeks before a picture drawing up sketch after sketch (having read the script first). If the script called for a rain sequence, he could count on making at least three copies of the dress. Rules stated that an actress could not be allowed to stay in wet clothes. If she was to fall in the rain, five to six copies had to be made.

Judy Garland for publicity for The Wizard of Oz
by MGM, 1939. Designer: Adrian

Marlene Dietrich in Desire
by Paramount, 1936. Designer: Banton

Polka dots were usually reserved for mornings. Their appearance on the screen almost automatically denoted informality. White backgrounds implied spring and summer, navy blue and black usually fall and winter. Marian Marsh posed in a fashionable petticoat dress from her cinema wardrobe. The black crepe dress exposed a black and white polka dot taffeta ruffled petticoat lined with black silk. The taffeta was repeated on a ruffled bodice flounce and dress collar and cuffs. Marsh's black taffeta hat had a wide stitched brim and white piqué bow matching that on the dress neckline.

To every rule there are exceptions, and the exception to the informality of dots was, not surprisingly, Marlene Dietrich. Her tailored suit with bursting dots could be worn to anything she chose, from morning to late afternoon. Edith Head once commented about the Banton-Dietrich team:

> That was a story. Don't forget Banton and Dietrich together built up almost a legend of an exotic, super high-fashion look, which on another person would have looked ridiculous. She could get away with it. It was almost a signature—the feathers, the veils, the furs, the glitter, the glamour.

Dots on Dietrich could be formal and dressy.

Fan magazines reveled in revealing delicious tidbits to support Dietrich's ultra glamorous image. *Photoplay* in May 1931 disclosed that Marlene Dietrich spent extra pennies on hose so thin you'd think she could get them for nothing but which actually cost $20 a pair. *Modern Screen Magazine* in November 1935 tittered that Dietrich wore real rosebuds for earrings. The fans loved it. Not that many tried to duplicate her style—that was impossible—but she certainly set high standards in the glamour game.

Carole Lombard in Love Before Breakfast
by Universal, 1936. Designer: Banton

Miriam Hopkins for publicity for The Old Maid
by Warner Brothers, 1939. Designer: Orry-Kelly

138

Plaids could be very tricky on the screen, and seldom did you see an actress entirely clothed in a highly contrasting pattern. Normally a vibrant plaid appeared for accent only, as on Mona Barrie. Royer designed her Scotch mist–blue wool tunic suit with blue-gray and black plaid highlights. The tunic suit had a bolera-type bodice which crossed over the scarf and fastened with a large triagular burnished silver button. The epaulets and Scotch kiltie hat gave this costume a regimental flair. Shoes and gloves were blue suede.

Although Miriam Hopkins's street suit was plaid, the subdued colors did not juggle the camera lens when she moved. The white hat, blouse, and large collar focused attention on her face. *Modern Screen Magazine* in June 1934 had this to say about Miriam Hopkins:

> Hollywood folk call Miriam "the human dynamo." She can accomplish more in one day than six women. She adores California in the daytime, but finds evenings boring. Hates bridge and night clubs and premieres. She'd like to smoke but can't learn how. She has one vice—forgetting appointments.

Carole Lombard's highly contrasting outfit was large checkerboard plaid in black and white necktie silk. Plaid also lined the scarflike sash and cape. The hat was white Baku with wool trimming in gray, black, and white. Such a bold outfit was probably mentioned in the script to attract an enormous amout of attention to the star. Travis Banton was borrowed from Paramount to design Lombard's clothes for this Universal picture. Successful stars could demand their favorite costumer for particular movies, whether that designer was with the studio or not. Adrian was borrowed by Mary Pickford to do *Secrets,* her last movie, at United Artists; Rene Hubert was brought from Paris to do Gloria Swanson's wardrobe in *Music in the Air.*

Mona Barrie in Mystery Woman *by Fox, 1935.*
Designer: Royer

Thelma Todd in After the Dance *by Columbia, 1935. Designer: Mayer*

A mainstay of the working woman in the Thirties was the ever-present, ever-popular little black dress. Real working women often made the wearing of the same old dress less obvious by using detachable collars and cuffs of various styles. In the 1940 movie *Kitty Foyle,* designer Renie made sure the basic black dress with white collar and cuffs was included in Ginger Rogers's working girl wardrobe for the 1930s sequences.

The cinema designers could make the impact of the basic dress utterly simple or, with just a little effort, add a dash of creativity and produce something moderately spectacular. Galdys Swarthout's ultraplain black dress had style interest centered on her white open-crocheted cuffs and collar. Because of the simplicity of the design, attention was riveted on Swarthout's face and hands. Swarthout was a famous opera singer who made a few movies in Hollywood. Following her second movie, *The King Steps Out,* she complained to every newspaper in the country that she was through with Hollywood because after singing three full days to a cow, the scene was cut.

The application of lace cuffs and collar on Olivia de Havilland's frock was an excellent idea to upgrade the basic dress into something suitable for late afternoon or an important luncheon engagement. Most of de Havilland's movies in the Thirties were period costume epics, so she wore contemporary designs for publicity only. Often, if a star were in a period movie, the studio would borrow outfits from the department stores, photograph them, and give the store credit. The cinema designer could also create a few fashion ensembles for publicity in the fan magazines. Sometimes a period movie would unexpectedly spawn a fashion vogue, as did *Mary of Scotland.* Walter Plunkett recalled:

> After filming it was discovered that all the Elizabethan ruffs were gone from the wardrobe department. Wardrobe girls and some actresses had taken them to wear with black dresses as collar and cuff sets because of their flattering effect. Ruffs were normally discarded. A manufacturer made up Elizabethan ruffs adapted from those worn in *Mary* and sold them commercially.

Thelma Todd's basic black dress could not be drastically modified. The hand-embroidered design was extremely stylish and easy on the cameras. This same costume was later worn by Rita Hayworth in Columbia's *Girls Can Marry.* It looked equally impressive even as a hand-me-down.

A decidedly distinct use of dark and light was worn by June Collyer. The dress was ridged blue crepe. The neckline and bow at the side and the two circular pieces that trimmed the sleeves were pink moire. The sleeves were said to suggest calla lilies. The blue and pink colors photographed black and white. The skirt was made with a tunic, and the rather wide belt fastened with two rhinestone buttons. The hat was blue crepe lined with pink.

Gladys Swarthout in Give Us This Night *by Paramount, 1936. Designer: Banton*

Olivia de Havilland by Warner Brothers, 1935.
Designer: Milo

June Collyer in Before Midnight *by Columbia,*
1933. Designer: Kalloch

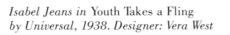

Isabel Jeans in Youth Takes a Fling
by Universal, 1938. Designer: Vera West

Claudette Colbert in She Married Her Boss
by Columbia, 1935. Designer: Kalloch

Janet Gaynor in publicity at Fox, 1935.
Designer: Hubert

One category of day ensemble that ebbed during the Thirties was the formal garden-party dress. An anachronism of the past, its ultrafeminine aura could not offset its total impracticality. The long day dress simply evolved into shorter styles, and the frilly organdy creations were relegated to fewer and fewer special occasions. For the screen, however, clothing an actress in a full-length, puffy garden frock for a snobbish, chatty tea party emphasized the social status and success of the screen character.

A really glamorous garden frock was worn by Isabel Jeans for her movie tea party. Navy and gray marquisette in broad alternating stripes was cut on the bias and looked like plaid when folded over itself. The short sleeves were an extreme version of draped melon sleeves, with the most fullness back towards the shoulder. Accessories were a wide-brimmed Milan straw hat with velvet crown and velvet bands under the chin and a three-strand pearl necklace.

The full organdy dress was often dubbed the "Ascot frock" and was usually accompanied by wide-brimmed straw or organdy hats. A charming garden party hat was worn by Janet Gaynor to complement her royal blue taffeta jacket and candy-striped nude-pink silk voile dress. The hat of natural leghorn had a brim edged with straw lace and a crown circled with a sash of blue taffeta. The garland of flowers echoed the colors of the one-piece dress.

Far more practical but no less feminine was the street-length outfit on Claudette Colbert. Crisp navy blue taffeta covered a sheer white wool skirt. Soft frills of organdy formed the neckline, with two gardenias adding a decorative touch. Of particular interest were the puffed sleeves of white organdy with a flange of taffeta. The bag, stitched hat, and shoes were also navy blue taffeta. When Gwen Wakeling was asked who took the longest fittings, she replied:

Claudette Colbert. And the most difficult. Not that she was bitchy at all. But whatever it was, you would do something and the neckline would be so and so and she would want it lowered, like an eighth of an inch. So you would lower it an eighth of an inch and she would want it raised again. That kind of thing. She was very pleasant, and I liked her, but she was a nit-picker.

143

Lilyan Tashman in Mama Loves Papa
by Paramount, 1933. Designer: Banton

Isabel Jewell in Day of Reckoning *by MGM,
1933. Designer: Adrian*

Some daytime engagements imposed formal requirements on a Thirties cinema character. Important teas or luncheons in town, a date that spanned late afternoon and early evening, or a prestigious social visit all demanded more notable attire. Lilyan Tashman was one of *the* clotheshorses of the early Thirties and always appeared on the best-dressed lists. Her navy blue and white taffeta style was an eye-catcher on the screen, with its unusual deep ruffles around the shoulders and waist and whimsical daisies around the glove cuffs and hat. Tashman's street-length ensemble would be appropriate for spring or summer teas or luncheons. Isabel Jewell's smart fall or winter formal suit allowed lush velvet to set its elegant tone. The sleeves appear tied to the dropped shoulders of the jacket bodice, and this idea is extended to the front of the jacket, which fastens by means of ties and two velvet bows. The upraised collar framed a lovely neck, and extralong sleeves emphasized Jewell's hands.

An exercise in how not to dress for that important afternoon date was presented by Omar Kiam for the movie *Stella Dallas.* Perhaps Kiam could be accused of overkill, but the role and script demanded instant recognition of Stella Dallas's lack of class. Even the most tasteless moviegoer could understand the basic conflict in the movie of Stella's refined daughter's having to live with her crass mother. Barbara Stanwyck displayed a significant amount of courage in exhibiting herself so unglamorously to her fans. However, because she was not yet typecast as a clotheshorse, and because of her enormous talent as an actress, Stanwyck was believable in the role. Other actresses such as Constance Bennett, Kay Francis, or Dietrich would never convince an audience they could be tawdry. Walter Plunkett remembers Stanwyck:

A charming woman. Cooperative with everyone on the set, always. There wasn't a person who didn't adore her. She looks even better now. Actually I think her inner beauty is obvious. You can see the beautiful mind, and the beautiful and generous personality. It shows.

For *Stella Dallas,* Omar Kiam designed 122 gowns, including thirty-three for Stanwyck and twenty-seven for Anne Shirley.

Barbara Stanwyck in Stella Dallas *by United Artists, 1937. Designer: Omar Kiam*

Fay Wray in Murder in Greenwich Village
by Columbia, 1937. Designer: Kalloch

Gail Patrick in Grand Jury Secrets
by Paramount, 1939. Designer: Head

Coats assumed many diverse forms during the Thirties. Some styles, like capes, always seem fashionable, while other styles, like coat-dresses or redingotes grow less popular each time they are revived.

Regarding capes, Gwen Wakeling commented:

Capes have never gone out of fashion. They are a very wearable item. Capes are ancient things which go 'way back to medieval and Roman times. They are so natural, move well on the screen, and conceal anything if you wanted to conceal something, yet you still have a sense of grace.

Frances Drake wore gray chiffon wool for her screen costume. The cape, with its epaulet shoulder treatment, revealed a pencil-slim dress with a V neckline trimmed with white silk piqué and a self-belt with nailhead clasp. Accessories were a black velvet profile beret and black suede gloves, bag, and shoes.

Coat-dresses combined the look of tailored coats with the comfort of a dress. Gail Patrick, who studied law prior to her film career, modeled a smart spring coat-dress that showed how chic and fashionable this style could be. Edith Head used flecked, pin-striped black and white worsted for this street costume with a novel application of black patent leather to highlight the pockets and act as an ascot. Black patent was further emphasized on a wide belt, pumps, and bag. The black felt hat was draped with deep red uncut velvet.

A redingote is a long, lightweight coat, unlined and open at the front, worn with a simple dress. The coat is usually not removed. Fitted redingotes ranged from very slender and summery to heavier fall thickness, as on Fay Wray. Fay Wray's outfit was designed by Kalloch for a busy morning in town. Of brown and beige sheer wool, it featured a fitted overcoat with epaulet shoulder treatment and diagonal pockets piped with the matching beige of the pencil-slim dress. The tiny Buster Brown collar was finished with a clip of diamonds and emeralds set in gold. The brown suede hat was topped with two pom-poms, one brown, the other bottle green. Accessories were brown suede.

Kalloch, of Scottish ancestry and American birth, designed for Pavlova and Irene Castle before his cinema career. A former employee of the prestigious couture store Lucille of England and Paris, he once commented:

It is my belief that American women are much more tastefully dressed than women on the Continent for the reason that they do not follow. slavishly, the edicts of any particular style but adapt new trends to their own personalities.

Eleanor Powell in Honolulu *by MGM, 1939.*
Designer: Adrian

Penny Singleton in Blondie Meets the Bo[...]
by Columbia, 1939. Designer: Kalloch

Madeleine Carroll in The General Died at Da[...]
by Paramount, 1936. Designer: Banton

Plain cloth coats were of course the mainstay of the average American woman. Their application on the screen, however, varied considerably. There were many instances where fur trim or lavish materials simply were inappropriate for star, story, situation, or character. But plain cloth coats did not necessarily mean *plain* cloth coats. Style and creativity were still factors, often in subtle ways.

Penny Singleton's herringbone tweed by Kalloch sported a fitted top, a black velvet collar, high revers, a wide leather belt held by loops, and a smartly flared skirt. The coat was appropriate for her role as Blondie, but still stylish.

In 1937 Kalloch suggested that movie fans use the colorful linings of their coats to create an interesting contrast to the rest of their outfits:

> Women make a big mistake by checking their wraps before entering a restaurant or cocktail bar. The coat to any costume is very important and should accompany the wearer for a harmonizing effect. Then, too, a cape or coat may be spread out becomingly to cover a divan or chair with a contrasting color, thus making a background against which the gown will be outstanding.

A resort favorite, Eleanor Powell's impeccably tailored white linen coat flashed electric blue for color contrast. The high collar was lined with blue to match the neckerchief, dress, and hat accents. The girdlelike belt tied with linen cord, and cuff flaps hid deep sleeve pockets. This type of coat, because of its color, was proper and popular for the spring and summer months.

Hardly flashy but decidedly chic is the coat costume worn by Madeleine Carroll. Black leather accents on belt, cuffs, and collar and the generous use of large black buttons provided the main style points. The polka dot of the dress collar was repeated as a bow on the small, close-fitting hat. This was an excellent coat for heavy drama. During the filming of this movie, *The General Died at Dawn,* the scene that took the greatest time was between Gary Cooper and Madeleine Carroll in which Cooper was to punch Carroll in the jaw. Cooper protested that he just couldn't do it, while Carroll urged, "Come on, hit me!" Finally lights went on, cameras rolled, and Cooper let go with a perfect punch in the Carroll jaw, then ruined the whole take by crying out, "Did I hurt you—did I?"

Simone Simon modeled a dull blue wool coat made interesting by scarlet embroidery. The embroidery appeared on the shoulders, down the front, and on the sash which fastened on the inside back of the coat and tied around the waist of the simple black dress. The obvious Chinese motif of the ensemble was applied to the beret hat of shiny black straw.

Simone Simon in Seventh Heaven *by 20th Century-Fox, 1937. Designer: Wakeling*

Norma Shearer in Let Us Be Gay *by MGM,*
1930. Designer: Adrian

In the early Thirties, Marlene Dietrich wore men's suits in public, trousers and all, and precipitated an exciting new vogue for women. Dietrich herself disdained any interest in being a style crusader and protested that she dressed just to suit her own individuality and was not concerned with what other women wore. Howard Shoup remembered that Dietrich created a sensation by wearing an identical man's outfit to match her escort when in public. The fashion world was shaken: although she really did look stunning, it simply was not done! While women hesitated to follow Dietrich to the extreme of matching their escorts' attire, the idea of a tailored suit for daytime became a hallmark of Thirties vogue. Tailored man-type suits had appeared on the screen long before Dietrich. Norma Shearer's daytime ensemble closely followed a man's double-breasted suit and typified the evolution of her screen character from a prim, homely wife to a vivacious woman of the world who could equal a man's sophistication. Dietrich's fitted, double-breasted sports jacket was worn over a plain white dress. Her role as a slick, international jewel thief required good taste with a minimum of frills—until the end, when she married Cooper. Note that both Shearer's and Dietrich's jackets, while copying the mannish look, still adhere to standard feminine buttoning on the left; men button on the right. Travis Banton complained to *Photoplay* in 1937:

> Marlene takes endless trouble about her picture clothes. She will fit the same dress four or five times. She is always perfectly charming about it, but at the end of a fitting we are all in a state of exhaustion. She challenges everything. Because a thing is good she does not let it go at that; she says "Let's see if we can make it better."

Dietrich was reported to play the violin to unwind after an exhausting movie; it is not noted what Banton did to relax after strenuous fittings with her.

Off screen as well as on, the wearer of a good tailored suit had to be at least moderately slender. Styling was usually a direct steal from a typical man's suit. Shoulders were only slightly exaggerated in their squareness. Notched lapels had buttonholes. There were trick pockets and a nipped-in effect at the waist. Single-breasteds had the edge over double-breasteds. In 1937 the cuff-length jacket, like a man's was smartest. The skirt was slender, with only pleats or tucks for detail. Suiting fabrics were hairline-striped worsteds, checks, tweeds, and worsted flannel. Navy was a favorite color.

Tailored mannish suits could be highly feminized, as the one worn by Barbara Stanwyck. This suit was designed for Stanwyck to help publicize her successful Western epic, *Union Pacific*. Note the sparkling diamond and sapphire pin on the navy blue silk blouse. Pins often substituted for ties or bows on this kind of ensemble. Gwen Wakeling worked with Barbara Stanwyck and remembered her as "very professional in her attitude. She felt that if the designer and the director thought that was the thing, that was the thing. She wasn't bitchy in the slightest. Easy to work with."

Barbara Stanwyck in publicity for Union Pacific by Paramount, 1939. Designer: Visart

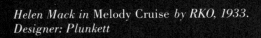

Helen Mack in Melody Cruise *by RKO, 1933.
Designer: Plunkett*

Spectator sports presented the cinema character with an opportunity for a wide range of casual-chic wear. Sports suits were extremely popular on screen and often doubled for less formal street wear. Checks and plaids were the most popular choice for sports ensembles. Although favorites for day fashions, checks and plaids were used cautiously by cinema designers. Walter Plunkett commented:

> If you got into a very busy black and white check, you avoided it because you knew it would not photograph well. If you wanted a check you would try to get it in two tones of blue that would soften it a bit, instead of black and white. You would be cautious about stripes that were too contrasting and would vibrate as you see them on television—just awful, shaking. But those are things you learn to deal with.

Helen Mack's sports ensemble by Plunkett was also considered appropriate for traveling across the water. The white wool costume had brown accents and featured wooden buttons tied onto the white swagger coat with strands of heavy string.

Alice Faye's cinema sports suit was coarsely woven crepe in white and plaid tones of gray, white, and wine red. The dress had a narrow cowboy collar which lapped over the yoked white jacket. A matching wine-red suede belt, attached to the dress's skirt, came through two large buttonholes and held the jacket front in place. Full long sleeves were caught by the white butcher-boy cuffs and large silver buttons. A beret of white felt was crowned with a red pom-pom. Faye's purse was red suede.

Adrian chose small and large checks for Dorothy Jordon's street-sports ensemble. The unusual cut of the jacket was matched in fashion interest by the toga-style cape of enlarged checks.

Shirley Ross in Devil's Squadron *by Columbia, 1936. Designer: Samuel Lange*

Florence Rice in Double Wedding *by MGM, 1937. Designer: Adrian*

Business suits were generally dressier and more serious than sports suits, although the fine lines between street, sports, and business clothes were often blurred. In 1937 Travis Banton summarized his ideas regarding Thirties business attire for *Motion Picture Studio Insider Magazine:*

> Simple clothes, well-cut and a bit streamlined for the speed of today's business, are well suited to the girl in the city. They should be fashioned for quick donning, and there is nearly always a place for the zipper.

The zipper, a relatively new clothing device at that time, was considered ugly by many couturiers. By 1939 zippers had become more popular. Barbara Stanwyck's dark green tweed midseason suit featured a collarless, long-sleeved bolero jacket that zippered up the front. The swirling, circular skirt, with extra fullness in front, was high-built to set off a narrow pigskin belt which matched a hand-knit sweater underneath. The hat was two-toned green felt, with a bandeau of two-toned green grosgrain ribbon across the forehead. Dark brown alligator shoes and bag were accessories.

Kalloch was forever mindful of backgrounds and colors and suggested that in an office a woman could suit the cut and coloring of her costume to the light and general coloring of the office as well as her own personal needs. If the office were drab, she could either choose similar colors and blend in like a chameleon, or dress with contrasting colors for attention. Kalloch commented:

> In designing clothes I strive for simplicity of line and clear, lovely colors. Even against a motley background your costumes will stand out and draw attention if they are classically simple yet beautiful as to color.

Exquisitely good taste is displayed by Adrian's lovely three-piece suit on Florence Rice. Softly patterned wool in this case was complemented by the accent of velvet. The jacket rose high in front to reveal blouse and vest, then dipped low in back for a stylish flare. The design lacked any form of flashy buttons or pins and relied on materials, cut, and color to carry the message of daytime elegance. Another classic in good fashion that is wearable today is the smart suit on Shirley Ross. Soft wool, finely checked in gray and white, was highlighted by a black velveteen ascot held by a large clip with a leaf motif. The suit blouse was also black velveteen. A black leather belt confined the otherwise loose jacket.

The versatility of a plain skirt paired with a smart, more colorful jacket was evidenced by its frequent appearance on and off screen. Black, especially black velvet, was the most popular skirt color to be paired with rich plaids and patterned tops. The expertly tailored suit on Nan Grey featured a jacket of imported tweed from Switzerland in soft tones of moss green, rust, brown, and yellow. This modern adaption of an English frock coat formed its square collars with light brown suede finished with saddle stitching. A deft touch of suede at the throat accented Grey's face. Double beige buttons fastened and decorated the jacket front. The solid matching brown skirt had a kick pleat in front for easy movement.

Nan Grey in Three Smart Girls Grow Up
by Universal, 1939. Designer: Vera West

Barbara Stanwyck in Remember the Night
by Paramount, 1939. Designer: Head

Joan Blondell in Gold Diggers of 1937 *by 1st National, 1936. Designer: Orry-Kelly*

Toby Wing in Torch Singer *by Paramount, 1933. Designer: Banton*

While the little black dress was the workhorse of the average woman, the black suit was even more versatile and every bit as popular. The black or dark suit was proper from afternoon through early evening and was always considered fashionably smart. Joan Blondell, called "Rosebud" by designer Orry-Kelly, modeled this daytime ensemble of black crepe with a bolero jacket and black ciré braid trim. According to Howard Shoup, who later costumed her, Blondell liked to try slightly more daring designs—a bit tighter here, a bit lower there. This demure, proper suit did not lend itself to a saucy bent.

Anita Louise's black velvet street costume took a different theme. The Eton jacket featured three-quarter-length peasant sleeves and a white taffeta blouse with black velvet cordings. The collar was held by a black velvet cord finished with black and white silk pompoms, which also adorned the black velvet hat. The plain skirt gained its fullness through gores.

As the white dress was generally relegated to spring and summer, so too the white suit. Although cameramen groaned whenever in all-white ensemble was to apear in a scene, sometimes its use could not be avoided. Quite simply, white has always been *the* proper color for summer. Joan Bennett's waffle crepe summer suit had black accents on the hat and shoes and black buttons, but the high contrast of the outsized collar and scarf were softened by dark blue.

An exquisite suit displaying great fashion style and restraint is the Banton creation worn by Toby Wing. The basically simple suit photographed white but was actually beige. Open and loose, the design permitted great freedom of movement. The three-quarter balloon sleeves focused attention on the diamond and sapphire bracelet. The dark brown silk blouse featured original diagonal lines and self-covered silk buttons, with a delicately draped scarf collar fastened in place by a large and lovely diamond clip on one shoulder.

The black or white suit looked expensive, but that was not necessarily a requisite for the well-dressed woman. In 1936, Adrian was quoted as saying:

> It is not necessary to dress expensively to dress well. The clever use of accessories and wise attention to restraint in business and street clothes will give you the beautifully groomed appearance which denotes a well-dressed woman. Often, if you watch the clothes of the stars on the screen, you will find a new way of wearing a belt—or a boutonniere—or an angle of tipping a hat which will suit your own personality perfectly.

He also stressed that the average woman should avoid harsh colors and intricately cut clothing that cluttered the lovely lines of a good figure. He though the simple three-piece black suit was the most versatile basic ensemble for a woman because it could be changed a hundred ways, with the addition of a tailored white blouse or a frilly pink one, detachable fur collar and cuffs, or a smart white vestee.

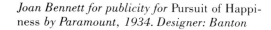

Rosalind Russell in Four's a Crowd *by Warner Brothers, 1938. Designer: Orry-Kelly*

Constance Bennett in Ladies in Love *by 20th Century-Fox, 1936. Designer: Wakeling*

The Thirties encompassed an exciting period of time for the fashion world. Many fads came and went, but a few basic styles lingered. Not always at the height of fashion, periodically they seemed smart, or at least acceptable. These classic styles were simple and changed the basic body lines very little, if at all. Gwen Wakeling has said:

> Any undue exaggeration of any part of the body has just turned out to be ugly and unpleasant and hard to live with. Maybe you can accept it for a couple of years when it is high fashion, but then you'll say "Oh, how could we possibly have worn a thing like that?"

The matter of good taste as well as good fashion was always tricky for the cinema designer. Designers constantly strove for classic lines and sophistication, but their costumes had to be glamorous, fashionable, and correct for the scene, too. George Cukor, the eminent director, feels cinema designers were not always successful in achieving all these goals, but he conceded they had to create costumes that were first and foremost good for the picture. Cukor commented, "Nobody always has the best of taste. I see French clothes now and they look ridiculous in some cases. No one hits it all the time."

Jacket styles changed constantly, but certain basic lengths returned regularly to the ranks of fashion chic. From *Four's a Crowd,* Rosalind Russell's toast and beige wool dress was flecked with gold and had a blouse treatment and large sleeves smocked in the shoulder. The full panel across the front of the skirt repeated the smocking. An antique gold mesh necklace finished the neckline. The bolero jacket, a darker shade of tweed, hung loose and avoided any real or faked buttons or clasps. The hat, bag, and gloves were dark brown antelope. Also loose-fitting was the longer style on Bette Davis. The high-waisted brown and black dress was topped by a simple jacket with slightly enlarged sleeves. Orry-Kelly once reminisced about Davis and Russell:

> Working with Bette isn't easy, but she's worth it. She's honest and outspoken. She's one of the very few actresses I know who can look in the mirror and tell herself the truth. Rosalind Russell was like that too. When I'm ready to give up and throw out a dress, she'll give it a hitch or a twist and turn it into something great.

Sometimes the difference between a jacket and coat was blurred. One example is the swagger style worn by Constance Bennett. The monotone beige woolen outfit featured a square-yoke, collarless jacket/coat outlined by stitched bands that simulated wide lapels. The square bodice of the dress and square white piqué collar repeated the block outline. The jacket was cut in a swallowtail style, with the sleeves slightly fuller at the top. The brown velour beret had red, yellow, and green highlights. Accessories were dark brown.

Bette Davis in Bureau of Missing Persons *by Warner Brothers, 1933. Designer: Orry-Kelly*

Joan Crawford and Spencer Tracy in Mannequin *by MGM, 1937. Designer: Adrian*

Greer Garson and Robert Taylor in Remember? *by MGM, 1939. Designer: Adrian*

Cinema designers tapped the world in their search for intersting materials and novel ideas. Maureen O'Sullivan's chic suit from *Stage Mother* shaped blue angora wool to look as soft as it felt. Adrian applied prominent and dramatic fins from wrists to shoulders and loose epaulets to create a high-style, original impression. Parallel stitching on all outlines infused more interest, but not ostentatiously. The little turban was angora.

Another noteworthy application of the unusual was the quilted black taffeta dress suit worn by Ginger Rogers. Very few women could carry the bulk of this material and still look slender and chic. Rogers's georgette blouse was flame red, and her hat was stitched black taffeta.

Gold thread enlivened an otherwise drab suit for Greer Garson. The peaked turban hat was borrowed from the Middle East and modified into one of the most stylish designs for the late Thirties and Forties.

Joan Crawford, when she married Spencer Tracy in *Mannequin*, wore this dark-colored bridal suit. The intricate embroidery of the bodice followed and emphasized the broadness of her shoulders and the narrowness of her waist. Adrian's bold composition of dark color, and even a dark veil, emphasized important points in the story: this was not Crawford's first marriage, and the marriage carried a dark cloud over it in the form of Crawford's first husband. Sixteen seamstresses worked on the twenty-eight different gowns worn by Crawford in *Mannequin* and the dozens of others modeled throughout the movie. Six wardrobe ladies kept all the clothing in perfect condition during filming.

Much has already been written about Crawford's broad shoulders and Adrian's brilliant exaggeration of them. The padded shoulder look became *the* vogue for the Forties, and Adrian and Crawford are credited with inspiring the world to wear them. Fellow designer Walter Plunkett commented:

> Paris had padded shoulders before Adrian took them. He was very smart. They had just come out in Paris and weren't very important yet, but Adrian saw their possibilities. And he saw them particularly as, What the hell do you do with a woman that has shoulders as broad as Joan Crawford's? Take this new fashion of pads, make them even bigger and set a fashion with them.

Maureen O'Sullivan in Stage Mother *by MGM, 1933. Designer: Adrian*

Ginger Rogers in 20 Million Sweethearts *by Warner Brothers, 1934. Designer: Orry-Kelly*

The formal black suit was extremely chic and always proper for that very important afternoon luncheon or appointment. When an actress appeared in such a suit on screen, she immediately set the image of rich sophistication, confidence, and impeccable good taste.

Binnie Barnes's very plain black velvet suit centered interest on a single large bunch of real violets. The severe simplicity of the ensemble relied on the long tunic jacket and white glove and hat accents for its style highlights. Mary Martin's black Lyons velvet suit publicized her role in *The Great Victor Hubert*. The outfit was a modern adaption of her 1900-period costumes. The jacket was inspired by the corseted waistline and puffed shoulders of the old gay days, with a Basque motif and a brief, rippling peplum. The full, circular skirt was topped by a frilly lingerie blouse of tucked organdy, copied exactly from one she wore in the movie.

Alice Faye's sophisticated afternoon costume was highlighted by an attractive sheer cape. A jewel-clipped neckline, bracelet, and circular, veiled hat were all the touches necessary to maintain a formal image.

Formal suits such as these—and many even more elaborate—were also worn by extras during party, luncheon, or even shopping scenes. Ladies sporting these magnificent clothes usually plucked them from their own closets. In the Thirties extras were rated according to wardrobe. Once a year every Hollywood extra joined a dress parade, held at a major studio. These girls and women sauntered before a critical board of judges and were classified according to the clothes they wore. The ''dress extra'' was the highest class and generally had a wardrobe many a star envied. Most were once wealthy women who lost everythng but their gorgeous clothes and now used them as a means of livelihood. The standard salary for a dress extra was $15 a day. Extras who spoke one word or seventy received $25 a day.

Alice Faye in On the Avenue *by 20th Century-Fox, 1937. Designer: Wakeling*

Gloria Swanson in Music in the Air *by Fox, 1934. Designer: Hubert*

Claire Trevor in Spring Tonic *by Fox, 1935.*
Designer: Hubert

Although scripts occasionally dictated that cinema designers create only a blouse or a dress top for a scene, more often they were required to produce an entire ensemble, two or even three layers deep, with hat, bag, and shoes. Two very different complete costumes are displayed on these pages, both designed by René Hubert.

It is realistically impossible for Claire Trevor to look so trim and slender in her powder blue wool dress-length coat when you realize she is wearing three layers of clothing—a dress, a jacket, and an overcoat. One secret to the lack of bulk is that the overcoat is sleeveless. The coat collar of angora jersey in blue, white, and rose stripes is the same material as the dress top, scarf, and jacket lapels. The Eton-type jacket is held in place by a white leather belt finished by a mother-of-pearl circle to match the coat buttons. The slim-fitting dress has a modishly full skirt. Accessories were a powder blue felt hat trimmed in blue grosgrain ribbon, white doeskin gloves, powder blue suede pumps with grosgrain ribbon bows, and a white leather handbag with silver clasp.

Hubert borrowed from the famed Tibetan Lamaists for Gloria Swanson's late afternoon winter costume. The one-piece black crepe satin dress was cut along straight lines. It featured a high front neck and was slit and open down the center of the back. The short sleeves were also slit along the top, and the skirt carried the "Hubert split" on the left side only. The dress alone was said to be proper for cocktails or dinner. For afternoon, a dress-length black and white plaid taffeta coat, with matching gloves, was added. The complete ensemble included a black hatter's-plush hat with eye veil, a muff of plaid taffeta with handbag and vanity inset, black suede pumps, and black velvet overcoat.

Martha Raye in Give Me a Sailor *by Paramount, 1938. Designer: Head*

Jean Harlow in Libeled Lady *by MGM, 1936. Designer: Tree*

Lavish use of fur was another hallmark of Thirties cinema vogue. Fur appeared on everything from evening gowns to pajamas. Even the little day dress received often generous and highly impractical amounts of fur. Gracie Allen, not known to her later television fans as a fashion leader, actually wore many lovely costumes created for her during her early days at Paramount. This beige day dress sported just enough fox on a brief attached jacket for the audience to recognize Allen instantly as a classy lady. Allen's brand of humor was such that goofy clothing was not only not needed, but would in fact not ring true to her basic character. Allen's grooming and clothing were always meticulous.

One lady whose beauty has been vastly underrated is Martha Raye. Possessing one of the best pairs of legs in Hollywood, Raye preferred the slapstick style of comedy and called attention to her mouth and loud voice. Much too curvy to be a fashion leader, she nevertheless wore some interesting cinema outfits, like this lavish fox-trimmed dress. The hem was slightly higher than normal and was raised even more for this publicity still.

One star who emphasized her good points, which were many, was Jean Harlow. This publicity still shows her with a 172-pound swordfish, supposedly caught by her mother. The ensemble was worn in the movie *Libeled Lady*. No longer the sleazy tart, Harlow changed her image from the Blonde Bombshell to simply a very sexy lady. Harlow, who weighed 112 pounds and measured 34-24-36, had a perfect complexion and was very superstitious. A news clipping reported that she took a chance with dice on her twenty-fourth birthday at Agua Caliente. She bet $2 on craps and let it ride eight times, winning $10,240.

Gracie Allen in International House *by Paramount, 1933. Designer: Banton*

Shirley Ross in Paris Honeymoon *by Paramount, 1939. Designer: Head*

Jeanette MacDonald in Monte Carlo *by Paramount, 1930. Designer: Banton*

A favorite style to show the status of an on-screen character was a suit trimmed with fur. Jeanette MacDonald's early Banton design shows the traditional application of platinum fox on the cuffs and collar of the jacket for her role as a countess. The three-piece costume was titled "the Basque suit" and made of gray Elizabeth crepe.

According to publicity, Shirley Ross's summer suit was to replace afternoon dresses in 1938. Edith Head's imaginative design in light blue novelty crepe splashed fur to highlight the interesting shawl idea. The slim skirt had a wide belt of self fabric, and covered buttons decorated the bodice and belt. The hat was matching blue felt, with a knotted treatment of deeper blue edging the brim. Edith Head once defined regular fashion designers as makers of clothing for the mass market, for a certain season, fabric, and economic level. She has said, "Actually I think the great one reason why I have never gone into fashion is because I think it is a ridiculously difficult idea to design a dress that will look just as good on a size 6 as on a 16." She thinks cinema designing is easier. "The main, basic factor in the bottom of all cinema designing is the script. The script actually can be interpreted in different ways, by the director, by the producer, by the star. But basically, that is the one factor that you have to follow definitely."

Very elegant for day was the charming bolero suit worn by Simone Simon. The obvious Spanish influence was accentuated by black Persian lamb trim on basic black broadcloth. Spaced bands of fur on the sleeves and a simple band on the skirt added weight and swing. The tassel on the sombrero-style black felt hat and the swathed sash over the white crepe blouse were both scarlet. The lamb pocketbook-muff was an important accessory style.

Simone Simon in Love and Hisses *by 20th Century-Fox, 1937. Designer: Royer*

Loretta Young in Second Honeymoon *by 20th Century-Fox, 1937. Designer: Wakeling*

Lucille Ball in Annabel Takes a Tour *by RKO, 1938. Designer: Renie*

If a dash of fur on suits added a touch of class to a cinema ensemble, then a cascade of fur should inundate it with elegance. Lavish fur for day costumes was the easy way to garner instant role identification, and audiences also loved to see such extravagance.

Lucille Ball, who wore many lovely outfits in her late-Thirties films, donned this classic style for one of her Annabel movies. A simple black suit swathed with luxurious fox was always fashionable and in good taste. The small, close-fitting hat sported a pink ostrich plume for accent. The jacket flared at the waist for a fashionable and flattering outline.

Miriam Hopkins's afternoon suit was pale gray wool dramatized by silver fox fur. Her small visor hat, handbag, and shoes were dark gray suede. Banton's fittings with Hopkins were most often frantic last-minute affairs, usually done at her home the day before shooting began. Hopkins was always surrounded by men at these madhouse meetings, and Banton would work hard to get her opinions and agreement on the armful of sketches he brought. Finally, Hopkins would merrily push a champagne glass into his limp hand and suggest he forget about business until the next day. For Hopkins there was always a tomorrow.

Travis Banton was well known among his peers for cinema costumes that expressed good taste, simplicity of line, and refinement of conception. Walter Plunkett feels Banton's strong point was his high style. "Travis Banton was actually nine-tenths fashion designer and one-tenth costumer. Even though the picture was two years in being released, his clothes were still good high style."

Decidedly glamorous was the prodigious fur on Loretta Young. Once again, black wool was the favorite choice of material, coupled this time with red fox. The thickness of the fox at the bodice concealed slit openings for handy pockets. The small, round puff of the fox hat was a neat balance to attract even greater attention to Young's exquisitely photogenic face.

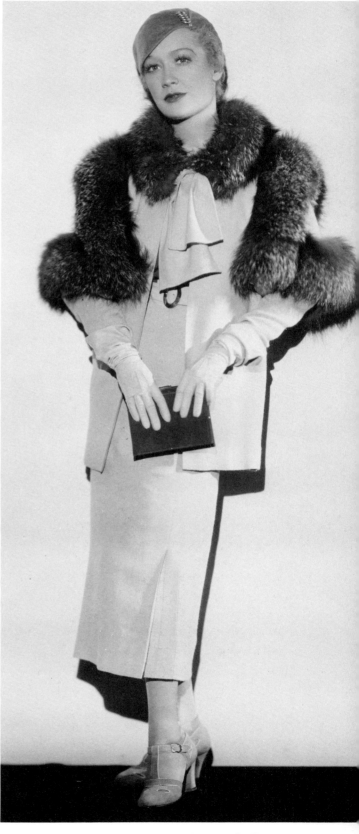

Miriam Hopkins in All of Me *by Paramount, 1934. Designer: Banton*

Kay Francis in Ladies' Man *by Paramount, 1931. Designer: Banton*

Ann Sothern in Don't Gamble with Love *by Columbia, 1936. Designer: Lange*

A few amazing examples of cinema glamour are shown by these exotic afternoon designs for the screen.

Marlene Dietrich's stunning full-length traveling suit was as amazing as her screen role of Shanghai Lily, the White Flower of the Chinese coast. Smothering her in black feathers as a symbol of evil or a sign of enchantment like a black swan, Banton made certain Dietrich's character as an expensive, experienced bewitcher in an exotic locale was not overlooked by the audience. According to publicity, the coq-feathered turban with nose veil was made feather by feather. The first feather was added near the left eyebrow and surveyed by Dietrich, Banton, a fitter, a tailor, and von Sternberg. It was moved and approved by the group, and the rest were added in similar fashion, one by one. Only Dietrich, with her unique glamour, could wear this outfit and be envied by the audience rather than laughed off the screen.

Kay Francis modeled a favorite formal afternoon combination—black velvet and white ermine. The white ermine muff and close-fitting black velvet hat completed an ensemble that was perennially stylish for winter.

Another extravagant formal idea for day wear was the all-fur suit. Most types of fur were too bulky, but galyak, or unborn lamb, was flat and fitting enough not to overwhelm the wearer. Hubert, shown here with Gloria Swanson, designed this tasteful gray galyak outfit with a short-waisted jacket, white silk blouse, and the famous Hubert slit on the left. Ann Sothern's striking black galyak afternoon suit had a wrapped skirt topped by a straight box jacket. The draped neckline of the black crepe blouse was held by a large diamond brooch. Twisted sables formed the semi-muff.

Although many Hollywood stars made fortunes during their careers and actually wore glorious outfits like these off screen, acceptance by the blueblood society was often out of reach. Several stars married titled men in an effort to break into polite society, but most marriages were a sham. One designer who often fitted stars in their homes remarked that he once went to the home of a newly married and newly titled star and found that her bedroom was an enormous and gorgeous thing. There was a dressing room, a huge bath, and vast closets. A little hallway led to a small, meagerly furnished bedroom where the ''prince'' slept. He entered her bedroom only on call and was paid an allowance by that star for services rendered.

Gloria Swanson and designer Rene Hubert for Music in the Air *by Fox, 1934.*

Marlene Dietrich in Shanghai Express *by Paramount, 1932. Designer: Banton*

Claire Trevor in Human Cargo *by 20th Century-Fox, 1936. Designer: Lambert*

Modern Screen Magazine advised its readers in April 1937 that caped suits were much better for travel and sports rather than active daytime wear in town. Despite this suggestion, capes, especially those with fur, were a popular choice for in-town wear on screen. The variety of capes for daytime was vast, ranging from a bit of fur trim, as on Claire Trevor, to the all-fur cape worn by Kitty Carlisle.

Claire Trevor's spring ensemble was made of gray-blue tweed, shadow-pleated in bright sapphire and white. Novelty fastenings at the neck and the belt repeated the three shades of the tweed. Deep gray fox fashioned the tuxedo collar of the cape, lined with sapphire blue. Accessories were dove-gray suede.

Gray was also the color of Dorothy Lamour's winter day suit. The straight skirt was made of novelty gray kasha, the cape was lined with gray crepe and trimmed with Persian karakul, which also fashioned the smart "jumper" and muff. The hat was matching gray suede, gloves and shoes bright blue antelope.

Very chic for the day was the black wool-and-fox-trimmed cape on Maureen O'Sullivan. A far cry from her "Jane" togs, this ensemble is classic in good taste and elegance and would be smart even today. The dramatic shadowing by studio photographer Stephen McNulty created a stunning publicity photo for a lovely star.

The all-fur cape was very common on the screen for the well-to-do to wear to all sorts of engagements. Paradoxically, it could be less formal than some of the other combinations displayed on previous pages.

A cool, early autumn afternoon in town was the cause for Kitty Carlisle to wear a black crepe dress topped by wide vertical bands of silver fox. The chic and shiny straw hat with a bold red quill on top was a reminder of the summer days just past.

Dorothy Lamour in Big Broadcast of 1938
by Paramount, 1937. Designer: Head

Maureen O'Sullivan in The Flame Within
by MGM, 1935. Designer: Tree

Kay Francis and Clive Brook in Twenty-Four Hours *by Paramount, 1931. Designer: Banton*

Although fur often swaddled suits and dresses, it seemed somehow more appropriate or standard for coats. Designers manipulated every kind of hair or fur imaginable on every type of style.

An unexpected arrangement of mink was executed by Royer for Sonja Henie. A detachable bolero of mink, matching a mink-edged turban, was the focus for Henie's fall coat of toast-colored duvetyn. Dark brown accessories complemented the mink.

Furred collars and cuffs were standard then as now. Leopard skin was considered the most colorful of furs and formed the wide panel on Irene Dunne's black leda cloth coat with broadened shoulders and dolman sleeves. Leopard also comprised the gauntlet gloves. Black accessories and a fetching felt cossack hat completed this striking outfit.

One of the most unusual furs seen on the screen or on the streets was Russian chipmunk, worn here as trim for Kay Francis's rather busy street costume. Francis became one of Hollywood's most envied clotheshorses after she stumbled onto Travis Banton's services. No star spent less time, money, energy, or thought on her wardrobe—initially, that is. Banton remembered that she wore a black lace dress for an entire season and a black felt hat for two years just becaue she hated to shop. Banton provided Francis with a new hat and coaxed her into the lead of Hollywood's best-dressed list.

Howard Greer commented to *Modern Screen Magazine* in 1934:

Kay is much taller than most people believe so she has to resort to a little trick to make her appear smaller in scenes with leading men. Her street dresses are always made an inch shorter at the back and when she walks on the set she literally slouches an inch off her height, but because the back of her skirt is shorter it hangs even with the front when she slouches.

Kay Francis was 5'7".

These designs were popular in the days before environmental awareness. The widespread application of exotic fur as a glamour item was a definite cause for many problems of endangered species today. The push of old Hollywood touting the extravagance and desirability of fur for fashion still haunts us. Fortunately, synthetic alternatives are available and just as glamorous.

Sonja Henie in Thin Ice *by 20th Century-Fox, 1937. Designer: Royer*

Irene Dunne in The Joy of Living *by RKO, 1938.*
Designer: Stevenson

Another rather conventional style lavished fur along the entire outline, collar, and lapels of a coat. The wider the band of fur, the better. The dresses accompanying this design were uniformly uncomplicated so as not to detract from the main feature and mood of the ensemble, simple extravagance.

For *The Princess Comes Across,* anyone would believe Carole Lombard was Olga, a Swedish princess, rather than the disguised Brooklyn showgirl she actually was. The excessively showy cape with its prodigal application of fur left no doubt in the audience's mind of Olga's real or imagined wealth or glamour.

Kalloch also designed Ida Lupino's spring street costume for dressy afternoons. Gray faille silk was the material specified by Kalloch's sketch of the outfit for *Weather or No,* the working title of the movie later released as *Let's Get Married.* The pencil silhouette dress was sleeveless, the three-quarter length coat had squared shoulders and was collared and banded with silver fox. The sketch described a self-fabric hat, but the tiny toque was actually made from black belting, the neckline was modified to feature a large jeweled pin, and the shoes and purse also were changed slightly. Kalloch specified a swagger back to this design, which emphasized his admonition to would-be fashionable fans, "Remember, with coats, that you are seen from the back also, and strive for a perfect fit through the shoulders and a swagger swing to the skirt."

Although Kalloch personally drew this sketch, most studio designers had at least one sketch artist who would translate the designer's initial scratchings and verbal directions into full working sketches. It saved the designer a great deal of time and explains why one designer's sketches sometimes vary considerably in style over time. Edith Head began her career as one of Travis Banton's sketch artists, and Bob Mackie, a gifted designer of the 1970s and 1980s, was once Edith Head's sketch artist.

Sketch for Let's Get Married *by Columbia, 1937. Designer: Kalloch*

Carole Lombard in The Princess Comes Across *by Paramount, 1936. Designer: Banton*

Ida Lupino in Let's Get Married *by Columbia, 1937. Designer: Kalloch*

Jeanette MacDonald in Broadway Serenade *by MGM, 1939. Designer: Adrian*

Frances Dee for publicity for Wells Fargo *by Paramount, 1937. Fur from Bullocks, Wilshire*

Irene Dunne in When Tomorrow Comes *by Universal, 1939. Designer: Orry-Kelly*

Fur jackets came in all shapes and styles. Some were created for a star, some borrowed from a store for publicity, some made specifically for publicity only.

Bullocks of Wilshire provided Frances Dee's bolero of mink for her fashion stills publicizing *Wells Fargo*. Neither the movie nor the role lent themselves to high-fashion features, so the studio photographed their star in a wide range of borrowed, modish clothing. The fans were happy, Dee was happy, and Bullocks appreciated the publicity.

It is a wonder why Jeanette MacDonald did not collapse from heat prostration while wearing this lovely white brushed lamb's-wool jacket for a musical number. Embroidered revers and pockets supplied the only color contrast. The overlarge beret was also lamb's wool, with a visor of heavy stitched felt. MacDonald's screen costumes always had extrawide emergency seams because of her fluctuating weight during filming. Between pictures she easily maintained a slim silhouette, but MacDonald believed a good voice for her screen roles required extra energy, and extra energy meant rich milk, malted milk, chocolate milk, etc. The extra seams handled the onslaught of the extra energy.

Irene Dunne's unusual seal fur and leather jacket was completed by an equally unusual gaucho hat and scarf, Argentine-style. When Dunne first achieved success in Hollywood, she was very definite about what was becoming to her and had a tendency to demand her way on all costumes. Walter Plunkett remembered that she insisted on seeing not only all sketches for her own cinema outfits, but also those of any other actress in the film. She later stopped that and impressed Plunkett as a delightful lady.

Irene Dunne and designer Robert Kalloch for
publicity for The Awful Truth *by Columbia,*
1937. Designer: Kalloch

Anita Louise in Here's to Romance *by Fox, 1935.
Designer: Hubert*

Fur for daytime was almost as common on screen as fur for evening. Yet by far the most popular fur for day was karakul, or Persian lamb. Various forms of karakul have already appeared as trim on suits, as skirts, as scarfs, but a glimpse of the variety possible in karakul coats is necessary when discussing Thirties fashions. Considered dressy and chic, karakul could believably be applied to a much wider range of wardrobes than the far more expensive mink or sable.

The stunning karakul ensemble on Norma Shearer displayed the curly form of gray Persian lamb—a fashion favorite. Adrian thoroughly enjoyed creating an overly dramatic wardrobe to match Shearer's overly dramatic screen character as a fake blonde Russian countess. Although the motif was Russian, the message was "rich."

Irene Dunne's very chic fall afternoon outfit, here inspected by its creator Kalloch, featured a high, delightfully mad hat and a brief, boxy coat. The white baby-lamb coat included draped sleeves boxed at the shoulders, a pert upstanding collar, and a large black and white corsage. The black felt hat reached for the sky and achieved its twelve-inch height through intricately cut points of fabric which swooped from the center, featherlike. For *The Awful Truth,* three exact copies were made of each garment Dunne wore: one for actual filming, one duplicate for wear and tear during rehearsals, and one for Kay Stanley, Dunne's stand-in. Usually the stand-in copy was only approximate to the star's.

White galyak fashioned not only the visible topcoat to Anita Louise's smart three-piece costume, but also the blouse beneath it. The attractive black velvet scarf of the blouse, brought over the coat, matched the black velvet skirt. A black metal mask clasp closed the coat at the waistline. Accessories were a white galyak beret, white doeskin gloves, black velvet bag, and black patent shoes with perky white patent bows.

Norma Shearer in Idiot's Delight *by MGM, 1939.
Designer: Adrian*

Irene Dunne in Theodora Goes Wild *by*
Columbia, 1936. Designer: Bernard Newman

184

As mentioned before, no designer shirked from using anything hairy to adorn his stars. All manner of furry beasts were susceptible to slaughter on the altar of fashion. Environmental consciousness was nonexistent during these Golden Days of Hollywood, and this ignorance sponsored some startling cinema styles.

For example, wild—definitely—was the long, hairy number on Irene Dunne, appropriate for *Theodora Goes Wild*. Of black monkey fur, this coat and hat grabbed the audience's attention and held it, particularly if fans recognized the fur. Joan Crawford wore an early fall sports coat made from snowflake weasel skins, with a double scarf collar as a throw. The coat was lined with apple-green polka dot jersey.

Ellen Drew modeled this eye-catching moleskin coat, which introduced a new elbow-length sleeve wth soft fullness at the shoulders. Williard-George, Limited, specially arranged the skins for maximum appeal and added a green velvet belt with a malachite buckle for the original design. Moleskin was no fashion favorite because it was so perishable.

Loaned from I. Magnin for publicity, Ann Sothern's casual coat was made from "exceptionally fine" black and white pony. The large hat of matching fur was lined and banded with sheer black wool.

Ellen Drew for publicity for Sing You Sinners *by Paramount, 1938. Designers: Willard-George Ltd.*

Joan Crawford for publicity at MGM, 1930. Designer: Adrian

Ann Sothern in Grand Exit *by Columbia, 1935. Designer: I. Magnin*

Dorothy Lamour in Swing High, Swing Low
by Paramount, 1937. Designer: Banton

One Thirties vogue that has fortunately not been revived is that of complete foxes and minks slung over milady's shoulders. Considered luxurious and comfortable at the time, the sight of poor empty feet and heads now looks barbaric and crude. In light of the elegance and beauty epitomizing cinema glamour in the Thirties, this fashion practice seems glaringly inappropriate. Fox skins nevertheless were popular on screen and off, for almost all seasons, and ranged from mangy-looking pelts to prize skins, like those on Dorothy Lamour.

Another regular feature of daytime cinema wardrobes was the full-length, all-fur coat made from mink, seal, sable, or ermine. The full mink coat was the goal of many a striving fan as she watched her favorite idols parade on the screen in their lavish and expensive wraps.

During Jean Harlow's early "gun moll" days, she was often swathed in outrageous fur coats to show her character's new-found, though often temporary, status as a nouveau riche. Later such ostentatious displays would be toned down as Harlow achieved a growing degree of sophistication in both her on- and off-screen wardrobes. Harlow's mink street coat may at first seem like overkill in the glamour department, but the script, the character, and Harlow's budding image all required it.

Frances Drake's dapper dark brown seal coat was perfect for shopping on that cool winter day. The braided leather belt, fedora, and stitched suede shoes all matched.

Jean Harlow in The Iron Man *by Universal, 1931. Designer: Vera West*

Frances Drake in She Married An Artist *by Columbia, 1938. Designer: Kalloch*

No matter how silly some people think hats are, during the Thirties it was impossible for an ensemble to be chic and fashionable without a proper chapeau. Something had to be on the head. Hats were the bane of many costume designers, who threw up their hands and sent for a salesperson from a local hat shop. Others, like Adrian and Hubert, considered the task an artistic challenge and delighted in creating millinery that was perfect and specific for a certain star or role. Many hats have already been seen in this chapter; many styles are absent. The following is a fleeting glance at a few of the reasons why hats, however maligned, were an important element in the completion of a glamorous image.

When the Thirties began, hats were generally close to the head, like the cloche on Marion Davis or the style on Myrna Loy. The still of Myrna Loy was totally, utterly simple as far as design and fashion are concerned, yet this very simplicity was the height of glamour when presented on Loy. Loy achieved her greatest fame as a comedienne and dramatic actress, but the reason she was typecast so long in her early career as a vamp—usually from the Orient—is because she carried such an exotic image so easiy. Sheila O'Brien often worked with Loy and remembers her as "... a nice gal. A real peach. You can sit down and talk with her about something more than who's doing what to whom and what's going on in the studio; you can talk politics."

Myrna Loy in Body and Soul *by Fox, 1931*

Marion Davies in Five and Ten *by MGM, 193*
Designer: Adrian

Hedy Lamarr in Algiers *by United Artists, 1938.*
Designer: Adrian

Greta Garbo in Ninotchka *by MGM, 1939.*
Designer: Adrian

Greta Garbo in The Painted Veil *by MGM, 1934. Designer: Adrian*

Garbo was a major factor in millinery fashions throughout the Thirties. Her costumes were often too elaborate to become fashionable, but anything on her head was copied. Among Garbo's most famous chapeaus was the cloche hat from *Woman of Affairs* which revolutionized millinery in the early Thirties and became known as "a Garbo." Also copied were the period hats designed for historical films such as the skullcaps from *Mata Hari,* the white panama from *Camille,* and, of course, the Empress Eugénie hat from *Romance.* During the height of the Depression, women everywhere walked around wearing various copies of the plumed Eugénie—a nineteenth-century costume hat with no relation to the rest of their ensembles. Garbo's contemporary cinema millinery was no less popular. She was the trend setter for hats because Adrian wanted to show off the fine lines of her face; he emphasized her unique beauty with unusual, simple hats.

The turban from *The Painted Veil,* the beret, the pillbox, the cap, the cloche all became tremendous vogues. Garbo herself originally designed the famous "Ninotchka" hat, although Adrian refined it a bit for the milliners. Garbo's white pillbox from *The Painted Veil* was corded felt with a jade ornament.

Adrian gave an interview for the September 1935 issue of *Photoplay* in which he was asked why he gave Garbo so many odd hats to wear and if she really liked them. He replied:

Garbo isn't very fond of the fashionable hat of the moment. Nor is she fond of the fashionable hairdress. As she does not wear her hair in a way that suits the current hats and is very fond of personal-looking ones, they are apt to appear rather unusual to the eyes accustomed to the prevailing mode. The combination of individualistic hat and hair arrangement often gives Garbo a rather extraordinary style effect, which, in itself, is not really extraordinary. I have noticed that these very hats usually become fashion "Fords" eventually.

As the Thirties ended, a new star burst onto the consciousness of movie audiences and generated fashion vogues in hair, hats, and image. After Hedy Lamarr first appeared on the screen in *Algiers,* drugstores experienced a run on hair dyes, and soon everybody, incuding starlets and established luminaries like Crawford and Joan Bennett, had changed their locks from blonde or brown to jet black. The Lamarr hair-do with the part in the middle and the total Lamarr look became the new standard of glamour. Shock waves were felt not only in personal beauty, but also in the realm of fashion, in particular, the hat. Somehow that three-letter word seems inadequate when describing what Lamarr wore in her first films. Lamarr veils, snoods, turbans, and such swept the fashion world, and millinery companies worked overtime to fill the hunger for the new cinema image. Not everyone could effect the Lamarr styles, but just about everyone tried. Turbans and snoods became *the* fashion for Forties headgear.

Hedy Lamarr in Algiers *by United Artists, 1938. Designer: Irene*

One romantic characteristic of many Thirties hats was the application of a veil or net. The cinema designer had to be careful, however, not to obscure the face if the scene called for obvious feelings and not to create too outlandish a design that would steal the whole show from the characters. Veiled hats were a fashionable item, but their appearance on the screen was often subdued, except for special effects. The veiled hats on these two pages are very low-key and do not include the overly exciting styles that did occasionally materialize in Hollywood movies.

Alice Faye wore a pert little turban called "the Princess Marina" because it was a favorite of the then-new Duchess of Kent prior to her marriage. This black felt hat had a silk cord that crossed the crown and was sparked with gold metal bands. The interesting veil underlined and emphasized Faye's eyes.

Delicate lace formed the swirled veil on the high dome hat modeled by Martha Raye. Posed alluringly for publicity to showcase Raye's lovely eyes, the veil was not as heavy over the face when it appeared on screen. Completely enclosing the head, Irene Rich's large net veil wrapped fully around the face and elaborately flowered hat, leaving only the very top open. This hat was ideal for more formal afternoon engagements.

Martha Raye for publicity for Tropic Holiday *by Paramount, 1938. Designer: Head*

Alice Faye for publicity for She Learned About Sailors *by Fox, 1934. Designer: Hubert*

Irene Rich in That Certain Age *by Universal,*
1938. Designer: Vera West

Betty Davis in Dark Victory *by Warner Brothers, 1939. Designer: Orry-Kelly*

Betty Furness for publicity at MGM, 1935. Designer: Tree

Hedda Hopper in Midnight *by Paramount, 1939. Designer: Irene*

Feathers and fur were favorite trims for afternoon hats. Many feathered styles were inspired by period or historical movies, while furred styles were usually more contemporary in origin. A designer was often forced to transgress the specific dicates of fashion in order for a scene to be properly photographed. Some actresses, like Claudette Colbert, flatly refused to be photographed on their "bad" side. If feathers on one side were *the* style, and there was a profile shot that would be blocked, the styles for the screen would have to be different from those on the streets. Notice that most hats tilt toward the right.

Ethel Merman's sporty white chapeau was made from the same heavy cotton as her dress collar. The long, lone feather reinforced the jaunty air of the ensemble and the screen character. A portent of things to come was the feathered frolic on Hedda Hopper. Known for her showy bonnets, Hopper's screen hat featured claret wool covered with red wings to complement her gray karakul ensemble.

Fur of all kinds decorated many cinema hats. The lavish use of fox on Bette Davis was important to estabish the wealth of her screen character. Some might say it looked untidy, others would call it glorious. Betty Furness's foxy black felt hat was said to be from her own personal wardrobe. The shape predated the similar "Ninotchka" design but dipped stylishly over the right eye. A baby fox head trimmed the high crown, and a long, curling shadow quill completed the design. On screen the crazy movement of the quill would seize and hold the attention of every person in the theater.

Ethel Merman in Strike Me Pink *by United Artists, 1936. Designer: Omar Kiam*

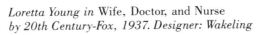

Loretta Young in Wife, Doctor, and Nurse *by 20th Century-Fox, 1937. Designer: Wakeling*

Joyce Compton in Artists and Models Abroad *by Paramount, 1938.*

Some hats were hilarious, some haunting. One popular style featured the wide brim, which became more fashionable as the Thirties progressed. Gwen Wakeling had these thoughts regarding hats in general:

> Hats were the biggest problem. Most were absolutely terrible. People really look better without hats. The only really good hats are like that big black one on Loretta, or a Russian fur hat. Or a watch cap, a knitted sailor's cap with a heavy cuff. Those three are the only decent hats. Others take away from the personality of the person. That was always a problem. Directors did not like hats. The big black hat was always romantic and Dietrich used to wear them a lot.

The big, bold, romantic black hat on Loretta Young was designed by Wakeling to complement her severe black frock. The major styling feature was the exaggerated length of chenille-dotted veiling Although cameramen and directors disliked the bother that these hats required, the effect of a large-brimmed hat tipped elegantly over a gorgeous head was stunning.

Less bold, more ethereal was the transparent brim on Joyce Compton's cinema chapeau. Worn for special effects in the movie, designs like this one appeared for teas in summer and were almost a standard accompaniment to "Ascot frocks."

If wide brims established a romantic mood, flat crowns produced something entirely different. The flat UFO shape on Isabel Jewell was interesting. Ernst Dryden, the designer of Jewell's pancake hat, introduced new fashion trends in *Lost Horizon.* The influence of ancient Tibet revived vogues in lounging pajamas, silk frog fastenings, oxidized metal buttons, two-color harmony, and the simple Chinese-collar neckline. Dryden advocated simplicity as the keynote to any wardrobe and cautioned great discretion in attempting adaptions of screen costumes to the demands of real life. He advised fans that it was always wiser to wait until the screen costume had been correctly interpreted for the public by fashion designers before attempting to use it in their own way.

Zasu Pitts's violet-covered pancake seemed pert and compatible with the star's zany but gentle screen image. Pitts was named after two aunts, one called *Eliza* and the other *Susan.*

Isabel Jewell in Lost Horizon *by Columbia, 1937. Designer: Dryden*

ZaSu Pitts in The Lady's from Kentucky *by Paramount, 1939. Designer: Head*

Modern stereotypes of Thirties millinery styles are most often limited to cloches for the early Thirties and wide brims for the mid years. The actual variety within various millinery categories—wide-brimmed, close-fitting, straw, feathered, flowered, etc.—was fascinating. One screen favorite was the adaption or feminization of male headgear, usually to complement tailored or feminized man-style suits.

Orry-Kelly went across the ocean for the theme to Dolores Del Rio's peaked black felt afternoon hat, which copied its cone shape from a Middle East turban. Marjorie Gateson's topper matched a braided band at the base of the crown with the plaid of her ensemble. This unpretentious yet dignified hat was extremely chic and fashionable.

Another adopted look was the sailor hat or schoolboy cap. Anne Shirley's pert chapeau boosted her image as a rising young star at the time. The hat had to fit or enhance the established or desired image of the wearer. Shirley's hat would look contradictory on Dietrich, for example, and the black cartwheel design previously seen on Loretta Young would be much too mature for Shirley's screen personality for this role.

Inspired by the British Navy, Wakeling discarded the band around the bottom of a seaman's cap and added a stitch-patterned wedge of felt to match Gypsy Rose Lee's coat while maintaining the felt body of the hat in the same color as her dress. Very simple, very stylish.

Dolores Del Rio for publicity for 20th Century-Fox, 1937. Designer: Herschel

Marjorie Gateson for publicity for Escape to Glory *by Columbia, 1939. Designer: Irene*

Anne Shirley in Meet the Missus *by RKO, 1937. Designer: Stevenson*

Lana Turner in These Glamour Girls *by MGM,
1939. Designer: Tree*

The variety of shapes that could conceivably be worn on the human head is infinite. Most cinema hats had to be subdued and not detract from action in the scene; a few, however, were deliberately outlandish to make a point instantly with the audience. The charisma and style of the star wearing these designs did influence fashion for better or worse, and many cinema hats reappeared on thousands of heads throughout the world.

Cinema designers drew on any idea, any motif, any shape to create a hat. Two doilies held on by velvet ribbon became something interesting when worn by newcomer Lana Turner. Jane Wyatt's minaret of black felt, with its gold ornament and black tassel, was adapted from a Chinese-inspired original seen in *Lost Horizon*. Jacqueline Wells, later known as Julie Bishop, modeled a favorite late Thirties–early Forties shape, with its stiffened crown of white heavy crepe. Simple engineering kept the style upright; a tied bow in back kept it on. The lines of the high-crowned black and white hat on Loretta Young are more identified with the late Sixties than the Thirties. The simplicity and elegance of this pharaoh hat design require little trim or decoration to establish a superb impression. Notice how the hat coordinates exactly with the dress, with its wedge cut, color scheme, and dots.

When a freakish fad swept the country, Hollywood was inevitably blamed, guilty or not. Travis Banton complained about this once in 1937 when he said that Hollywood was given undeserved credit for eccentric styles frowned upon by Paris designers. He did admit that the movies sometimes began disturbing vogues—like going hatless. Banton thought the hatless fad started in Hollywood generally because of the great weather there and the healthy hair of its stars, and specifically by Carole Lombard in *Swing High Swing Low* when she entered a restaurant and removed her hat before starting lunch. This act shocked the fashion world at the time.

Julie Bishop for publicity for Frame Up *by Columbia, 1937. Designer: Kalloch*

Chapter Four

Glamour at Home

When asked if he had a favorite screen costume, director George Cukor responded:

> No. It was always what suited the scene that was the best. And I think if you had a costume that knocked your eye out, it wasn't good for the scene and it was not good for the picture.

Despite this belief, many of Cukor's pictures were "women's" movies that featured dramatic wardrobes (many by Adrian) which did indeed knock the eyes out of most fans. Cinema negligees and hostess gowns offered special opportunities for unparalleled Hollywood glamour. If the script allowed, an eccentric or wealthy character could be swathed in all manner of lavish materials in the guise of nightgowns, slips, and robes.

One of the most publicized negligees created in the Thirties was the silver beaded design with twenty-two-inch-long ostrich-frond cuffs that Jean Harlow wore in *Dinner at Eight*. To this day, lavish, excessive Hollywood glamour is epitomized by this garment. When asked whose idea it was, George Cukor, the director of the film, said:

> Maybe Adrian. We all thought that she should knock them in the eye. And also the consideration was with the actress with a perfectly beautiful figure. You see, if the actress who played a role had a bad figure, you might have to cover everything up, but she had a spectacular figure, and Adrian just dressed her to her best advantage.

an Harlow in Dinner at Eight *by MGM, 1933.*
signer: Adrian

Mary Carlisle in Lady Be Careful *by Paramount, 1936. Designer: Banton*

Marlene Dietrich, one of the exemplars of Thirties glamour, wore this ensemble as a daytime hostess gown. Made of white chiffon with shimmering satin, the fox-bordered circular cape was draped to resemble a coat. The gown was softly shirred at the neckline wth a jewel clasp. Banton reminisced once about Dietrich and presented a paradoxical image of a cinema queen who grew tired and bored with a gown after it had hung in her closet for a week and who flushed with pride when he sampled and praised the magnificent torte cakes she delighted in making from scratch.

The maribou-trimmed robe on Mary Carlisle featured voluminous yards of taffeta, with a finely pleated front panel in the skirt. The wide-open, low-dipping décolletage was executed in the best of taste and presented Carlisle as a sweetly sexy, glamorous star.

Clara Bow, shown in a lace and sable negligee, was another star dressed by Banton. Her inexhaustible energy continually turned his creations into rags because she never remembered what was on her back. Sequin trains were ruined when dragged through muddy studio streets, satin robes littered dusty floors, and exquisite lace met its fate at the paws of Bow's enormous, friendly Great Dane, Duke. It took Travis Banton quite a while to overcome his aversion to this two-hundred-pound constant fitting-room companion.

Gwen Wakeling's opinion of glamorous fur-trimmed negligees was, "You're not supposed to take those things seriously."

Clara Bow in Hoopla *by Fox, 1933. Designer: Kaufman*

Marlene Dietrich in Desire *by Paramount, 1936.*
Designer: Banton

Jean Arthur in History Is Made at Night *by United Artists, 1937. Designer: Bernard Newman*

Loretta Young in Three Blind Mice *by 20th Century-Fox, 1938. Designer: Wakeling*

Carole Lombard in My Man Godfrey *by Universal, 1936. Designer: Banton*

Brocade, metal cloths, and printed taffeta represent only a small sampling of the rich fabrics which constituted cinema garments to wear around the cinema house. An eccentric but wealthy scion of a socially prominent family might go a bit Middle Eastern for her private attire, as Carole Lombard did in *My Man Godfrey*. Her lounging gown of heavy Gobelin silk was embroidered in golden plumes. Under this were golden trousers tightly fitting at the ankles. The gold belt clasped with an antique gold buckle, heavily jeweled. Lombard was one of the best-loved actresses in Hollywood. Film crews could count on her unfailing humor and generosity. For a Lombard picture, she usually ordered cases of Coca-Cola delivered on the set for everyone to drink; she also enjoyed giving other gifts to cast and crew for any reason.

Bernard Newman's stunning pajama ensemble modeled by Jean Arthur worked finely pleated gold lamé into harem trousers topped with a belted coat of gold lamé scattered with tiny, colorful flowers. Less flashy but still spectacular was the taffeta print hostess ensemble on Loretta Young. Vivid red and yellow orchids on a gray background provided the basis for Young's Middle East motif ensemble, complete even to her red open-toed leather boots. The unusual caravan pants and long train made a striking screen entrance mandatory. In 1936 Loretta Young was recuperating from a serious illness. While filming *Unguarded Hour* at MGM she ate a half dozen ice cream cones every day, and at ten-thirty every morning shooting was halted by doctor's orders so she could have a second breakfast.

As already stated, it was not unusual for a garment to be used over and over by a studio on different actresses. What was highly unusual was seeing the same item on two top stars. In a rare display of leg art, Mae West wore a dazzling dressing robe of gold metal flowers on a black background. The full sleeves, tight near the shoulders, and black satin lining were simple style details which had originally caught the eye of Marlene Dietrich. Whether the same gown was worn by two such distinct personalities is unsure—note the cuffs on Dietrich—but the same material and basic design did grace the forms of Paramount's top two stars.

Plain lamé, if lamé can ever be said to be plain, lent itself to less magnificent but still impressive robes and negligees. Adrian's intricately cut dressing robe for Greta Garbo was extremely subtle in its Chinese theme. The lounging pajamas on Margaret Sullavan combined blue velvet and gold lamé to suggest Russian origins. The sleeves were left open at the bodice top in a manner usually reserved for dance dresses. A sash of bright blue satin tied at the waist.

Howard Greer, in his biography *Designing Male*, stated that Banton had an amazing aptitude for creating photogenic clothes. Despite this obvious talent, when Banton first arrived in Hollywood in the mid-Twenties, he was very certain that designing for a studio would be a jolly lark and that all female stars were sweet-natured, although misunderstood, young ladies who would be enchanted to have him correct their abominable taste in clothes. He later learned that many actresses had developed definite ideas about what they would and would not wear. He also had to contend with armies of people who often accompanied various stars, as well as with personal superstitions. Mae West had an admirable list of taboos that Banton had to remember. For instance, West disliked pearls because they meant sorrow, refused any Sunday fittings no matter how far behind schedule production was, thought peacock feathers brought bad luck, refused to permit stitching on any gown she was wearing while filming a scene even to repair a rip, and of course forbade whistling in the dressing room, open umbrellas in doorways, and black cats. And then there were West's ever-trailing skirts, which Banton considered simply unfinished. West insisted no matter how much Banton resisted.

Greta Garbo in Grand Hotel *by MGM, 1932. Designer: Adrian*

Mae West in Night After Night *by Paramount, 1932. Designer: Banton*

Marlene Dietrich in Morocco *by Paramount, 1930. Designer: Banton*

Loretta Young in Shanghai *by Paramount, 1935.*
Designer: Banton

When it came to creating glamorous lounging attire, few designers could resist the built-in exotic quality inherent in the Oriental motif. Elaborate designs and lavish embroidery never looked overdone, and a simple Chinese note here or there evoked instant fascination.

Garbo wore this dramatic Adrian creation on screen to lie around the house while in China. The turban, of course, made fashion history, but the elegance of the entire ensemble was also not overlooked by either fans or fashion designers.

Elissa Landi's black satin Chinese lounging pajamas were sheer perfection and were made for her by Banton, supposedly for her own personal use. Stars often purchased favorite items from cinema wardrobes; few were given them outright.

Loretta Young's ornate Chinese costume was vibrant with richly colored embroidery. Said to be a totally authentic Chinese outfit, the meaning of the designs was hidden from Occidental minds. Young was known for her great knowledge of all facets of moviemaking. Between takes of her movies, she did not retreat to her dressing room as most actresses did, but kept the crew busy answering technical questions on everything from lighting to costumes. According to a 1937 studio publicity release, Young felt:

> The reason why so many stage actors fail in Hollywood is because they expect to find the stage set for them as in the legitimate stage. Each successful motion picture star is really a one-man or a one-woman business. It's just like running a little store in a small town, you have to know every branch of the business. Giving a truly great and artistic performance isn't sufficient. A Sarah Bernhardt could fail in Hollywood if she just thought of her performance and ignored the details that make it posible to carry over that performance through the film to the audience. . . . For every hour that I've spent before the camera or waiting on the set or studying the script, I've devoted three to chats with executives and interviewers, in posing for photographs, in attending to personal business concerned with films, and in taking care of a thousand little matters that either make or break an actress.

Elissa Landi in publicity for Paramount, 1934.
Designer: Banton

Greta Garbo in Painted Veil *by MGM, 1934.*
Designer: Adrian

If Oriental mean exotic, and velvet meant wealth and sophistication, the combination of the two should have been memorable, and it was.

There is an old maxim which states that if the human mind can imagine something, somewhere it must exist. Therefore, wasn't it possible that stars like Dietrich or Crawford really did entertain at home wearing black velvet with ornate hand-beaded trim? Fans wanted to believe it because it was a dream shared by all and achieved by a few on the screen. In 1936 alone, Hollywood spent $175 million making movies and another $17 million to advertise their stars and products. The studios gave the people what they craved—glamour, fantasy, and entertainment. Credited screen players in 1936 earned a weekly salary of $1 million, extras made $3 million for the year. Hollywood was big business.

The opulence that Hollywood could produce, faked or real, was staggering. The attention to detail and professionalism of every member of cast and crew was meticulous. The drape of Kay Francis's train and shoulder panels was very carefully staged to maximize appeal and show off the gown. The gown itself followed Orry-Kelly's commandment, ''Drape the body rather than squeeze it into forms of distortion.'' Loretta Young's head was precisely positioned against the background plant for an excellent composition. She was perfectly posed to display the main style feature of her hostess gown, the splendid sleeves and dropped wide shoulders, trimmed with large brilliants in an elegant design.

The exacting work of beading all these ensembles was performed by highly skilled seamstresses, and no mistake or error was tolerated. This did not mean that the studios did not have thrifty streaks. The exquisite hostess ensemble on Gladys Swarthout, photographed in 1937, appeared sans belt and turban that same year for publicity on Mady Correll. Tight gold trousers encased the legs and were visible when the front of the gown swirled apart. Notice how Banton considerately left a ring of soft velvet about the beaded neckpiece so the wearer would not scratch herself when she turned her head.

Kay Francis for publicity for Mandalay *by Warner Brothers, 1934. Designer: Orry-Kelly*

Gladys Swarthout in Romance in the Dark *by Paramount, 1938. Designer: Banton*

Velvet hostess gowns were popular on the screen and ranged from seductive to simple. The overall effect, however, was uniformly stylish and smart. Marian Marsh's elegant black hostess gown with puffed three-quarter sleeves was functional for teas or dinners. On screen, the upraised white collar showcased Marsh's face, and the shortened sleeves were practical for unencumbered dining or sipping.

Claire Trevor's noteworthy hostess gown was coral transparent velvet with chocolate satin-back crepe undersleeves which crossed in back and tied in front, leaving skirt-length sash ends. A pin of emeralds, garnets, and sapphires held the neck drape in place. Bracelets were matching stone medallions.

Norma Shearer's lovely velvet-topped two-piece hostess ensemble was only one of several amazing Adrian creations for the *Riptide* role. The shirred sleeves and central panel were simple lines that slimmed the body but did not detract from the focus of attention, the collar and face. Regarding her on- and off-screen wardrobes, Shearer once said, ''The dress has to fit you mentally as well as physically. You must imbue the clothes with your own personality.'' One fetish Adrian could indulge when designing hostess gowns was his extreme dislike of fancy shoes. He admonished Shearer fans never to let people be conscious of their feet!

Hurrell, the famous still photographer, once commented that he could not pose Shearer for photographs unless she could scrutinize herself in a large mirror while he was shooting. It was difficult to catch spontaneity and a natural mood while she was so preoccupied with how she appeared to the camera.

Marian Marsh in Counterfeit *by Columbia, 1936. Designer: Anthony*

Norma Shearer in Riptide *by MGM, 1934. Designer: Adrian*

Claire Trevor in Dante's Inferno *by Fox, 1935.*
Designer: Royer

Irene Dunne for publicity for RKO, 1931.
Designer: Jessie Turner

Ann Harding in Devotion *by RKO-Pathé, 1931.*
Designer: Wakeling

Luxurious velvet was not reserved for public or semipublic use; the Hollywood cinema boudoir also saw an ample amount of this expensive material. Negligees presented the most extravagant application of velvet because only the wearer, her lawful husband, a few close female friends, and her maid would ever see these elegant styles.

Fans were delighted when the prying eye of the camera revealed Ann harding's velvet gown of rich red, far too elegant to be wasted on only a few souls. Gwen Wakeling remembered Ann Harding and the early days at RKO:

> Ann Harding was difficult to dress at that period only because
> she had so much hair on her head and people wore hats.
> Wonderful woman. Her hair was long enough to sit on, and
> people wore little cloche type of hats; we had one hell of a time
> with hats. Not very clothes-conscious, but a wonderful actress.

Irene Dunne's unusual pale green velvet negligee featured extraordinary sleeves that were very full from the shoulder to the forearm, then gathered snugly at the wrist. Gold thread embroidery trimmed the shoulder yoke and bodice design, and a gold lamé belt finished the gown.

Kay Francis was a favorite of the costume designers because she rarely questioned anything they made for her. She never told Orry-Kelly to change a line or redo the skirt folds. Kelly once commented on professional stars like Francis to *Motion Picture Magazine* in December 1937:

> They know that I know my business, which is to make them
> look superlatively well on the screen. They understand to the
> point where they know, too, that if they look badly on the
> screen, if their clothes fail to bring them distinction, that they
> are not as much at fault as I am. And that this failure is going
> to re-act more on me than on them in this one brief badly-
> gowned appearance. I endanger my reputation as a designer.

His reputation was secure with the velvet negligee worn by Francis. Black panne velvet was trimmed with white and featured a low, low back. Kay Francis was queen of the matinee audience in the early and mid-Thirties. Women would stand in line, come rain or shine, to see what their favorite star wore because it was terrifically important to them. Outfits such as this one on Francis kept them coming back for more. It was Hollywood glamour, and moviegoers loved it.

Loretta Young in Private Number *by 20th
Century-Fox, 1936. Designer: Wakeling*

*Margaret Sullavan, James Stewart, and Walter
Pigeon in* Shopworn Angel *by MGM, 1938.
Designer: Adrian*

Totally feminine as evening gown material, satin became even more lovely in the home. Satin tended to flash back at the camera because of its tricky highlights, but the professional still photographer could emphasize the effect and create a fantastic still like the one of Frances Drake. The ice-green hostess gown had a closely fitted bodice, full sleeves, tight wrist bands, and a long, narrow train. Large satin roses at the shoulder and on the wrists gave this garment an absolutely superb flair.

White ostrich plumes and white satin made a very chic combination, especially on Margaret Sullavan. The crossed bodice panels formed a long, stylish train, and the slit overskirt disclosed a seductive lace-trimmed satin slip.

Silver-threaded satin formed the stunning hostess gown from *Private Number.* Delicately pleated, the ancient Greek motif was obvious from the blue and white waist and bodice banding, intricately designed and beaded. This same banding also appeared on the neckline of the exquisite pale blue chiffon cape. Young's favorite colors were blue and white. In fact, many other stars preferred blue. MGM used five hundred more bolts of blue material than any other color every year because it was so popular.

Styles in at-home wear floated in and out of vogue just as other categories of clothing did, but Orry-Kelly felt that any style was "out" if unbecoming and always "in" if it enhanced an actress's appearance. If Paris dictated that all skirts would be fourteen inches from the floor to be proper and an actress looked better in a twelve-inch length, Kelly—and all other costume designers—would choose what looked best on that body. They designed for individuals, for unique personalities, not faceless masses.

Betty Grable, Fred Astaire, and Edward Everett Horton in Gay Divorcee *by RKO, 1934. Designer: Irene*

Dolores Del Rio in Flying Down to Rio *by RKO, 1933. Designer: Irene*

Marion Davies in Bachelor Father *by MGM, 1931. Designer: Adrian*

Informal satin pajamas were far more casual than satin hostess ensembles. The outfits on these two pages were for relaxing and lounging.

"Exquisite" and "elegant" must be used to describe Ida Lupino's glamorous black and white satin pajamas. The Russian motif predominated, but the mood was pure Hollywood. Notice how even the slippers echo the braiding of the flat gold belt and sash.

Lamé and chiffon satin fashioned the beautiful pajama outfit on Marion Davies. A very early Thirties design, lounging pajamas like Davies's with their ultrawide trouser cuffs, have always returned periodically to fashion heights.

Dolores Del Rio wore this handsome coral satin jumpsuit for *Flying Down to Rio* in 1933. Publicity at the time touted it as the new epaulet pajamas. Apparently the style was long-lived because the same garment appeared on Betty Grable for her number in *Gay Divorcee* in 1934 and also on Grace Bradley in *Old Man Rhythm* in 1935. These pajamas looked vastly different on each woman. On Del Rio they were exotic, sultry, chic; on Grable they were vivacious, for fast dancing; and on Bradley they were appropriate for a college dormitory. In filming *Flying Down to Rio*, actual footage of Rio was shown for background shots, with Malibu Beach used for fill with cast members. The big airplane scene was filmed in a hangar and took four weeks to complete.

Ida Lupino in Let's Get Married *by Columbia, 1937. Designer: Kalloch*

If satin is considered sexy for sheets, satin negligees must be the height of sensuousness. Negligees today are described as loose-fitting dressing gowns. To a Thirties costume designer they were not always loose-fitting and were not limited to something worn before dressing.

One could hardly wear the glamorous negligee on Madeleine Carroll to bed, yet the boudoir was the locale for its use. Delicately sequined lace formed the train and open sleeves on this stunning pink satin design.

Rose satin and matching maribou produced the charming negligee on Shirley Ross. The robe was cut in a princess line with balloon sleeves of maribou; the nightgown beneath was double rose chiffon, the slippers rose satin mules.

Satin loveliness describes Shirley Temple's provocative pale blue two-piece negligee, which was suitable both before and during slumber. The embroidered trim outlining the bodice created a fashion sensation with its chic white bunny. Stylish dark blue and white striped yarn framed the neckline and reached perfection when completed by matching pom-poms. Accessories included a cuddly white duck with contrasting red and white checked bonnet.

Shirley Temple in Curly Top *by Fox, 1935.*
Designer: Hubert

Madeleine Carroll in The Case Against Mrs.
Ames by Paramount, 1936. Designer: Taylor

Mary Ellis in All the King's Horses
by Paramount, 1935. Designer: Banton

A favorite complement to satin in the boudoir was rich, delicate lace. No large jewels could imply femininity better than the dainty frill of a lace collar or trim. Even today satin and lace are an unbeatable combination in the glamour game.

Rosalind Russell wore a beautifully graceful pink negligee to entice Willian Powell. The accordion-pleated lace jabot, with a dot of a diamond, balanced the lace inset of the skirt. The sleeves were wide above and tightly fitted below the elbows. The only fastening was a jeweled clasp at the waist.

June Collyer's lovely lace negligee had long, fitted sleeves and was trimmed with a roll of twisted satin at each shoulder. The robe fastened on one side, and a satin sash matched the slim underslip and shoulder rolls.

Satin and rare lace fashioned Marlene Dietrich's cinema nightgown in a soft fleshtone. The elaborate side trim of the skirt and neckline was all hand-done. Her short-sleeved bed jacket was a deeper tone of maribou. Paramount did not allow the extravagant wardrobe budgets that were a trademark at MGM. Only for Dietrich's cinema costumes was Banton able to secure carte blanche from the finance department. Off screen also, Dietrich's clothing tastes were costly and deliciously reportable. According to publicity, Dietrich's expensive ($20 a pair) and ultimately sheer nylons were worn only once. (Garbo wore a size 9½ nylon, Anita Louise size 11.)

Chiffon negligees were at their best when a profusion of material was sent swirling around a wearer with a graceful walk or a becoming swing of an arm. Mary Ellis was the central focus in a remarkably romatic yet delicately sensual still. Backlighting and the sheer chiffon and lace negligee combined to cover just enough of Ellis to be ladylike while revealing just enough to be memorable.

June Collyer in Before Midnight *by Columbia,*
1933. Designer: Kalloch

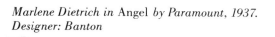

Marlene Dietrich in Angel *by Paramount, 1937.
Designer: Banton*

Rosalind Russell and William Powell in
Rendezvous *by MGM, 1935. Designer: Tree*

Grace Moore in When You're In Love
by Columbia, 1937. Designer: Newman

Jean Harlow in Dinner at Eight *by MGM, 1933.*
Designer: Adrian

Ruffles in the bedroom were not the same frothy, youthful style points seen on some evening dresses. They could still be gay and light, but they could also be serious if necessary.

Feminine and dainty to complement the wearer was the charming style on Janet Gaynor. Not one to carry a Dietrich type of glamour, Gaynor's delicately printed chiffon nightdress combined maribou with stiff chiffon ruffles. A satin sash also featured ruffle flowers.

Only a studio wardrobe woman would have the patience to keep long ruffles, such as the multiruffled sleeves on Jean Harlow's bed jacket, ironed and fresh. Becasue most of the scene in which this costume appeared was shot from the waist up, Adrian concentrated all style details to that area and supplied Harlow with eye-catching ruffles, beads, and lustrous satin necktie. The role was flashy, the blonde was flashy, and the clothes simply continued the theme.

Grace Moore's striking satin and chiffon negligee was highlighted by a neckline and cape of lavish rows of ruffles. Pearls were not worn to bed, but jewelry often appeared on cinema bedroom attire. It was amusing and entertaining to have a very wealthy character emerge from her bath wearing emerald and diamond bracelets.

Janet Gaynor in Adorable *by Fox, 1933.*
Designer: Kaufman

Frieda Inescort in If You Could Only Cook
by Columbia, 1935. Designer: Lange

Gail Patrick in The Lone Wolf Returns
by Columbia, 1936. Designer: Lange

When it came to hostess gowns, it was often difficult to separate them from negligees, lounge wear, robes, or sometimes evening gowns. Hostess gowns carried elements of all categories. They could tie in front like a robe or have low backs as on Frieda Inescort. They could be modest like morning dresses or exotic like negligees, serious or gay. There were really no hard-and-fast rules for absolutely defining or confining a hostess gown. The solution appeared in the context of the movie itself.

The stately beauty of Frieda Inescort influenced the design of this gray crepe Roma gown. The pleated panels were caught in front at the neckline with a jeweled clip, giving a caped effect. This gown was elegant enought for evening wear in public.

Rosalind Russell's fashionable hostess ensemble combined Oriental novelty with stylish flair. The slight flare of the sleeves mimicked the lines of the tunic top, as did the high military collar and the self-belt.

Another pleated hostess gown appeared on Gail Patrick. The graceful lines of this magnificent blue crepe Roma gown, bordered in white, would be tasteful and stunning in the evening setting.

Joan Bennett posed in a luscious crepe Roma hostess gown featuring a two-toned color scheme of wild rose pink and crushed raspberry. The padded shoulders were emphasized even more by meticulous draping and the lighter-colored shoulder top inserts. Bennett's new look for the Forties was exotic and sultry and very different from her previous fragile, innocent blonde image.

Rosalind Russell in Craig's Wife *by Columbia,*
1936. Designer: Anthony

228

Joan Bennett in Housekeeper's Daughter
by United Artists, 1939. Designer: Irene

Gertrude Michael in Murder at the Vanities
by Paramount, 1934. Designer: Banton

Lilyan Tashman in Mama Loves Papa
by Paramount, 1933. Designer: Banton

Hostess gowns did not have to be frilly, or pleated, or simple, or stunning. They were all created to match the mood, personality, and circumstances of the screen character, and that meant the variety was endless.

Gertrude Michael donned a black crepe hostess gown inspired by the age of Romance. Stitched white faille collar and cuffs drew on the Elizabethan theme, while a belt of gold cord accentuated the waist. Notice the unusual dropped sholder before the full sleeves. When asked what his impression was of Gertrude Michael, Walter Plunkett replied, "Fun. I remember that I liked her very much. Used to love to go to the set and tell jokes and have a good time."

Adrian interpreted another black and white version of a hostess ensemble for Jean Harlow. Although Harlow's charisma would shine on the screen even if she had been in burlap, this impressive ensemble featured a full black skirt overlaid by a full white three-quarter-length jacket. The special sleeve detailing, in particular the ruffled elbows, were relatively subtle style points done in eminent good taste.

A more classic example of the typical hostess dress is worn by Lilyan Tashman. This design was conceived in 1932 for a 1933 movie but remained smart for years due to its lack of faddishness and its enormously pleasing lines. The full sleeves, slightly puffed at the shoulders and caught by long, elegant cuffs, and the Chinese frogs combined with an English tied neckline to make an ensemble fashionable even today. Tashman was a woman who had a frank and lusty interest in clothes and worked seriously and intelligently toward retaining her best-dressed title in the early Thirties. Her friend and ally toward this goal was Travis Banton. Only a few weeks before her untimely death from cancer, Banton received the following letter from the East coast:

> Dear Travis: Just had to write and tell you this—went the other night to a very swanky party at the Embassy, and the most chic woman there was dressed in—what do you think? An absolute copy (not a good one, of course) of my first dress in "Girls About Town." Am so proud of you and tell everyone about you and your great talent. My love to all, Lilyan Tashman.

Loretta Yong modeled an Oriental-inspired hostess pajama dress in royal blue crepe. The sides of the looped trousers were outlined in green crepe, the same color that outlined the slit in the bodice. Sparkling colored stones in rose, sapphire, aquamarine, and pale green formed the interesting collar and cuffs. On the set of *Café Metropole,* Young served hot coffee and doughnuts first thing every morning to everyone on the set, from prop men to "juicers" (electricians). Consumption of doughnuts eventually reached fifteen dozen a day. In appreciation, the crew gave her a coffee set with doughnut saucers for the cups.

Loretta Young in Cafe Metropole *by 20th Century-Fox, 1937. Designer: Royer*

Jean Harlow in Bombshell *by MGM, 1933. Designer: Adrian*

Katharine Hepburn in Break of Hearts *by RKO, 1935. Designer: Newman*

Jean Parker in Life Begins With Love *by Columbia, 1937. Designer: Kalloch*

Housecoats were less formal than hostess gowns, dressier than robes, more public than negligees, and more casual than morning dresses. It seemed that on the screen a woman changed her clothing fifteen times a day to suit every activity from brushing her teeth in the morning to removing her make-up at night. When Walter Plunkett was asked if women really dressed so formally and had so many changes during the day, he answered:

> I suppose there were groups and classes of people in New York and the big cities who did, but I don't think the average woman did it. I think it was expected of a movie star, it was expected of the story, the fairy tale that was a movie. I don't think people ever expected a film to be real in those days as you do now. You question anything that is out of the normal way of living in the modern film. In those days you only questioned it if it was out of the normal way of doing a motion picture; bracelets up to the elbows when you come out of the bath, waking up in the morning with your hair gorgeously dressed.

The housecoat on Billie Burke was made along traditional Revolutionary American lines. The outlined-button cut of the bodice was an interesting fashion note, and the vertical lines of the pleated look helped reduce the thick effect from the bulky material.

A lovely taffeta turn-of-the-century–inspired housedress was modeled by Jean Parker. The large leg-of-mutton sleeves, the raised waist, the self-fabric round buttons, and the full, graceful skirt may have been part of history, but modified by a cinema designer they also became contemporary fashion hits. Jean Parker made her first dollar by selling her own oil painting at the tender age of ten.

Unusual but stylish was the housecoat ensemble on Katharine Hepburn. Patterned after a man's smoking jacket, the velvet and wool design became feminine yet dramatic to match Hepburn's screen character. This particular outfit was extremely futuristic and would be as perfectly appropriate and comfortable in the 1980s as it was in the 1930s. The lounging ensemble was dull gold metallic wool with rust velvet quilted cuffs and revers.

Billie Burke in The Bride Wore Red *by MGM, 1937. Designer: Adrian*

Claire Trevor for publicity at Fox, 1935.
Designer: Hubert

Joan Davis in Holy Terror by 20th Century-Fox,
1937. Designer: Herschel

The term negligee was often applied to what we know as the plain old bathrobe. Most cinema robes, however, were far from plain for the lead female star. She would never appear in the same robe twice in a movie, no matter how many mornings or evenings were depicted. The male star, however, always wore a good old favorite, sometimes in more than one movie.

Rose crepe satin produced Claire Trevor's charming night robe ensemble. The nightgown was trimmed with Alençon lace, and the robe featured a Japanese theme with its butterfly-decorated kimono sleeves. Swansdown buttons dotted the front closing, and a rose satin sash circled the waist.

Joan Davis posed in a striking house robe of heavy moire silk. This practical, stylish garment had no train and tied comfortably in front.

Fabulous and drmatic was the two-piece quilted satin robe design on Loretta Young. The easily detachable top and bottom revealed a blue satin and chiffon nightgown underneath. The full circular bottom of the robe was lavish in its proportions, just as the bolero top was thrifty in its. The beautiful and elegant Loretta Young had one tiny flaw that endeared her even more to her fans. In January 1937 Merle Potter reported that Young would rather walk under a thouand ladders than wear shoes in a picture. She always wore an old pair of bedroom slippers unless the camera angle caught her feet. In fact, *Love Is News* was later publicized as the most superstitious set because director Tay Garnett wouldn't shoot a scene unless he had a cane in his hand, Tyrone Power had to park his car exactly in his "lucky spot" in the studio parking lot, and Young wouldn't shoot a take if her feet didn't show unless they were in her frowzy and ancient pair of lucky bedroom slippers. Finally, in August 1937, the crew of *Love Under Fire* chipped in three cents each to buy Young a new pair of blue slippers because they were tired of seeing her prehistoric pink ones.

Loretta Young in Eternally Yours *by United
Artists, 1939. Designer: Irene*

Ethel Merman in We're Not Dressing
by Paramount, 1934. Designer: Banton

Loretta Young for publicity for Love Under Fire
by 20th Century-Fox, 1937. Designer: Wakeling

Regular, less exotic robes also had their place in cinema wardrobes. Luise Rainer wore her pleasing white negligee in *Ziegfeld Follies,* a period movie. Yet this style was far from dated and shows how a classic design can span many years without losing its fashion punch. Rainer's subdued but appealing robe perfectly demonstrated a clothing maxim attributed to Gloria Swanson: "Actresses are not mannequins displaying gowns. Gowns are to display actresses." A cinema design was unique to the star for whom it was made, as well as the character in the script.

According to publicity, the demi-negligee modeled by Ethel Merman was the newest item for a lady's boudoir. The white *peau d'ange* robe, with its double-breasted coachman effect, was said to be almost formal enough to serve as a summer evening wrap and was the ultimate in a lounging robe.

Taken from her "personal" wardrobe, Betty Furness modeled her pale blue velvet studio-made negligee to publicize her latest MGM movie. The design featured wide lapels and glass buttons of the same shade of pale blue. Just prior to this, Furness co-starred with Irene Dunne in *Magnificent Obsession* at Universal. That movie took sixteen weeks to film; shot 467,000 feet of negative which was cut to 10,000 feet, or 330 reels cut to ten, employed 4,300 extras and forty-two sets; and created thirty-eight costumes for Dunne and twenty-seven for Furness.

A glimpse into Loretta Young's private home was afforded by a series of publicity stills made for *Love Under Fire.* This one, shot in her French and Venetian inspired sitting rooom, showed Young in a padded antique-ivory quilted robe fastened with a quaint cameo. The exquisitely furnished room incorporated a rose marble and bronze fireplace topped by a French candelabra and clock, an antique-ivory velvet and rose rug, a Directoire chair, and a stunning Venetian mirror. Note also the impeccable attention to detail: the photographer has placed Young so precisely that her image is centered in the Venetian mirror. Such professionalism and exactness was a hallmark of Thirties still photography.

Luise Rainer in Ziegfeld Follies *by MGM, 1936. Designer: Adrian*

Betty Furness in Three Wise Guys *by MGM, 1936. Designer: Tree*

Clara Bow for publicity for Paramount, 1931.
Designer: Banton

Joan Crawford for publicity for Possessed *by MGM, 1931. Designer: Adrian*

Fashions for the bedroom sometimes included very revealing garments, which meant that the censors worked overtime to insure modesty in negligees and night wear. Every now and then, and especially before 1934, a star appeared terribly sexy despite all Hays Office efforts.

Backlighting an actress dressed in a thin, gauzy material never failed to delight audiences. The degree of sophistication and good taste varied considerably, however. The elegant appeal of Joan Crawford's still was preserved by good judgment and professionalism. Crawford revealed a significant amount of chest in her nightgown ensemble, but she could hardly be ashamed of it in later years. Backlit, but only to highlight the transparency of the robe, the low-cut but simple costume on Crawford showcased a great star.

As revealing and sensuous as Garbo ever became was the still of her in her Mata Hari working dress, filmed before the 1933 Censorship Code was enforced. There was nothing artificial to mold or trim the figure, and almost all of it was bared. Despite the stunning nudity of this costume, sensuousness was heightened by the prudent draping of material. While much of Garbo was unadorned, much was also seductively concealed. Adrian realized that yards of exposed skin are not as exciting as that which remains barely hidden.

Clara Bow's pouting still showed she had "It" in the early Thirties. Professional photography expertly maximized star, setting, and ensemble. Satin pajamas were crowned by a sheer lace top with strategically cut satin backing. Pearl seedlings shaped a self-belt. Bow probably added the bodice pin herself. Banton would have to get up at dawn to beat Bow to her dressing room and remind her not to ruin the effect of a design with spangles and heavy jewelry. To this, Bow would smile enchantingly and always agree. Once when rushes revealed a pendulous earring dragging down her ear lobe and counteracting the simplicity of an otherwise elegant evening ensemble, Bow protested innocently to Banton, "Why, Travis, darling, you said that *two* earrings were not right. Just to please you I wore only *one*."

Greta Garbo in Mata Hari *by MGM, 1932. Designer: Adrian*

239

Joan Crawford in Our Blushing Brides *by MGM, 1930. Designer: Adrian*

Jean Harlow and Clark Gable in Red Dust *by MGM, 1932. Designer: Adrian*

Jean Harlow for publicity for Hell's Angels
by United Artists, 1930. Designer: Greer

Plain cheesecake shots were often required of studio stars, but the tone depended on the status and personality of the star, the movie, and the role.

Virginia Bruce struck a haughty stance for a publicity shot for *The Great Ziegfeld*. Seductive though she was, there were no garters showing, no cleavage, and no belly button. The Hays Office was in full control. New actresses in particular routinely appeared in leg art to catch the eye and interest of the public and studio executives in pre-code days. Such was definitely the case with Jean Harlow, whose reputation as a sex-symbol made leg art mandatory for early publicity shots. This pose from *Hell's Angles* appeared on lobby cards introducing her as the ''Blonde Bombshell''—an appellation coined by Howard Hughes. Many other actresses had curvaceous figures like Harlow, but her personality and zest for life endeared her to her fans, as did her natural, exciting earthiness.

It was not necessary for established stars like Carole Lombard to pose for conspicuous cheesecake, but Lombard's enthusiasm and charisma lent themselves to ''semi-cheesecake,'' refined yet sexy stills like this one. Only the outline of the Lombard figure is actually revealed, and the censors could say little, but the shot is highly provocative and utterly sensual. Lombard was a favorite of the cast and crew in all her movies. After filming *Love Before Breakfast*, the crew at Universal gave her a huge wooden egg mounted on an axis and inscribed ''To Carole, a good egg; from her gang.''

Ginger Rogers's captivating publicity still was enchanting, winsome, sexy, and sensational. Her role as the Purity Girl of the Air in *Professinal Sweetherat* called for her to affect an air of childish innocence for her public while in reality being a temperamental spitfire with a taste for romance and wild excitement. Designing for this uproariously satirical movie was one of Walter Plunkett's favorite assignments.

Virginia Bruce in The Great Ziegfeld *by MGM, 1936. Designer: Adrian*

Carole Lombard for publicity at Paramount, 1933. Designer: Banton

Ruth Hussey in Rich Man, Poor Girl *by MGM, 1938. Designer: Tree*

Chapter Five
Glamour at Play

Cinema designers were not confined to glamorous evening gowns, smart day ensembles, or beautiful hostess costumes; sports and playtime received a great deal of attention also. Fans wanted to know what their favorite star wore to relax after a hard day making screen love to Gable or Grant or Cooper. The fact that not many stars really had the opportunity or time to spend days at a plush resort or idle away hours sailing around Malibu or Catalina did not hinder interest in what gorgeous outfits Hollywood thought appropriate for such times. On the screen designers were still restricted by black-and-white film limitations and the script, but for off-screen publicity cinema designers created many colorful, sporty, and casual outfits for the stars' ''personal'' wardrobes.

More pants than skirt was the Arabian trouser outfit designed by Gwen Wakeling for Loretta Young's personal wardrobe. Fine white toweling striped in broad bands of blue and orange with narrower stripes of maroon and gray composed the trousers and hooded bolero. This ensemble was ideal for after swimming at the beach.

The demand for stills of every star, rising or dimming, was insatiable. Stills in 1936 were either free or cost twenty-five cents each. Sporty and casual styles were favorite publicity features for fan magazines, and designs ranged from highly fashionable and chic to obviously show biz.

Loretta Young in a publicity still for Love Under Fire *by 20th Century-Fox, 1937. Designer: Wakeling*

Frances Langford in Broadway Melody of 1936 *by MGM, 1935. Designer: Adrian*

Toby Wing in Mr. Cinderella *by MGM, 1936.*

Perhaps one of the most innovative fashion occurrences during the Thirties was the gradual acceptance of pants into public life. The originator of this was, of course, Marlene Dietrich. She was the first star to wear slacks in public in 1931 in Hollywood, although everyone wore them on the studio lot. It is ironic that a woman renowned for her femininity would launch a new vogue of fashionable masculinity. Howard Shoup remembered he was still working at Bonwit Teller in New York when Dietrich caused a great commotion by arriving to shop attired exactly like her escort, an actor. "She looked stunning, but the entire schedule and work program of the store was disrupted as everyone flocked to see her. It was sensational." Despite Dietrich's enormous impact on the fashion world, slacks functioned mainly as casual or informal attire.

For *Lost Horizon* Ernst Dryden preferred to combine two distinctly different colors such as black and beige or wood brown and dawn pink for a balanced and harmonious effect, and he also researched the costumes of the locale for the movie. Each piece of jewelry seen in *Lost Horizon* was an exact replica of an ancient Tibetan piece copied from an authentic collection. The pants ensemble on Jane Wyatt was designed as a cinema costume to be worn as foreign attire in the movie, but the obviously comfortable lines merged with the choicest styling of the day to produce a popular casual outfit that helped pants join the public fashion parade. Note the shoes Wyatt wears. Dryden borrowed the great thick soles from the Chinese. The studio conducted an extensive search for "authentic-looking" Tibetan extras for *Lost Horizon*. The Mission Indians on the Pala Reservation in San Diego County looked and photographed most like Tibetans. Their costumes were furnished by the Western Costume Company.

More public and less sporty was the white crepe pants suit on Toby Wing. The full lines of the slacks became even more popular in the Forties, although the width of the pants legs and cuffs narrowed a bit to conserve material. A white-dotted navy blue silk blouse was attached to the pants to avoid unsightly darkness below the waist as well as unglamorous blouse lines which might clutter the smooth lines of the pants. Also white, but producing a far different mood, was the exceptional pants suit on Frances Langford. Again, the Oriental theme lent an air of fascination and intrigue, but the Adrian touch was evident in the imaginative, symmetrical arrangement of points and counterpoints in the frogs and pockets. A matching red scarf was natty, and everything combined to form a clean, sophisticated ensemble entirely glamorous, on screen and off. Thanks to Dietrich, Bette Davis could wear her chic pants costume for many public daytime engagements. The full-cut pants were not quite paluzzo, the three-quarter coat a bit too tailored to be swagger, the entire effect sensational and superb.

Jane Wyatt in Lost Horizon *by Columbia, 1937. Designer: Dryden*

Bette Davis in Golden Arrow *by Warner Brothers, 1936. Designer: Orry-Kelly*

Joan Crawford for publicity for Grand Hotel *by MGM, 1932. Designer: Adrian*

Ann Sheridan for publicity for Crusades *by Paramount, 1935. Designer: Irene Brury*

Loretta Young in Second Honeymoon *by 20th Century-Fox, 1937. Designer: Wakeling*

Resort wear, on or off screen, meant terribly, terribly chic beach wear. The resort that Ginger Rogers visited in *Top Hat* was a far cry from anything the masses would ever see. Her fully coordinated sun ensemble matched not only the purse to the jacket trim and sunsuit, but also the shoelaces to the purse handle and belt. More down-to-earth was the beach or bicycle costume on Ann Sheridan. The divided skirt and halter top were made from aquamarine cotton crepe, while the large beach hat was in a slightly lighter shade. This ensemble appeared extensively in publicizing Sheridan and her role in *The Crusades*. The period costumes in that movie did not lend themselves to fashion layouts, so nonstudio designs were borrowed for fashion features in magazines. This particular outfit became Modern Screen Pattern 748.

Loretta Young's white sharkskin three-piece suit forecast what the smartest women would be wearing during the coming resort season in Palm Springs in 1939. Fabric lacings on the slacks belt and bolero-brassiere top were repeated on the three-quarter-length coat (not shown). Copper disks formed the unusual necklace, which was inspired by an ancient Mayan design.

Publicity for *Grand Hotel* included this fashion shot of Joan Crawford in a pajama suit for resort wear. Fitting snugly over waist and hips, it flared in a not-too-exaggerated line towards the pants hem. An abbreviated bolero jacket accentuated the snug body line, while bold diagonal white stripes created a striking contrast to the dark red shade of the suit.

248

Ginger Rogers in Top Hat *by RKO, 1935.*
Designer: Newman

Mary Brian in Charlie Chan in Paris *by Fox,*
1935. Designer: Lillian

250

*Gail Patrick for publicity for Paramount, 1934.
Designer: Banton*

Of course every Hollywood star had a huge yacht and spent most of her time relaxing on board, while en route to another exotic party locale. Such was the stuff the studio publicity machine touted to bolster the fascinating aura of stardom. The truths of early make-up calls, long hours, and a regimented private life were far from glamorous and thus rarely discussed.

Yachting was one of the luxurious symbols of glamour and success. It still is. And yachting ensembles were favorite publicity subjects. Carole Lombard wore *the* classic yachting design. All such costumes appeared nautical, of course, usually red, white, and blue, and all sported stripes somewhere. Despite these unwritten requirements, the variety was still delightful. Gail Patrick's red, white, and blue ensemble of nubby cotton knit featured comfort as its main objective. No fitted blouse, no fastenings to bind the jacket, and the definite inclusion of easy, roomy slacks.

A slim-skirted design was part of Mary Brian's Cossack sailor dress. Less practical, but more interesting for the screen, this costume had yard-wide full sleeves on a Russian blouse with a pointed sailor collar that stood stiff and high, which, like the cuffs, pockets, tab, and double ascot, was trimmed with a triple border of silk braid matchng the slit scarlet skirt. A scarlet silk scarf with anchor, a knitted white topless fez tasseled and stitched in red, and red suede oxford shoes completed this ensemble.

Carole Lombard for publicity for Paramount, 1933. Designer: Banton

Marion Davies in The Floradora Girl *by MGM, 1930. Designer: Adrian*

Cinema designs were often called upon to remold an actress for the cameras. Correctly designed clothes can add or subtract many pounds, and figure faults or virtues can be emphasized or minimized. That was one of the primary jobs of a cinema designer, to make the actress look not just good, but great. Bathing suits, however, presented a special problem. If the script called for swimming, perhaps with a run into the ocean, hiding stubby legs or fat arms became the work of the cameraman and director because there was little a costume designer could do. Many designers often wished they could impose swim suits like the one Marion Davies wore. This style could hide any number of faults, if necessary, and, modified here or there, could still reveal or at least hint at a good figure. Still publicity shots fortunately allowed the studio to retouch and erase unwanted inches and pounds.

In 1933 Travis Banton thought the ideal screen actress should weigh 109 pounds, be 5′3″ tall, and measure 32½–25–34. Those figures matched Claudette Colbert exactly. Bette Davis's waist was 21″, bust and hips 34″. Davis was considered too busty, and her waist much too small. Today, actresses would kill for such a figure. Garbo measured 35–27–38.

Colbert's perfect screen figure and lovely legs were deliciously displayed in *Bluebeard's Eighth Wife,* a rare occurrence after her Cecil B. De Mille epics. This swimsuit became a popular style for publicity and appeared on more than one starlet.

Cinema designers were not concerned with just the clothes on an actress's back or how they looked on the screen. They also were acutely aware of background coloring and the relation of a costume with the set. A long quote by Kalloch from *Motion Picture Studio Insider* in April 1937 focused on this detail:

This problem of background is best brought forth now that summer is upon us and sea and sky make the setting for beach clothes. In regards the colors on the beach, did you ever consider the problem of *contrast*? For instance, there your bathing suit ensemble is seen against blue water, blue sky, and beige sands. A blue suit merges too completely with the general color scheme, though if you are inclined to plumpness this is the way of making the figure less conspicuous. However, if you wish to stand out against this natural scenic backdrop, the contrast of cool green or vivid scarlet will attract all eyes toward you. This simply, is the psychology of working with your background for effect.

Claudette Colbert and Gary Cooper in Bluebeard's Eighth Wife *by Paramount, 1938.*
Designer: Banton

Rochelle Hudson in Mr. Skitch *by Fox, 1933.
Designer: Kaufman*

Jeanette MacDonald in Sweethearts *by MGM,
1938. Designer: Adrian*

Olivia de Havilland for publicity for Anthony Adverse *by Warner Brothers, 1936. Designer: Milo Anderson*

Paulette Goddard in Pack Up Your Troubles *by MGM, 1932. Designer: Adrian*

If an actress became bored with getting her feet wet yachting or swimming, she could always take to dry land on horseback. Riding was another glamorous leisure-time exercise practiced during the Depression by the dirt poor in rural areas or by well-to-do urbanites who could afford to feed and stable living symbols of luxury. If a script called for a riding habit, Hook Ltd., tailors and habit-makers, probably made the actual outfit. The cinema designer chose fabric, color, and general style, but the actual creation of a beautiful English riding habit was the exclusive reserve of a professional, experienced, authentic English tailor.

It is amazing how many actresses during the Thirties were raised on horseback and enjoyed a romp through the woods every day. According to publicity Olivia de Havilland was one such person. Shown here in the "woods" of a Warner Brothers set, she looked lovely and very stylishly sporty in her beige and brown checked jacket and jaunty brown felt hat. Rochelle Hudson wore this informal riding costume on screen, but publicity said she also used it every morning for a brisk autumn canter. The beige and brown sweater complemented the brown pants and dark brown accessories.

It is also a wonder how cool and dry actresses always appeared on screen. Even when they were strenuously exercising, no hair fell out of place, no sweat formed on the forehead, no make-up ran, and, of course, no telltale perspiration ever stained her tailored ensemble. Two sports where one might expect to see some physical train were calisthenics and tennis. Paulette Goddard, as a beautiful platinum blonde, wore this snappy exercise suit for early publicity shots. Jeanette MacDonald's cool-weather tennis ensemble was designed by Adrian and exhibited restraint, good taste, and, on MacDonald, a high degree of charm.

Ann Harding in Biography of a Bachelor Girl
by MGM, 1935. Designer: Adrian

Actresses were not limited to just yachting, beach, and tennis wear. Any sport or leisure-time activity presented the opportunity for a smart costume. Some sports were more glamorous than others, but stars and starlets were photographed doing everything from practicing archery to studying the zodiac. Of course every hair was once again in place, make-up was perfect, and the attire eye-catching.

Looking unusually chic, Ann Harding modeled the stereotype ensemble of a painter. This velvet-highlighted design was not envisioned to be besmirched by a single drop of paint.

For brisk days on the links, Marguerite Churchill wore this golfing costume designed by Kalloch. The feature was a leopard belt and shoulder piece. The hand-knit cocoa brown sweater topped a natural-color, hand-sewn antelope skirt.

Marion Davies wore this standard pilot's costume in the early Thirties. The fur-lined jacket was needed for warmth in open-cockpit planes; the pants borrowed from riding stables because women's pants were still not acceptable except as pajamas for around the house. The greenery in the background of the Davies shot presents another problem studios had to handle—live plants. When a company remained for weeks on a set in which greenery formed a major part of detail, all of the living plants had to be removed after four or five days and replaced with "doubles." The intense heat and lack of ultraviolet light killed them. Deterioration of plants for the street scene in *Babes in Toyland* cost $200 per week, plus two men to provide constant care for the live plants.

Marion Davies in Bachelor Father *by MGM, 1931. Designer: Adrian*

Ida Lupino for publicity for The Light That
Failed *by Paramount, 1939. Designer: Head*

Janet Gaynor in Adorable *by Fox, 1933.
Designer: Kaufman*

Stars did not hibernate during the winter months. Even though the only snow they saw in Hollywood came from the prop man and the temperature rarely dropped below just plain hot on the sets, nevertheless an actress would don winter woolies and pose prettily for publicity while baking in the hot, glaring California sun, or attempt to shiver while filming a wintery scene when actually sweltering under blazing klieg lights. The more realistic the winter garb, and therefore the heavier, the better the chance that filming would have to stop to wipe the bands of sweat from a star's forehead. To achieve the frosty breath called for in some scripts, although set temperatures usually were above 90°, MGM made actors and actresses chew a trick gum-and-menthol concoction which produced the required chilly-looking exhale.

Janet Gaynor's fashionable beige wool skating ensemble was trimmed with sable. Her little cap was also beige wool; the boots were brown leather. The leg-of-mutton sleeves and profuse buttons indicated the turn-of-the-century inspiration.

Alpine skiing was growing in popularity in the Thirties, though one wonders why when considering the primitive equipment at the time. Sonja Henie's sensible one-piece ski outfit was not as warm as a real slope might require, but any more bulk would have been unacceptable for the screen.

Ida Lupino's distinctive white ski costume, with its pristine boots and skis, was created to complement the white slopes of California—and the unmelting "snow" of a Paramount back lot. When Edith Head designed the open jacket, open cuffs, and light sweater underneath, she wasn't thinking about snow, only the primary purpose for this outfit—to make a great publicity shot. In 1936 Paramount received fifty unsolicited applications monthly for Edith Head's job as assistant designer. At MGM seamstresses were laid off two to three months every year. A good dressmaker made $22 to $29 a week plus overtime. Twenty seamstresses worked at MGM, and there were two hundred applications on file for their jobs. One a year was hired to fill a vacancy.

Sonja Henie in Everything Happens at Night *by 20th Century-Fox, 1939. Designer: Royer*

Chapter Six
Epic Glamour

Fay Wray in Behind the Make-up *by Paramount, 1930. Designer: Banton*

The studio costume designer in the Golden Days of the Thirties contributed much to the enjoyment of films and added a certain artistic elegance to the image of the movie colony, on screen and off. The designer was devoted to the glorification of feminine charms through the medium of clothes within the restraints of script, director, and actress. Stage costumes were constructed for both comfort and endurance, movie costumes for sheer appearance.

Many historical costumes in particular appeared dazzling on the screen, but were so cumbersome, heavy, expensive, and delicate they should only have been worn for short periods of time. In fact, filming a historical epic required the actress to be in costume for many hours a day, for weeks at a time.

The cinema costume designer's first priority was appearance and authenticity. Period pictures required a great deal of research on the part of the designer. He might interpret his findings in more pleasing colors and lines to fit the actress, but the costume had to remain essentially true to the period it depicted. Fanciful dramatizations of the lives of kings and queens drove keepers of archives to despair, but the characters were garbed in authentic clothes. Publicity loved to report this preoccupation with pictorial realism as a factor that made many an otherwise merely entertaining picture vastly educational for the discerning eye.

Despite the months of research that preceded most historical movies to provide the required illusion of authenticity, the costume designer had to remember his two most important goals, to make the star believable in the role and to make her appear as beautiful as possible. As Gwen Wakeling commented:

> You don't ever make anything exactly true to life with the average character. If you are doing a mother struggling to raise her children, not a famous character, you will struggle to be true to life. But when you do a famous figure like Fanny Brice, you'll take some license, and you must consider the star playing Fanny Brice. If one star plays it you might go one way on it, if another star plays it you'll go a little different.

Just as each item of contemporary clothing seen on the screen was designed for a particular actress in a particular part, so too were historical costumes tailored for the star and mood of the movie. Walter Plunkett elaborated:

> I think you took the period thing and knocked off an awful lot of things that truly dated it and then blended in a little of what the modern eye would accept as smart. Of course in doing any biography of an actual person, you took what they had worn or were painted in as a basis because it had to look like that. Then maybe soften the things that to the contemporary eye looked ludicrous about a period and substitute a blend of modern. Or if you have a comedy character you emphasize the ludicrous things of the period. For instance, in *Singing in the Rain*, at first Arthur Fried was furious with me because I insisted that the skirts be about that much shorter (two to three inches) than they actually were in the late Twenties, the period of the film. The average woman was wearing her skirts at the bottom of the knees, a few were wearing them at the mid-knee level, and a very, very few were wearing them just above the knee. But I pushed them all up there, above the knee, because it was a comedy, you were making fun of the period of the Twenties, so I wanted the thing to look absurd. Now when the film is shown it isn't funny at all because skirts have gotten so

much shorter, but at the time when they threw in the fashion show number, that "Beautiful Girl" thing, the audience roared and yelled. A wedding dress with the knees showing! Things like that were absurd and it was one of the biggest laughs in the whole film. But now it is no longer funny. You let contemporary feelings and tastes influence you to make a thing good or bad.

Months spent at research were matched by weeks of designing and completing the costumes. Generally the finest materials were used for the major stars' wardrobes, with extras and bit players in reworked hand-me-downs. Big budget spectacular productions like *Marie Antoinette* allowed everyone seen on the screen to be uniquely fitted with a stunning new costume requiring almost the same lavish care as the stars'.

Times of course have changed. Most stars of television epics, for example, are now dressed by costume companies, the slim, brunette star fitted into something resembling the period originally designed for a curvy blonde. Edith Head has survived the transition from Thirties glamour to today's less golden methods and can compare television production routines with those of a major Thirties studio. Her comments:

> You cannot compare television, which is done under great pressure and low budget, with even a low-grade "B" picture. For *Gable and Lombard* I had three months to design clothes, unusual. I would say we had at the most two or three weeks to design for a television show. For De Mille pictures in the Thirties we would have as long as thirteen to eighteen months. A terrific amount of research. The average picture we would have six weeks to two months at least. Also, in those days we knew exactly who the stars were under contract to the studios. Banton knew he was going to dress these people. He knew what looked good on them. At that time each studio had a store. In other words, they, the great fabric people, Bianchini, Dushon, all the great French, Swiss, and Italian fabric people would come over with their samples, and each studio would say I will take a bolt of that hammered satin, I'll take a bolt of velvet. And when we did a dress we would say, "Oh, there is that beautiful brocade, there is that beautiful lamé in the store," because we knew were going to do pictures and we knew who was going to wear them. Today, we go out to a [regular commercial] store and try to buy something, and we don't know until the last moment who is going to be in the film.

Costumes seen in this chapter include not only the magnificently detailed and exquisite gowns worn in historical movies, but also the imaginative designs created for musical numbers, costume balls, westerns, fantasies, exotic locales, and unusual clothing not appropriate elsewhere in this book. All costumes in a movie, contemporary or historical, received the same care. Someone was in charge of the finished wardrobe, and almost always a cleaning crew went over the costumes worn that day and pressed them and cleaned them every night and had them ready for the morning. Sometimes if a beaded dress had a few beads hanging loose, it went into the workroom for a repair job. After the picture was finished the wardrobe crew made sure the costumes were hung properly or boxed and laid in tissue.

The complexity of caring for costumes was staggering. In 1935 alone, MGM produced 2,600 dresses using 23,000 yards of material. Keeping track of accumulating cinema wardrobes was an enormous job.

Sylvia Sidney in Madame Butterfly *by Paramount, 1932. Designer: Banton*

Vivien Leigh in Gone with the Wind *by MGM,
1939. Designer: Plunkett*

Perhaps one of the greatest movies ever made, and surely one
of the most enduringly popular, was *Gone with the Wind*, or
GWTW to its many fans. Appearing as a brilliant finale to the
decade of the Thirties, *GWTW* was a tour de force for costume
designer Walter Plunkett. Having already earned an enviable
reputation from *Mary of Scotland, The Little Minister, Little
Women, Quality Street,* and others, Plunkett was considered *the*
designer for the job. As on any set, problems arose and were solved,
and new ones took their place. Researching the costumes took
months, but actual execution of Scarlett's wardrobe was delayed until after filming had begun.

David Selznick instructed Plunkett to follow Margaret
Mitchell's descriptions as precisely as possible. The clothes were
designed, the fabric selected, and the wardrobe department was
ready to go. Some details such as proportion of collars had to wait
until the actress to play Scarlett was officially chosen. When Vivian
Leigh was announced and finally fitted, the wardrobe department
worked in a mad rush to keep ahead of filming.

Only Selznick had costume approval. There were two women
cutter-fitters and a separate crew for aging fabric and costumes.
Two men made gloves and hats for male cast members, and a crew
of milliners completed hundreds of hats for the women. Forty per-
cent of the cloth was custom-made for large scenes.

Although Vivian Leigh had a lovely figure and twenty-three-inch
waist, she also presented a major problem. Plunkett explained:

> A figure problem as far as Selznick was concerned. He was
> looking for cleavage, which the censors wouldn't let us use
> anyway. But she had no cleavage, and that was because she
> had a chest in which the bones went outward, called pigeon-
> breasted. Her breasts were normal, but it was very difficult to
> get cleavage for her.

Vivien Leigh in Gone with the Wind *by MGM, 1939. Designer: Plunkett*

Olivia de Havilland and Walter Plunkett for Gone with the Wind *by MGM, 1939. Designer: Plunkett*

For scenes which required cleavage on evening dresses or low necks, Leigh's bust was taped into position, a little padding added to the sides to look more natural, and the whole upper torso wrapped in adhesive as if she had pleurisy. She was extremely uncomfortable. As Plunkett put it, "It was horrible!" But you can never see a hint of the physical pain Leigh was experiencing in any moment of her superb performance.

Plunkett had other problems. The censors refused to allow any sign at all of pregnancy. In one critical scene Melanie was fainting and just on the verge of miscarrying. Unless they had read the book, few fans were aware that she was almost at term. Plunkett said, "I could only have great big long shawls and scarves to hide her figure, she could not wear a pad to look pregnant. I guess the censors figured it showed men and women slept together occasionally and that was so wrong."

An elegant but often overlooked costume was the gown Scarlett wore in the dramatic ending scene. Plunkett again:

I designed it with a large cameo, and there wasn't one in the department. I had bought one for my mother in Italy, and so I asked my mother and she let us borrow it for the film. When my mother died I gave it, the sketch of the costume, and a still of the dress to the Hollywood museum—it never got off the ground. I understand that the cameo has been stolen and is lost.

GWTW required over 5,500 costumes. The laundry bill alone was $10,000. Scarlett's white and green barbecue dress is periodically displayed at the Academy of Motion Picture Arts and Sciences as an example of costume designing at its best. The negative cost of *GWTW* was $3,957,000, of which $98,154 was spent on the women's wardrobe and $55,664 on the men's.

Vivien Leigh in Gone with the Wind *by MGM, 1939. Designer: Plunkett*

Unknown in The Great Ziegfeld *by MGM, 1936.*
Designer: Adrian

The Great Ziegfeld was a fantastic tour through a Hollywood fantasy, and Adrian was the perfect designer for it. His dramatic flair, follies experience, and vivid imagination combined to produce a movie whose extravagant costumes are awesome even today. Sheila O'Brien worked with Adrian in her early years at MGM, and she remembers him as extremely versatile. In 1938–39 he worked on *The Wizard of Oz, The Women, Remember?,* and *Lady of the Tropics* all at the same time. O'Brien commented:

> He had no assistants—he designed for all players. He had marvelous cutters and tailors, fitters, beaders, milliners. He had a crew that was unbelievable. I don't think he got his inspiration from Paris; in fact, I think he exerted some influence on Paris. . . . In *Ziegfeld,* Adrian had to design thousands of costumes. You couldn't do that show today. First of all I don't know where you would get those things made. I don't know where you would get all those marvelous helpers; they have all faded out of the industry.

O'Brien began her career working in the sewing room. It was hard work, with long hours, but she said it was fascinating to see the dress emerge from the sketch. Her pay was $16.80 per six-day week, less than janitors at the same studio. As a wardrobe girl or costumer, her first assignment was working on *Ziegfeld.* For fifteen hours a day she placed girls on the set and made sure their costumes were complete. Again O'Brien, recalling the scene with the huge staircase to heaven:

> That stairway went miles; up and down the stairs for fifteen hours a day. We just came down to go to the bathroom or eat. We used to go up there and get the girls placed, and every time you turned around one of them had gone up without her shoes, so you asked her what size shoe she wore and she would tell you a six, so you go up with a seven and she couldn't get it

Group in The Great Ziegfeld *by MGM, 1936.*
Designer: Adrian

Virginia Bruce in The Great Ziegfeld *by MGM, 1936. Designer: Adrian*

on, so you go back down and she may wind up wearing an 8½. Or someone would leave part of their costume behind. We'd have to get them all ready, all the costumes and the curtains, and be sure everybody had their clothes on exactly right. We worked hard.

The Great Ziegfeld started at Universal and after a year's preparation was acquired by MGM, which required six more months' preparation and six months to film. Two years and a production investment of $1,500,000 finally produced the movie. The program for the movie lists seven musical numbers, but actually there were twenty-three. For example, the Ziegfeld roof sequence had five subdivisions, the circus number had ten component parts. *Variety* in April 1936 commented that Adrian had captured the Ziegfeldiana of traditional good taste and skill in dressing up his girls rather than undraping them.

Adrian hired one hundred extra seamstresses for two months to work on *Ziegfeld;* they worked in crews, day and night, sewing the costumes. A carload of ostrich feathers was ordered from Australia. Despite the lavish materials and styling, the costumes were uncomfortable. Luise Rainer swore she never drew a breath all the time she wore hers on the set due to iron stays which girded her waist. Virginia Bruce wore one gown with a glass headpiece weighing twenty-two pounds, and the train was wired so it weighed an additional forty-six pounds. It took three men to carry her up the steps to pose in one scene. She also wore a costume with an incredible ostrich-plume train that cost $20,000.

The successful construction of the massive sets for *Ziegfeld* and other MGM extravaganzas prompted an appropriate footnote in history. Hanging in the MGM office of the superintendent of construction was this sign:

IT CAN'T BE DONE. BUT HERE IT IS.

Two of the greatest fantasies ever created for the screen were *Midsummer Night's Dream,* a critical success but a box-office disappointment, and *The Wizard of Oz,* which made money for the studio only after it was sold to television.

Midsummer Night's Dream's costumes and sets were remarkable. Anita Louise as Titania wore a costume with a train that required 91,000 yards of cellophane. According to publicity, moonlight for lovers was made wth 650 ten-watt bulbs; part of the city of Athens was built with 1,100 barrels of plaster; the moonbeam on which fairies danced weighed seven tons and included in its structure 750,000 yards of cellophane; and the woodland set required a stage 175 by 375 feet and extended over the top of another stage.

The book *The Wizard of Oz* was purchased by MGM for $75,000 (Selznick paid $50,000 for *Gone With the Wind*). Preparation for the movie started in summer of 1938, tests in August, and actual work in September. Actual filming began October 12, 1938, and ended March 16, 1939, with the cast and crew working the normal six days per week. Ten writers worked on the script, and four directors on the movie. The budget was set at $2 million, but the movie actually went $777,000 over budget. Director LeRoy originally wanted Gale Sondergaard to play a sequined, vampy Wicked Witch, but the studio insisted on an ugly old one. Ed Wynn and W.C. Fields turned down the part played by Frank Morgan because both thought it much too small.

According to studio publicity, 3,210 costumes were designed, 8,428 separate make-ups devised, and sixty-eight sets made; 350 lights on one set generated enough electricity to light 550 five-room houses with two sixty-watt bulbs in each room. The three hundred inhabitants of Emerald City worked for four days and earned a total of $44 each.

Adrian followed illustrations in Baum's book done by W.W. Denslow for Dorothy, the Scarecrow, and the Tin Woodsman. Billie Burke appeared quite different from the Little Old Woman described in the book. The Munchkin costumes were designed with large-scale vests and collars to make the actors appear even smaller. The Munchkin costumes were difficult to put on and wear because of the extraordinary number of flowers, tassels, bells, bows, and ribbons attached to add charm and cuteness to the characters. Everything about the Munchkin costumes was done in felt, even the shoes. The Munchkins were 124 Singer Midgets mixed with children. They worked for nine weeks and were paid $50 a week plus expenses. MGM's make-up department normally consisted of five or six artists, but forty extra were hired for *Oz*. The first make-up man would arrive on the set at five-thirty, the Munchkins would appear at six, and all would be made up by eight-thirty.

Buddy Ebsen, the original Tin Woodsman, left the picture after nearly suffocating to death from an allergic reaction to the aluminum powder make-up he wore. Most make-ups of the main characters took two hours to apply and at least one to remove. The Emerald City horses, Bill and Jake, "wore" different colors of Jello-powder for their big scene, but they kept licking it off.

Olivia de Havilland in Midsummer Night's Dream *by Warner Brothers, 1935. Designer: Max Ree*

Anita Louise in Midsummer Night's Dream
by Warner Brothers, 1935. Designer: Max R

Judy Garland in The Wizard of Oz *by MGM*
1939. Designer: Adrian

Gorgeous, cool Madeleine Carroll, the epitome of exquisite British beauty, was born Marie Madeleine O'Carroll in Birmingham, England; her father was Irish, her mother French. She was one of the few stars in Hollywood with a Bachelor of Arts degree, hers from Birmingham University, with a major in diplomacy and international relations and a minor in French language and literature.

A crack hockey player when at the University, the 5'4", 115-pound blonde had a passion for blue and insisted on civilized tea time at four o'clock every day. A maid would bring a tray of Carroll's personal blue tea service to the set, and she and whoever else would relax for a few minutes before continuing filming. Gwen Wakeling remembered Carroll as "lovely, elegant, beautiful, warm-hearted, honest and straightforward, and a lady. No figure problems."

Carroll did not have a "bad" side photographically, but she often remarked to cinematographers that the studio could get two actresses for the price of one because her right side and profile looked like a different woman. Cameramen like Joseph LaShelle agreed and avoided all right profiles when possible.

Although not pertinent to the Thirties, it should be noted that Madeleine Carroll won the Woman of the Year humanitarian award of the National Conference of Christians and Jews in 1948 for her outstanding war work with orphans (she adopted and cared for two hundred) and war wounded, her efforts in civic relations, and her overall unselfish service in World War II when she lived in France.

Many of Carroll's Thirties movies offered less dramatic meat for her talents and more showcase for her incredible beauty. Her costumes for *The World Moves On,* for example, were designed by Lambert, who copied and modified gowns actually worn by ladies of the period. The green moire gown, for example, followed one shown in an old engraving of Lola Montez, ex-Empress of Bavaria. The billowing sleeves, fichu collar, tiny peplum, and tiers of small bows were stylish in the early nineteenth century. The green silk moire picture hat with its chiffon veil was particularly appealing.

Perhaps Carroll's best-known Thirties role was as Princess Flavia in *The Prisoner of Zenda,* and her best-known gown this creation by Ernst Dryden. The gown was peach chiffon velvet, richly banded with mink and elaborately embroidered with crystal beads and ostrich feathers. The skirt alone contained over a dozen yards of material. Two petticoats helped fashion the princess lines true to the high styling of 1896. The first petticoat covered a twenty-one-inch waist corset and was made from dozens of yards of ruffles in pink taffeta brocade, occasionally caught in scallops by narrow blue satin ribbon bows. Over this was a peach taffeta slip cut on the same lines as the dress. As with most period costumes the dress was heavy, the corset breathtaking, and the overall effect stunningly magnificent.

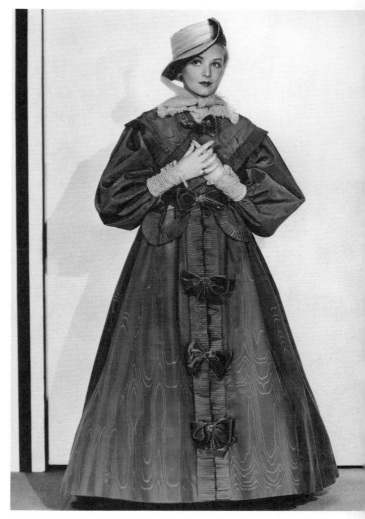

Madeleine Carroll in The World Moves On *by Fox, 1934. Designer: Lambert*

Madeleine Carroll in The Dictator *by Gaumont,*
1935. Designer: Strassnen

Madeleine Carroll in Prisoner of Zenda
by United Artists, 1937. Designer: Dryden

To audiences who missed the Thirties and became fans of Claudette Colbert because of her Forties and Fifties movies, Colbert presents the image of a totally refined, modestly attired, impeccably groomed, and morally spotless lady. It is quite a surprise, therefore, to see her bare, lovely, and wicked for De Mille epics like *Cleopatra* and *Sign of the Cross*. For *Sign of the Cross* in particular, Colbert played an evil woman whose moral standards were shocking, to say the least. Despite the unarguable fact that Colbert possessed one of cinemaland's most perfect figures, she thought her hips too big and preferred to call attention to the chest for her revealing costumes.

Sign of the Cross was filmed in the worst days of the Depression for film studios. Budgets had been slashed, and big productions were few. Cecil B. De Mille, however, had insisted to skeptical studio executives that he could produce the movie at a minimum budget and on time. To suggest vast crowds, cameraman Karl Struss (who worked on the silent *Ben Hur*) employed a prism lens which in effect doubled the size of the crowd. Mitchell Leisen, the set and costume designer, worked for $125 a week rather than his usual $600 a week. Over a four-month period, four hundred workers made a miniature Rome, which was burned while Nero plucked his harp. Thirty lions were used, twelve males and eighteen females for the final martyr scenes. They were furnished by the A.B. Barnes Circus and the Selig Zoo. Of 4,500 extras who worked on *Sign of the Cross*, half had also worked on De Mille's *Ten Commandments* thirteen years before. *Sign of the Cross* took eight weeks to make, at a cost of $650,000. Filming was stopped by De Mille in the middle of the last scene when the budget ran out. He was determined to keep his promise to the studio.

Colbert also had her problems on this movie. One costume weighed thirty-five pounds and was made of finely woven silver chain mail. Because she had to stand for most scenes with it on, she lost five pounds just carrying it around. Her famous milk-bath scene took too long to film. After bathing in milk for two days, Colbert—and the crew—complained that the bath was turning to cheese, smelly cheese.

At the end of the Thirties Colbert made another costume film, this one far less revealing. For *Zaza,* a cancan sequence was cut by the studio and a less controversial dance inserted in its place. The movie was considered shocking by many Colbert fans because the main character was far too naughty, despite the zeal of studio self-censorship that continually watered down the script. Edith Head designed most of Colbert's wardrobe, but Colbert asked Banton to design a spectacular costume when Zaza becomes the toast of Paris. According to Banton, it was a typical princess dress embroidered lavishly with diamonds, with an enormous hat, towering with birds of paradise, and a boa of bird of paradise around her shoulders. As Banton described it, "It's an extravaganza, and purposefully so, frankly vulgar."

Claudette Colbert in Sign of the Cross *by Paramount, 1932. Designer: Leisen*

Claudette Colbert in Cleopatra *by Paramount, 1934. Designer: Banton*

One of the most spectacular movies of the Thirties was the Cecil B. De Mille production of *Cleopatra.* Claudette Colbert was stunning as Cleopatra, and the costumes were designed to maximize that effect. Yet the gowns seen on the screen were not those originally designed for the movie, and that fact created a very tight situation for Travis Banton. De Mille had already started shooting *Cleopatra,* but Claudette Colbert refused to wear the gowns made for her. De Mille had his own staff at Paramount, and Banton was not to be responsible for the wardrobe for the movie. When shooting starts on a picture of such magnitude, any delay costs the producer thousands of dollars. When Cleopatra did not appear on the set, Banton was called in to design an entirely new wardrobe for her, and the very next day he had the first dress ready for filming. In fact, according to publicity, he produced one of the most extravagant wardrobes seen on the screen on a day-to-day basis while the cameras recorded scenes of ancient Egypt as seen through the imagination of Cecil B. De Mille.

Henry Wilcoxon presented such a handsome, manly Anthony that, to De Mille's delight, two hairdressers and a script girl fainted on the set the first time Anthony kissed Cleopatra. Filming *Cleopatra* was very hard on the cast, however. Colbert was sick during most of the production; she had never really fully recovered from an attack of appendicitis while making *Four Frightened People* and the health problems acquired completing that movie in primitive jungles. Colbert's stand-in, Gladys Jeans, rehearsed scenes and lines because Colbert could only stand for a few seconds at a time. She collapsed several times on the set. In one interview she said temperatures had to remain at 86° so the feathers on her costumes would not molt, and one costume had a veil that weighed seventy-seven pounds.

For the all-important final scene when Cleopatra dies clutching a snake, De Mille knew Colbert was deathly afraid of snakes and kept this scene as the last to be filmed. When the time came, De Mille approached Colbert with a large boa snake wrapped around his shoulders and, after scaring the wits out of her, produced a small garden snake that looked like an asp. Colbert felt sorry for the poor little thing, and the scene was filmed in one take.

Costumes depicting ancient Egypt, Rome, or Greece had to fulfill a multitude of requirements. They had to give at least the illusion of being historically accurate for the character, and they had to fulfill the expectations of the audience—an audience educated by previous movies. For example, every Egyptian queen since Theda Bara has appeared in a black page-boy bob with bangs. Proper Egyptian ladies actually shaved their heads and wore heavy wigs molded into stiff shapes with fat and glues. Social tastes change, but to present a Cleopatra or Nefertiti in historically correct headgear would simply be unacceptable to audiences long accustomed to Claudette Colbert, Anne Baxter, and Elizabeth Taylor in their uniform "Egyptian" hair styles. The same is true for "classic" Greek costumes, which are seen carefully draped and stitched into place on both men and women. In fact, Greeks donned geometric pieces of material which they draped into new shapes every time they wore them. There were no sleeves or armholes; belts and string held them on.

Claudette Colbert in Cleopatra *by Paramount, 1934. Designer: Banton*

Marion Davies and Adrian in publicity for Operator 13 by MGM, 1934. Designer: Adrian

Mary Pickford in Secrets by United Artists, 1933. Designer: Adrian

The Thirties was an era of splendid parties on a grand scale. Weeks were spent in planning, and cost was no concern. Many get-togethers rivaled anything seen on the screen. Two premier hostesses were Mary Pickford and Marion Davies, two ladies of far different background and experience.

Marion Davies's career in motion pictures was given a tremendous boost by her association with William Randolph Hearst. First cast in more serious and overtasking dramas, Davies was best as a comedienne, when her wit and charm were showcased. Later, Davies dropped her flagging theatrical career and concentrated on being a hostess with few peers. Although she initially wanted only to be a schoolteacher, in 1934 Marion Davies gave a charity ball with 1,200 invited guests. She handled this production as easily as if it were tea for six.

While on the MGM lot, anything Marion Davies wanted, she got. Davies thought it would be nice if she had her own private projection room, so one was built in her dressing bungalow, the only one of its kind in Hollywood. Davies left MGM because Thalberg refused to give her the leads in *Marie Antoinette* and *The Barretts of Wimpole Street.*

The other grande dame of the social scene was the incredible Mary Pickford, the most successful actress ever seen on the screen. Pickford's last film was *Secrets* in 1933, and she supervised every detail. The film spanned fifty years, from 1860 to 1910, and won this acclaim from its star:

> When I finish a picture I am always reluctant to talk about it. I can say this about *Secrets,* however. There is no one place in it when I feel embarrassed. It is the first picture I ever made to which I have had that reaction. Not once do I want to hang my head. I have great faith in *Secrets.*

Production for *Secrets* required that an old Salem homestead be reproduced to the last detail on a set. The house was surrounded by a synthetic garden, with birch trees built from tissue and oak trees made from plaster of Paris. Even some flowers were set in cement so they would break off when picked by Mary.

Secrets was not the crashing success Pickford had hoped for, so she concentrated on managing United Artists, her charitable works, and enjoying the benefits and responsibilities that her great fame and wealth offered her. She confided in one interview for *Photoplay* in March 1933:

> Irving Thalberg once told me that you can't always be right but you can always be busy. No one's judgment is infallible but it isn't the mistakes you make that down you, it's the inaction. No one can stand still and go ahead. And you can't move forward and look backward. You go in the direction you look.

Marion Davies in The Floradora Girl *by MGM, 1930. Designer: Adrian*

Bette Davis in Private Lives of Elizabeth and Essex *by Warner Brothers, 1939. Designer: Orry-Kelly*

When Bette Davis first came to Hollywood for a short contract with Universal she was called the Little Brown Wren. Universal let her go after one year's try, a top producer saying of her, "She has no sex appeal. No one will believe that a fellow would walk to the corner to get her." On the advice of her agent, she dyed her hair to honey blond and a few days later met George Arliss, who was looking for a honey blonde "with dignity" to play opposite him in *The Man Who Played God* at Warner Brothers. After this movie, Warners offered her a standard contract, and history was made. Six years later the producer who said she had no sex appeal was helping his father market self-heating hot dogs, and Davis was a $3,500-a-week star.

One of the most important movies Davis made in the Thirties was the elaborately costumed *The Private Lives of Elizabeth and Essex*. To insure authenticity, Bette Davis shaved her hairline back a few inches to look really bald, and her face was coated with chalk-white make-up. Her eyebrows were also completely plucked.

Orry-Kelly designed the costumes, but director Michael Curtiz thought the hoops and ruffs too big. Unbeknown to Curtiz, two sets of costumes were made. Davis tested in scaled-down gowns but wore larger, historically correct clothes to film. All available seamstresses worked on the costumes because so many of them were gem-encrusted, quilted, or embroidered. The grandeur and sumptuousness of the costumes and settings for this movie were captured on Technicolor film, an additional consideration for Orry-Kelly in designing the wardrobe.

Bette Davis in Private Lives of Elizabeth and Essex *by Warner Brothers, 1939. Designer: Orry-Kelly*

Bette Davis and Errol Flynn in Private Lives of
Elizabeth and Essex *by Warner Brothers, 1939.
Designer: Orry-Kelly*

According to publicity in *Photoplay's* November 1939 issue,
Orry-Kelly researched the period for a year before he ever drew a
sketch, and he visualized not only the clothes of the period, but also
their adaptability to contemporary times. He saw the long, fitted
bodice with its petite waistline, the full skirts standing out from the
hips, the heavily detailed virago sleeves, the padded shoulder wings,
the stomacher, the luxurious fabrics, the bold, rich colors, and the
expensive embroidery all as modern possibilities. One gown, a
model of elegance in spite of being the simplest in the queen's
wardrobe, combined an overdress of rust-colored velvet and a petticoat, or underdress, of red, rust, and gold moire metal cloth. The
velvet virago sleeves were heavily embroidered in gold, split to
reveal a tight metallic-cloth sleeve beneath, and caught by gold
bands to form a series of diminishing puffs from shoulder to wrist.
At wrist and neck were fluted ruffs of white cellophane net. The
long, molding bodice ended in a long, slim waistline marked by a
wide girdle of gold and jewels. Topping her chestnut wig was a tiny
cap of velvet, elaborately embroidered in jewels. The wide skirts of
the period were held out by a hoop and padded bolster at the
hipline; Davis reported the style far more comfortable and wearable
than the hem hoops of the Civil War period which she wore in
Jezebel, Juarez, and *The Old Maid.*

Most of the collars and ruffs of the period were enormous.
Davis's collars were so wide, she used a cigarette holder a foot and
a half long so she would not burn her costume. Embracing Errol
Flynn was also a trick.

Bette Davis in Jezebel *by Warner Brothers, 1938.*
Designer: Orry-Kelly

When Bette Davis became a full-fledged star on the Warner Brothers lot, she inherited Kay Francis's dressing room, which had five rooms, two baths, and a real fireplace. Davis very nearly had her acting career ruined when she was still a child. Her face was badly burned at age ten when she was playing Santa Claus and a candle on the Christmas tree torched her cotton costume. Only her mother's heroic efforts prevented major scarring. Every fifteen minutes for fourteen straight days and nights her mother, Ruth, moistened the burned area with a boric acid solution. The dampness prevented the burns from healing and making scar tissue until new skin could form. Davis's hair was burned off, and her eyes remained red and inflamed for three months, yet the only major effect from the burn accident was a slight protrusion of her eyes which made them appear larger. Davis's hard-working mother had at least one premonition that saved her daughter's life and two that launched her career. Ruth Davis was a remarkable woman in her own right.

Due to contract problems at the time, Bette Davis refused the part of Scarlett O'Hara in *Gone with the Wind*, and later she declined a second offer when she thought Errol Flynn was to be Rhett. *Jezebel* was Warner Brothers' answer to *Gone with the Wind*; it was budgeted at $1.25 million and was Davis's first big-budget movie with all the trimmings. *Jezebel* took a mere three months to make. Conflict in the story centered around the color of dress Davis would wear to a debutante ball. In real life the color of her wardrobe also caused concern. White was the proper color of the second main dress in the story, and Davis insisted on white, with all its attendant glare, instead of the pink gown already created for her. She got her way, and the cameraman modified the glare of white to produce a lovely image of Davis. The dress worn to the ball in the movie was red, according to the story, but black-and-white film was tricky. Red usually photographed deep black, so the red dress in *Jezebel* was actually brown.

Juarez was another exquisite period feature for Bette Davis. The movie took one and a half years to write, one year to research, and six months to prepare for the cameras. There were 1,186 supporting players, fifty-four sets, and an eleven-acre "Mexico" in Calabasas. Director William Dieterle was a staunch believer in astrology, so he shot the first scene three weeks ahead of schedule, two hours before usual call, and waited by a telephone on the set for his astrologer to tell him the exact moment to begin.

All the fourteen dresses Davis wore in *Juarez* were simple and very regal. Beautiful materials were brought from French looms because very heavy moires and taffetas were not made in America. Only one dress was fussy, the coronation gown, which was white satin beaded with tiny pearls. Jewels were important to the costumes of the times, and these were brought from Europe and Mexico City. Orry-Kelly's costume sketches were discussed with Davis and Dieterle. Davis loved them. Orry-Kelly played up the insanity of Davis's character by presenting her first in a white dress and then progressions of gray until she was in black at the end. Dieterle suggested this idea. After the sketches were discussed, the costumes were made on padded muslin models of the stars. Usually camera tests were made of costumes, but everyone was so satisfied with the sketches, only half were actually tested. Orry-Kelly once said of Bette Davis:

> The intelligence of Bette Davis was a great help to me in designing her costumes, for her first thought is always to be realistic. She doesn't start out to cheat the period by adding a soft touch here and there. Most actresses won't make sacrifices for their parts. In one scene, Bette wore a white lace mantilla which was so heavy it almost broke her neck. Half a dozen stars wouldn't have worn it.

The budget for *Juarez* was $1.5 million; the wardrobe budget was two and one half percent of that.

Bette Davis in Juarez *by Warner Brothers, 1939. Designer: Orry-Kelly*

Dolores Del Rio in Madame Du Barry
by Warner Brothers, 1934. Designer: Orry-Kelly

Dolores Del Rio's exquisite and flawless beauty has charmed audiences for generations. Even today the lovely lady appears as beautiful and vivacious as women half her age. In one interview she confided, "The secret of youth is work, keep busy, and never be bored." She also loves dancing and creating dances, herb teas for sleep, herb and dried-fruit masks, and herb medicines. She drinks thirty glasses of water a day. Del Rio feels inner harmony is absolutely necessary because any disharmony or stress will be etched in the face.

Christened Lolita, she was educated in a convent and maintained the surname Del Rio from her first marriage. Her whole existence can be described as a gracious life surrounded by people who loved her. She speaks seven languages.

Del Rio's worst experiences were dealt to her by various studio executives whose choices for her films were unfortunate and whose subsequent lack of consideration was offensive. Her first and best picture at Warner Brothers was *Wonder Bar*, in which her role was expanded at the expense of that of Kay Francis, the alleged star. Because of the enormous potential apparent in their lovely new star, Warner Brothers exempted Del Rio from the frantic pace usually suffered by others who completed ten or more movies a year on the Warners lot. Del Rio was reserved for a proper follow-up to her *Wonder Bar* success. Del Rio and her husband Cedric Gibbons, the brilliant stage designer at MGM, were most definitely a part of Hollywood in its heyday, and her infrequent studio demands left ample time for her other interests as a popular hostess.

The movie Warners chose to continue her success was *Madame Du Barry*, a costume film which starred Del Rio in a series of opulent and breathtaking gowns. The movie was not as successful as Warners had planned, and its intent was misinterpreted by the public and critics.

Director Dieterle is quoted in the book *Close Up: The Contract Director* by Jon Tuska, as saying:

> In Europe it was just torn to bits. They had no fun with it. They thought because Madame Du Barry was decapitated it had to be all serious. But her life was such a farce. Other directors got away with historical farces. . . . I don't think my *Du Barry* can be compared with Lubitsch's *Du Barry*; mine was not meant to be a big epic but a nice historical farce. I thought Dolores played it just right.

Another problem arose because the film was made prior to enforcement of the new Hays Office Code. When *Madame Du Barry* was finished, it virtually had to be remade to conform to the new code.

Dolores Del Rio in Madame Du Barry
by Warner Brothers, 1934. Designer: Orry-Kelly

Olivia de Havilland. Even the name was a publicist's dream. The reality was that de Havilland, a gentle, lovely actress with a perfect photographic face, was in period costume far more often than modern dress during the Thirties. As the romantic foil to a gallant Errol Flynn, she molded an image of the ideal heroine, beautiful, intelligent, charming, desirable, stubborn when necessary, possessed of a reserve of strength to tide both herself and the hero over in a crisis, and, above all, a lady.

Although she had pursued a career in teaching, de Havilland began her rise to stardom as the understudy to the understudy (Jeanne Rouveral) of Gloria Stuart, playing Hernia in the Hollywood Bowl presentation of *A Midsummer Night's Dream*. Stuart and Rouveral coached de Havilland, and when both left for other film commitments, de Havilland stepped into the part letter-perfect. Spotted and signed by Warner Brothers, de Havilland played Hernia for the screen and then catapulted to instant success as the co-star in *Captain Blood*. She was then only nineteen years old.

The financial statistics for *Captain Blood* give interesting insight into the costs of a Warner Brothers costume epic in 1935. The total budget for the film was $760,534. The budget for wardrobe was $34,000; the actual costs for outside rental were $13,102, for outside purchases $166, for studio charges $5,155, and for wardrobe labor $5,462. Thus, wardrobe used only $23,885 out of its $34,000 budget. In comparison, the director received $17,600; cameramen and assistants, $10,866 ($8,228 budgeted); cast, $99,118 ($77,438 budgeted); extras, $27,410 ($38,808 budgeted); musicians, $2,045 ($15,800 budgeted); and electricians, $25,479 ($11,185 budgeted). Location expenses were $10,642 ($3,894 budgeted). Seven ships were built, and research for de Havilland's costumes took six months.

The Adventures of Robin Hood was another costume movie which generated its own unique problems. The entire company spent one month on location at General Bidwell State Park near Chico, California, because the director wanted only real settings for this early Technicolor production. Location costs were $25,000 a day. According to publicity, ten carloads of props, costumes, and equipment were hauled to Chico by special train, including fifty horses. Milo Anderson, the costume designer, had his problems. The chain-mesh armor made for knights and soldiers in action sounded like the Navy weighing anchor. A realistic substitute was devised of woven string sprayed with metal paint. The statistics are endless on costume films. *Anthony Adverse* used 131 sets and 1,600 players, and the studio built eight types of coaches.

Through it all, de Havilland kept her wits and humor. Horseplay was a necessary element on a set, and tense moments were frequently broken by the surprised shriek of a cast or crew member. Once, during the filming of *Dodge City*, the scream belonged to de Havilland, who finally discovered the garter snake Errol Flynn had planted in her pantaloons.

Olivia de Havilland in Adventures of Robin Hood *by Warner Brothers, 1938. Designer: Milo Anderson*

Olivia de Havilland in Anthony Adverse by
Warner Brothers, 1936. Designer: Milo Anderson

Olivia de Havilland and Fredric March in
Anthony Adverse *by Warner Brothers, 1936.*
Designer: Milo Anderson

Marlene Dietrich in The Scarlet Empress
by Paramount, 1934. Designer: Banton

Marlene Dietrich as Catherine the Great of Russia in *The Scarlet Empress* presented the audience with a gorgeous symphony of costumes. As a rule, the cinema wardrobe should serve as background and not attract any special attention to itself, but sometimes it must have the opposite effect and emphasize the character of the wearer; that is when cinema clothing takes on a special dramatic quality. Russian court life in the time of Catherine as interpreted by Travis Banton produced some of the most sumptuous costumes, both in line and coloring, of any period in European history seen on the screen. Publicity for the movie quoted Banton as saying:

> Miss Dietrich's costumes in that picture represented perhaps the finest and most beautiful collection of clothes I've ever had the pleasure of designing. They were expressive of the period's fashions, without being mere stereotyped copies of sketches found in books. Rather, I placed myself mentally in the position of a designer of the middle eighteenth century.

Inspiration for much of the wardrobe came from Catherine the Great's own memoirs. For the journey from Germany to Russia, Dietrich wore a sable cape edged with complete skins, a sable hood, and sable gloves. Her wedding gown was silver cloth with a full court train, all very heavily embroidered in silver threads, pearls, and diamonds. Banton explained:

> In several scenes, like the wedding ceremony in the cathedral, I strove for somewhat barbaric effects with sables, furs, jeweled headdresses, black and gold combinations—but the average spectator, of course, missed many authentic details over which I had worked days and weeks. They just added to the general glitter.

One exquisite gown was of handmade rose-point lace purchased from a Russian woman who needed money desperately. This lace was originally made by a township in Russia and presented to the last czarina. The facts of its origin and subsequent history were well authenticated in the documents that accompanied it.

Marlene Dietrich in The Scarlet Empress
by Paramount, 1934. Designer: Banton

The Scarlet Empress cost $900,000. Director von Sternberg himself wrote the screenplay, selected the statuary and icons, and chose the music. Dietrich was thirty-four years old when she played Catherine from her early teens to her late years.

Von Sternberg was not a director beloved by the cast. In filming *The Scarlet Empress* he insisted on take after take to achieve his idea of utter perfection, ignoring the suffering of the actors, and particularly Dietrich, in their hot and heavy costumes. The dinner scene was refilmed so often, a boar's head on the table decayed and stank up the whole set. According to the book *Marlene* by Charles Higham, Sam Jaffe had already made thirty-seven takes of one of his scenes and refused to be further badgered by von Sternberg. In a friendly little talk between actor and director, von Sternberg said, "Mr. Jaffe, I wonder if you have any idea how important I am. Why, I have seventy million followers in Japan alone!" Sam Jaffe replied, "That's wonderful, Mr. von Sternberg. Christ had only twelve." Von Sternberg routinely took twenty, forty, even sixty takes of one scene. With Dietrich, he often went beyond seventy.

The Scarlet Empress was visually fascinating, but box-office receipts were very disappointing.

Marlene Dietrich in The Scarlet Empress *by Paramount, 1934. Designer: Banton*

Marlene Dietrich in Devil Is a Woman
by Paramount, 1935. Designer: Banton

Variety in 1935 had this to say of *Devil is a Woman*:

Not even Garbo in the Orient has approached, for special effects, Dietrich in Spain. With fringe, lace, sequins, carnations, chenille, nets, embroideries, and shawls, Miss Dietrich is hung, wrapped, draped, swathed, festooned. . . . Miss Dietrich emerges as a glorious achievement, a supreme consolidation of the sartorial, make-up, and photographic arts.

Devil is a Woman was the biggest box-office disaster of the Dietrich–von Sternberg films. Dietrich played Concha the Savage, the toast of Spain, and the public refused to accept her as the cruel, inhuman creature she portrayed under von Sternberg's direction. Concha was the only woman Dietrich played who took pleasure in wanton destruction of a man without any logical explanation.

Dietrich has said that *Devil is a Woman* was her favorite film because she felt she never looked better. The costumes for *Devil* were incredible and the most bizarre created by Banton. Von Sternberg tried to make Dietrich look different in each movie, and for *Devil* he hardened her make-up and lit her face to emphasize her strong bone structure. This gave her a much harsher appearance than in any previous movie. Flashy costumes and gaudy jewelry completed the image of a lower-class woman who demonstrates remarkable social mobility. The most exquisite costume was white lace with an authentic antique pattern. The ruffled sleeves and combination cape and scarf were typically Spanish, and in place of a mantilla, she wore a dramatic hat of lace wired to effect a brim. The broad-brim lace hat was accented by a row of pink carnations, the only coloring in the outfit beside white.

Dietrich's sudden rise in the Hollywood firmament was aided by massive publicity. Moviegoers thirsted for any knowledge about this unique new star, and fan magazines delighted in disseminating little bits of information here and there, such as Dietrich's weakness for hats and the assertion that she often purchased as many as thirty at her favorite milliner's in New York, Lilly Daché. Even the talented but unknown people who assisted the glamorous image occasionally received a gleam or two in the spotlight. *Photoplay* reported that Willys de Mond, the only Hollywood hosiery stylist for the stars and known simply as Willys, created sandal foot hose for Dietrich, ombre (two-toned) hose also for Dietrich, complete lace heel and toes for Ginger Rogers, and peek-a-boo hose (with the toes cut out to vie with open-toed shoes) for Lily Pons. According to Willys, the perfect leg had to measure eight and one half inches at the ankle, twelve and one half at the calf, and nineteen and one half at the thigh. Six stars met his criteria: Claudette Colbert, Ginger Rogers, Alice Faye, Eleanor Powell, Betty Grable, and Marlene Dietrich.

Dietrich's knowledge of the technical aspects of moviemaking was legendary. She knew which lighting was best for her face (overhead) and used her status to insist on the best. Her salary for *Song of Songs* was said to be $200,000 to $250,000, plus what she earned from the cameramen who gave her a penny each time she gave them a good tip on lighting or camera angles.

Irene Dunne in Sweet Adeline *by Warner Brothers, 1935. Designer: Orry-Kelly*

Consistent is a word that perfectly describes Irene Dunne and her career in motion pictures. From her first successes on the stage through her later films into the Fifties, Dunne projected the image of a hard-working, well-adjusted, likable lady.

Born Irene Marie Dunn—she later added the "e"—her parents were German and Irish. Dunne had voice, dance, and language courses at the Indianapolis Fine Arts Academy and the Conservatory Division of the Chicago Musical College. Although blessed with a fine voice, she failed her audition for the Metropolitan Opera Company in 1920. Paramount publicity claimed Dunne was a lyrical soprano who sang with the Met "for a time." Dunne appeared in several stage musicals, including Florenz Ziegfeld's production of *Show Boat* in 1929. At that time RKO wanted a new ingenue for the musical comedies then in vogue. She was thirty years old. Hired to sing, Dunne found her first film was changed to a nonmusical. She later co-starred in the 131-minute western epic *Cimarron* and earned her first Academy Award nomination. Dunne's reputation was established by consistently good performances in weepy, sudsy movies. RKO loaned her out at a profit to themselves for *The Secret of Madame Blanche*, a role rejected by most MGM stars. Dunne played an American chorus girl in 1890s London, and the movie was successful. While intrastudio wars raged politely between Ann Harding and Katharine Hepburn for supremacy on the RKO lot, Dunne kept plugging along and kept her mouth shut. *Stingaree* was set in 1874 Australia and allowed her to use her voice for the first time in four years at RKO. *Sweet Adeline* was another loan-out, this time to Warner Brothers. She is best remembered musically for *Show Boat*, for which she received $100,000.

High, Wide and Handsome was a musical epic that cost $1.9 million. Comparisons, even to the gowns worn, have been made with Jeanette MacDonald's more successful musicals produced at MGM. *High, Wide and Handsome* was set in Pennsylvania in 1859 and was a so-called popular musical that did not attempt to imitate grand opera but sought pure entertainment for the masses instead. For the 1937–38 season, fifty popular musicals were scheduled for production by the major studios.

The production dollar for movies like *High, Wide and Handsome* in 1937 was divided up as follows, according to *The Film Daily*:

> ... the cast received 25%; extras, bits and characters, 5%; director, 10%; director assistants, 2%; cameraman and crew, 1.5%; lights, 2%; makeup, hairdressers, and supplies, 0.9%; teachers, 0.2%; crew and labor, 1.2%; story preparation, 7%; story costs, 5%; costumes and designers, 2%; sets and art directors, 12.5%; stills and photographs, 0.4%; cutters, 1%; film negative, 1%; tests, 1.2%; insurance, 2%; sound-engineering and negatives, 3.1%; publicity, transportation, research, technical, and miscellaneous, 2%; and indirect costs, 15%.

In 1937 Hollywood's total annual payroll was $91 million, with 28,000 employed in the production colony. About seventy percent of the world's movies originated in Hollywood.

Irene Dunne in Secret of Madame Blanche *by MGM, 1933. Designer: Adrian*

Irene Dunne in High, Wide, and Handsome
by Paramount, 1937. Designer: Banton

Alice Faye in Now I'll Tell *by Fox, 1934. Designer: Kaufman*

Alice Faye in In Old Chicago *by 20th Century-Fox, 1938. Designer: Royer*

Alice Faye in On the Avenue *by 20th Century-Fox, 1937. Designer: Wakeling*

Alice Jeane Leppert was born in New York City in 1915; her parents were Irish and French. She chose the name Faye for no particular reason except that it went well with Alice. Faye was a protégeé of Rudy Vallee, who in the beginning paid her salary as a singer with his band out of his own pocket. Thanks to several ironic quirks of fate, Faye co-starred in her first movie, *George White's Scandals*, and was never billed below third in her subsequent thirty-one films. She retired voluntarily in 1945 when her star was at its peak. For her first three years in Hollywood, Faye was molded to follow the then-popular Jean Harlow image. On Faye the platinum hair, thin lips, and plucked eyebrows appeared hard and artificial. However, Harlow was originally cast for the female lead in *In Old Chicago*, but her death the summer before filming allowed look-alike Faye another boost in her career.

In Old Chicago, co-starring Faye's own protégé Tyrone Power, was a major production with a budget of $1.8 million. The twenty-minute fire sequence alone cost $750,000 and took three days to film. To rebuild Chicago and imbue it with life and reality for the period 1854–71 took one and a half years' research. Daisy, who played Mrs. O'Leary's cow, received $2,000 for her histrionic activities and even had a stand-in. For a musical number in *In Old Chicago*, Faye wore a pair of jeweled stockings that cost $2,500. These were the same pair she wore briefly for publicity for *On the Avenue*, though this time they were embellished even more with butterflies. A pair of mesh hose of 14-karat gold thread to match a lamé dress cost $1,100.

By 1937 Alice Faye was receiving marriage proposals by mail. A wealthy Argentine cattle baron offered her a 500,000-acre ranch and 10,000 head of cattle as a wedding present if she would marry him. A Frenchman offered jewels and a castle in the Alps. Faye seldom wore jewelry; her passion was said to be furs.

Opening scenes in the movie *You Can't Have Everything* called for Alice Faye, hungry, to eat three plates of spaghetti in an Italian restaurant. Bravely she ate her way through a lot of real spaghetti for the two days it took to shoot the scene, finally swearing she was off spaghetti until 1939. Next day, the crew gave her a birthday party in the studio café. The *pièce de résistance* was a gorgeous white birthday cake. Thrilled, Faye cut into it to discover that the studio publicity people had filled it with spaghetti. Incidents about the glamorous stars and ingenues of the Thirties filled not only fan magazines but newspapers, ladies' magazines, fashion magazines, and all manner of mass communications as well. Fascinating trivia were an important part of a star's publicity campaign, and the studio disseminated them by the mile. Whether the publicity was rock-true or slightly embellished made little difference to the fans.

Greta Garbo in Mata Hari *by MGM, 1932.*
Designer: Adrian

Greta Garbo in As You Desire Me *by MGM, 1932. Designer: Adrian*

Greta Garbo's fame was in her exquisite face. Her body was trim enough to wear many styles, but one way or another her dresses and gowns were designed primarily to direct attention to the face. One excellent example is the severe black gown from *Queen Christina.* The stiff white collar presents the Garbo head as on a platter, with little else to detract from it. This interesting neckline created a mini-vogue, and adaptions of the white square collar were sold at stores like Macy's Cinema Shop for $15 to $35. They were also *Modern Screen Magazine* patterns.

More unusual was the sight of a blonde Garbo clad in tight velvet pants. Self-conscious about her legs, Garbo usually balked at displaying them, so this pants still from *As You Desire Me* and the glamorous pose from *Mata Hari* are among the few glimpses allowed.

Garbo's wardrobe for *Mata Hari* was sensational, and Adrian spared no effort to encase her in the most sumptuous, glamorous costumes he could devise. Despite the phenomenal opulence of the designs, it was the simple jeweled skullcaps which caught the public's fancy and earned a favorite niche in the fashion world. The *Mata Hari* wardrobe was sent on nationwide display at various large city department stores for publicity. Unfortunately, the wives of studio executives decided the costumes would look just marvelous on them, so little by little the collection dwindled as it journeyed around the country until there was nothing left to return to Hollywood.

According to Hedda Hopper in 1955, Garbo started at MGM at $250 a week only because the studio wanted Mauritz Stiller, a director, and he would not come to America without her. After their first picture, Stiller was forgotten and Garbo soared to $300,000 per picture. Clarence Bull thought her greatest characteristic was her punctuality. She was always on time or ten minutes early. Her regular garb was an old pair of slacks, turtleneck sweater, men's socks, and sandals. The only trouble with Garbo's cinema wardrobe was length. She wanted them clearing the floor, but her feet would show and Adrian didn't think that pretty. One secret to Garbo's glamour was that, if she liked a costume, no matter how eccentric, she gave it an air of authority by the unself-conscious way she wore it. She did not like décolleté, so Adrian designed long sleeves and high necks which became fashionable. Adrian created fourteen beautiful, glamorous gowns for Garbo for *Two Faced Woman,* but the studio refused to let her wear them because they wanted her to become a real American sweater girl. Adrian and Garbo both quit motion pictures after that.

Greta Garbo in Queen Christina *by MGM, 1933. Designer: Adrian*

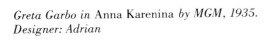

Greta Garbo in Anna Karenina *by MGM, 1935.*
Designer: Adrian

Greta Garbo in Camille *by MGM, 1936.*
Designer: Adrian

Garbo, the legend, donned many feminine, lavish costumes for *Camille, Anna Karenina, Conquest,* and *Romance.* Very frilly, authentic but modified, the styles seemed somewhat incongruous with her own character when frothy and ruffled but beyond compare in the less cluttered designs. For example, the severe black evening gown from *Anna Karenina* is sublime elegance. Of all the costumes Adrian designed for Garbo, he felt those in *Romance, Queen Christina,* and *Anna Karenina* interested her most of all.

Only the finest materials were used for Garbo, even for her intimate underthings, and real jewels as well as museum-quality replicas escalated wardrobe budgets. *Conquest* reportedly cost $3 million in 1937. On the set Garbo drank a broth of spinach, carrot, celery, and parsley juice for energy in order to be able to carry some of the heavy gowns.

Camille was set in the 1850s; for it Adrian designed eighteen costume changes for Garbo, fourteen for Robert Taylor, twenty-seven for the male supporting cast, three hundred fifty for male extras, and three hundred for female supporting cast and female extras. An evening coat she wore in the movie was silver bengaline, very heavy, lavishly embroidered in real gold thread and sprinkled with brilliants and emeralds. The uneven hem was bordered with fifty-five yards of mink banding. According to publicity, during one torrid love scene with Robert Taylor in *Camille,* Garbo's dress and Taylor's pants caught fire because an extra had tossed a cigarette over a wall and into the garden set, where it landed in Garbo's dress. Production was halted until another pair of pants and another gown could be made. Also during filming Taylor became so flustered after his first screen kiss with Garbo that he dropped her to the floor. She was unharmed, and production continued.

Garbo kept a print of every photo taken of her, and not out of vanity. She always kept the radio on in the still-photo gallery, except when posing for tragic mood shots, for which there was total silence. Clarence Bull was able to take three hundred pictures per six-hour setting with Garbo. There were no forbidden angles or sides.

Garbo was diligently punctual. At 7:55 A.M. she arrived at the studio and at six sharp she dropped everything and went home. When the crew saw her maid approach her at six o'clock with a glass of water, they knew that was it for the day—even if they were in an important scene.

Much has been rumored about Garbo's big feet. In fact she wore a modest size 7AA shoe. Her favorite color was red.

Although many fashion trends did not originate in Hollywood, many were given a great boost when viewed on the charismatic personages created by Hollywood's stars. Garbo's flattering version of the up hair-do seen in *Conquest* helped make it very smart in 1938. Her odd little pillbox hat in *The Painted Veil* caught on soon after the movie and reached a style peak in 1935. The delicate, romantic evening gowns Garbo wore in *Camille* turned evening clothes from sophisticated sheaths to more feminine, frothy frocks.

Greta Garbo in Anna Karenina *by MGM, 1935. Designer: Adrian*

Sonja Henie in My Lucky Star *by 20th Century-Fox, 1938. Designer: Royer*

Sonja Henie worked hard and planned well for her assault on Hollywood.

Before Henie came to Hollywood, she launched her publicity campaign in New York by staging public exhibitions of her skating talent; her showmanship and abilities drew standing-room-only crowds. On the strength of this, a representative of Paramount offered a screen test in New York; Henie did not like the test—there was no skating. She was to walk onto the set, pick up a magazine, sit down, and look sad. After the test, the representative said her nose was too small and her face too round. After arriving in Los Angeles, Henie rented the only skating rink in Southern California and again produced skating exhibitions. Her first was for the press, and her second was for the large crowds drawn by favorable reviews by the press. Darryl Zanuck then offered her $15,000 to star in a movie (she always said she would never take anything less than star billing); she told Zanuck she wanted $300,000 for her first picture. They reportedly settled on a cool $1 million for five pictures.

Henie's grandmother was Irish, and that is why her eyes were brown and not Swedish blue. She always had a rabbit's foot for good luck while making her first film, *One in a Million*, in 1936. Henie did not smoke and kept in rigid training for this movie. A special rink was built on a sound stage with real ice, no artificial substitutes. The rink took three days to freeze solid, then the cameraman noticed that the refrigeration pipes showed. The rink had to be unfrozen and drained. Skim milk was poured and frozen for the first layer to hide the pipes, and then another layer of clear ice was formed on top. A new job was even created for this and all subsequent Henie films: before every take, an "ice inspector" went over every square inch of the rink to make sure that no hair pins, nails, matches, or anything else would get under Henie's skates. For the first time, 20th Century-Fox used a super-slow-motion camera that took 11,060 exposures a minute so that blurring would not be a problem in her fast-action skating numbers.

One in a Million was so successful that Henie received $125,000 plus overtime for *Thin Ice*, an unheard-of sum at the time for such a new star. The studio believed she was worth every penny.

The white fur-trimmed skating outfit from *Happy Landing* is generally considered to be her most famous skating costume. Sonja Henie is credited with influencing several fashion trends; perhaps her most famous was the fur hood she wore in the picture *Thin Ice* which turned up on everybody's head the next winter.

Sonja Henie in Happy Landing *by 20th Century-Fox, 1938. Designer: Royer*

Sonja Henie in Thin Ice *by 20th Century-Fox, 1937. Designer: Royer*

Katharine Hepburn in Mary of Scotland
by RKO, 1936. Designer: Plunkett

Mary of Scotland created a fashion sensation in 1936 because of the elegance and style of its period costumes. To this day the gowns are acknowledged as some of the finest made in the Thirties.

The star of *Mary of Scotland* was Katharine Hepburn, whom cast and crew never fail to praise, including Walter Plunkett: "Katharine Hepburn is a very well educated, intelligent woman who knows what she is doing in every part that she plays. She researches it, she knows who that woman is, and she knows how to feel like that character." Hepburn did have a phobia about exposing her long neck, which she always insisted be covered. Plunkett thought her neck beautiful but designed around Hepburn's one quirk.

The elaborate costumes for *Mary of Scotland* demanded that RKO hire an additional fifty seamstresses. No detail, no matter how small, could be overlooked. The gorgeous lipstick-red Lyons velvet gown shown here on Hepburn featured gold-plated thistles, all made to order by Joseph, a jeweler. Although Elizabethan ruffles became *the* fashion accessory for black day dresses, and *Mary* sleeves a new vogue, Plunkett did not design them to be fashionable or to create fashion but to be authentic and harmonize with the personality and figure of the actress. Authenticity, however, sometimes created its own problems. For example, regarding the hunting hat for Mary, shown here, Plunkett recalled:

Katharine Hepburn in Mary of Scotland *by RKO, 1936. Designer: Plunkett*

> To exploit the film the studio had a manufacturer in New York make these things. This is a real eagle feather [in the movie]. We had terrible trouble with the government over that. But finally they agreed and let me borrow an eagle feather, I've forgotten from where, but I know it was listed and we had use of the feather only in the film because I insisted it could not be anything else because the Queen of Scotland would only have a real eagle feather. But that beret was copied with turkey feathers and sold in Woolworth's, I think, hundreds and hundreds. All the school kids wore them for a while.

Although elegant in the extreme, the *Mary of Scotland* costumes were bulky and very heavy. One hot day Hepburn got fed up with her heavy velvet gown and so for lunch ripped it off, got into breeches and a sweat shirt, and, still wearing her queen's headdress and crown, stalked into the RKO café.

An original painting of Mary of Scotland was used by Plunkett to authenticate one of Hepburn's screen costumes. Notice how the original was only slightly modified for compatibility with the cameras and Hepburn.

Thanks to *Mary of Scotland* and Katharine Hepburn, Walter Plunkett stayed on in Hollywood and became noted for retaining the authenticity of a historical costume while adding an intriguing bit of originality to make it and the star emerge with beauty and charm. It almost never happened. In 1935 Plunkett quit RKO because the salary was absurdly low. He remembered:

RKO would not give me a raise, would not give me screen credit. As I remember, the salary was $75 a week. I went to New York immediately and got a job with a manufacturer for $150 a week, with the understanding that I was being tried out. RKO called me and said they wanted me back to do *Mary of Scotland*. I said, "Not on your life because I'm enjoying New York and making twice as much as before." And they said, "But Miss Hepburn wants you and you have to come back." I said I would talk to my bosses and they said that the collection was finished and that there would be eight weeks' rest for the designers, so if I wanted to go for eight weeks to go ahead. So I told RKO if they would pay me $300 a week and guarantee that I would be finished in eight weeks to go back to New York, I would take it. If they did not finish in eight weeks with me, they would have to double that salary to $600. They agreed. I came out and in the sixth week they had a script so I could start the thing, so I went to $600.

He stayed because the studio wanted him to do *A Woman Rebels*, *Quality Street*, and others. When Plunkett was asked who his favorite actress is, he replied, "Kate Hepburn. The woman's magnetism, her talent, her intelligence—all of it. She would give you feelings about things and not need to say exactly what she wanted."

When designing for a period movie, Plunkett first began with detailed research, sometimes taking months. He felt he had to learn all he could about the proper dress of the time or the film story. He then made a visual reading of the script, picturing the people and the clothes as he read. Then there was a second reading during which he made thumbnail sketches as he went along. Next he visited the stockroom and selected the proper fabrics so he could proceed to draw the necessary sketches. From each sketch a muslin pattern was produced on the actress's clothes dummy. Plunkett then made the required corrections in the pattern and cut the material, and finally the actress was called in for a fitting. He said, "There must be a complete balance in costume for pictures. The most important character must have the most important costumes."

Quality Street was Hepburn's first period movie in which the skirts were slim and revealed the shape of the lower body. Plunkett stated, "I attempted not only to present the costumes of the Empire but tried to reflect some of the feminine, whimsical quality of Barrie's play." For *Quality Street* one set had to age from 1805 to 1815. The research department discovered that a rose bush had to grow two stories and a stone stoop had to show foot wear. In *The Little Minister* a riot staged between the soldiery and the townspeople near the picture's close actually ended in several casualties. In the melee Reginald Denny's white horse reared, causing an extra armed with a pike to leap back, his pike butting John Beal in the eye. Katharine Hepburn became so excited she fell off a make-believe cliff and sprained her ankle.

Plunkett sparked many mini-trends with his historically accurate yet contemporarily beautiful styles. *Little Women* motivated a fashion for tiny muffs and veils; *A Woman Rebels* made jackets more important.

Jeanette MacDonald in San Francisco *by MGM, 1936. Designer: Adrian*

Jeanette MacDonald, one of the most beloved screen luminaries, was also known professionally for her flaming temper, and when strained or provoked she could swear up a storm. MGM director Robert Z. Leonard nicknamed her "The Red Volcano" and said working with her was never dull. Despite the reported temper, MacDonald was a lovely combination of intelligence, stubbornness, charisma, practicality, beauty, discipline, charm, unselfishness, energy, and talent. She was prim and proper on screen and off and was always treated with the respect and affection she deserved. Her film work spanned twenty years (1929 to 1949), and she was never less than co-star. In the age of total studio control of careers, Mac-Donald's contracts were remarkably in her favor and even included unique clauses granting her the right to choose a script or reject one offered. She used her considerable intelligence to guide her own career and create wonderfully popular operettas that are still enjoyable today.

Despite the level of professionalism in cast and crew for her pictures, things did not always go smoothly. For example, the earthquake scene in *San Francisco* called for Clark Gable to be trapped under falling debris. The scene was shot several times, and three tuxedos were ruined as falling plaster, bricks, and furniture covered him. On the fourth take the bricks hit him so hard that Gable, in a rage, left the set—but returned the next day. Most of *San Francisco* was shot at MGM, except for one scene at Sunland and the finale at Lafayette Park in Los Angeles.

For *Maytime*, a movie started twice at MGM, with the second version far more lavish than the first, the script called for a romantic scene in which apple blossoms fall on MacDonald and Nelson Eddy. According to studio publicity, even though it was midwinter, MGM prop men found fifteen blooming apple trees, transplanted them to the set, and rustled them with a wind machine. Each studio did things a little differently. Over at Paramount for *High, Wide and Handsome*, apple blossoms were also required for a scene. The California frost had done away with real blossoms, so a corps of Paramount technicians worked overnight peeling rosebuds down to the size of apple blossoms and sticking them on bare apple trees with maple syrup to simulate an orchard.

Jewelry appearing on the screen was not only taken from the studio's own treasure chest, but also made specially for an important film, borrowed from other movies or other studios, or rented. The film appearance of a $5,000 emerald, pearl, and silver necklace created by Adrian for Garbo in *Camille* was left on the cutting room floor. However, Jeanette MacDonald wore it in *Maytime* and later Lily Pons in *Hitting a New High* and Raquel Welch in *Myra Breckinridge*. A set of necklace and earrings made for Norma Shearer in *Marie Antoinette* was an authentic reproduction of the queen's own jewels. Because the movie was shelved for three years, MacDonald, Mae West, and Joan Bennett wore them before Shearer did. Ginger Rogers donned a $9,600 diamond bib in *Flying Down to Rio*; it also appeared on Ona Munson in *Shanghai Gesture*, on Tallulah Bankhead in *Royal Scandal*, and on a "Mission Impossible" episode. Many stars copied their fake screen jewelry in real gems because they liked them so much.

Jeanette MacDonald and Maurice Chevalier in
The Merry Widow *by MGM, 1934. Designer:
Adrian*

Jeanette MacDonald and Nelson Eddy in
Maytime *by MGM, 1937. Designer: Adrian*

Jeanette MacDonald in The Firefly *by MGM, 1937. Designer: Adrian*

Jeanette MacDonald's career as a motion picture star was extremely long. The average star sparkled for five years; MacDonald shone for twenty. During her screen appearances she wore many lovely and often fabulous costumes designed for her by Adrian. In fact, he did her wedding gown when she became Mrs. Gene Raymond. Adrian's favorite costume for MacDonald appeared in *The Firefly* during a night club scene. She wore a vein of diamonds up one side of a provocatively slit gown.

Exuding the image of a happy, cheerful woman on the screen sometimes took great acting; filmmaking, especially on location, could be trying. For example, during the six weeks *Rosemarie* was filmed at Lake Tahoe, the fifty cast members awoke at four-thirty A.M. and were in bed by nine P.M. MacDonald heartily disliked the conditions, hours, and bugs, as did everyone else.

Costumes often created their own problems. MacDonald wore many petticoats on a Dutch costume for a scene in *Sweethearts*. She was singing with Nelson Eddy, and in the background was a Christmas tree. Unnoticed, the dress short-circuited the wire of the Christmas tree lights and started a fire. MacDonald didn't see it, but Eddy did; without breaking the take, he beat out the flame and continued singing.

MacDonald's singing voice was first noticed and applauded before she was six years old. She lost her voice completely at age nine and did not regain it until she was fourteen. During this time she learned arias listening to records and became a good dancer, first performing on a New York stage when she was thirteen.

MacDonald was fitted for her beautiful costumes in Adrian's spacious "office" on the MGM lot. The huge oval fitting room had buff-colored carpets, pale walls, and oyster-white furniture, all designed by Adrian to set off the lavish creations he designed. An enormous mirror lined one whole wall, while the other side presented a series of windows facing a busy studio street and shaded with white venetian blinds. Adrian was a modest and intelligent man who dressed himself as well as he did others. He was the artistic head of the wardrobe department, which numbered 178 people in late 1938. He never used a sketch artist. Even in those days the average cost of a cinema dress ranged between $500 to $1,500. All costumes were cleaned and pressed at night. MGM worked twenty-four hours a day, six days a week. Beaded and chiffon dresses were cleaned by hand, extras' costumes by a cleaning service. It is said that Adrian's hobby of painting graceful, flowing animals in wild and exotic backgrounds contributed directly to the flow, grace, and exotic quality of his designs for the screen. *Photoplay* in September 1939 quoted him as saying:

> If you aren't pretty, make no attempt to be pretty. Be ever so smart. France remains the fashion center of the world because her women, unable to depend upon their looks, use their brains to do interesting things with their appearance.

Jeanette MacDonald in Maytime *by MGM, 1937.*
Designer: Adrian

Jeanette MacDonald in Broadway Serenade
by MGM, 1939. Designer: Adrian

Norma Shearer in Marie Antoinette *by MGM,*
1938. Designer: Adrian

For *Marie Antoinette* Adrian journeyed to France and scoured the Continent, returning with authentic velvets and laces, paintings of actual dresses, and pictures of jewelry, wigs, and accessories. Only the finest materials were used, and the expense was enormous. Fifty yards of white satin were used for Marie Antoinette's wedding dress, and her white plumed ball gown weighed fifty-two pounds.

The movie was budgeted for $1 million, and the studio spent five years planning it; $500,000 was spent even before all the players were cast. Research was meticulous and turned up many fascinating tidbits, such as the fact that Louis XV bathed only seventeen times from cradle to grave and that Marie had holes in her shoes as she knelt at the guillotine. Adrian went to Vienna and unearthed every known Hapsburg portrait of Marie's generation. In Paris he roamed the streets and visited hairdressers whose ancestors had trimmed the wigs and curled the coiffures of the courtiers. He combed knitting mills in France for weavers and found long-forgotten samples of gold cloth and brocade. He dug up copies of Marie's jewels. Even the prop man came back from Europe with $100,000 worth of antiques. Irving Thalberg, Shearer's husband, began the project but died before it could be completed. Some felt that the loss of his guiding hand in such an ambitious spectacle was a factor in its less-than-stunning box-office success.

Marie Antoinette took sixty-seven days to film and ninety-eight sets. Adrian designed for 1,250 extras and two poodles; there were over 4,000 costumes; 5,000 wigs were used and reused; and director Woody Van Dyke downed 1,340 cups of coffee. The wardrobe department worked around the clock in three shifts. Adrian produced fifty to seventy-five sketches a day in pencil and watercolor. Despite the turmoil, Adrian's favorite films were *Marie Antoinette, The Great Ziegfeld*, and *Idiot's Delight*.

Every day for three months prior to filming, Norma Shearer would be fitted and refitted for forty Adrian gowns, learn court dances, and help devise a special white make-up to give her an alabaster beauty. Shearer actually wore thirty-four costumes for *Marie* and eighteen wigs, one of which weighed twenty-five pounds. Gold lace, Lyons velvet, antique gilt braid and buttons, and antique embroidery were more common on the set than cotton in a western. Marie's skirts were too heavy to catch, and Shearer could not grab through to the steel hoops because of her petticoats, so loops of ribbon were fastened to the hoops and passed through the skirts so she could hold them up and walk.

After filming ended, all the incredibly gorgeous costumes were returned to wardrobe and reused again and again. Anita Louise's chinchilla cape reappeared in *New Moon*, then the fur was removed and it was used again, then it was shortened and Agnes Moorehead wore it in another movie.

Gladys George in Marie Antoinette *by MGM, 1938. Designer: Adrian*

Norma Shearer in Marie Antoinette *by MGM, 1938. Designer: Adrian*

Norma Shearer in Romeo and Juliet *by MGM,
1936. Designer: Adrian*

Romeo and Juliet was an epic MGM production guided by the golden touch of Irving Thalberg. Although Shearer was far beyond the tender teens envisioned by Shakespeare for Juliet, the production was hailed as an artistic and dramatic success. MGM publicity disseminated many fascinating bits of information about this picture. Budgeted at $2 million, *Romeo and Juliet* took ten years to plan and film. Cameramen were sent to Italy to photograph crooked little streets and castles and cathedrals for reproduction back in Hollywood. MGM rented a hundred nearby acres and built a miniature replica of the whole city of Verona.

Oliver Messel, a noted authority on fifteenth-century costumes, was imported from England to do the costume designing. Adrian asserted his right to clothe the main character of Juliet, and Shearer supported him. Two costumes were made for each of Shearer's scenes, completed costumes, and at the time of filming she decided which one she wanted. Rejects were either put on extras or not worn at all. Shearer made every decision.

Messel spent two months in Verona studying, sketching, and photographing works of art, architecture, costumes, and hairdresses in museums. An extra 500 women were employed for several months to sew 1,250 costumes, and 125 tailors did men's costumes. Most required all hand work and hand stitching because sewing-machine stitching would be too noticeable on the screen.

The entire movie was first shot against a black background so the director and actors could study the acting without the distraction of scenery. The set was strictly closed. Despite all precautions, Barrymore, Howard, and Rathbone were all hurt during film duels. And Leslie Howard, a cameraman, and director George Cukor were reported to have helped deliver a lamb during filming—the offspring was named Romeo.

The statistics for the movie are staggering. MGM technicians planted thirty trees on the set and used or employed 90,999 flagstones, 200 tons of cement, 75,000 feet of lumber, 300 barrels of paint, eighty books of gold leaf, 500 yards of carpet, 500 feet of garden hose, thirty crates of grapes, 100 gallons of kerosene for torches, 300 pounds of ginger roots for parakeets, twelve milliners, twenty-five knitting machine operators, twelve bootmakers, thirty embroiderers, twenty-five dyers, 500 painters, 100 paving workers, 150 mill workers, and 30,000 miles of film.

Norma Shearer had been a star for some time before *Romeo and Juliet* and was the acknowledged queen of the MGM lot, with first pick of choice roles. Her father had been a prominent businessman in Montreal, Canada, but the aftermath of World War I caused financial reverses for the family. At the age of fourteen Norma Shearer left school. Her family sold an heirloom piano so Norma, a sister, and her mother could set sail for New York and find work in acting.

Violet Kemble Cooper in Romeo and Juliet *by MGM, 1936. Designer: Messel*

Katherine De Mille in Romeo and Juliet *by MGM, 1936. Designer: Messel*

Mae West was an enigma of the Thirties. When other stars were svelte and wore any style, West's healthy hourglass figure was adorned by clothing suited and fashionable only for West. She was a magnificent, elaborate exaggeration in her long, long dresses encrusted with diamonds and lavished with furs and laces. Edith Head remembered her experience with West this way:

> I did a picture called *She Done Him Wrong*. Travis Banton was on vacation in Paris. Mae West came to the studio. We could not wait for him to come back, so I did the clothes. They not only became a style, but it was the only time that Paris admitted that there was a Hollywood. They didn't mention the designer, but they said, *"le style Mae West, c'est magnifique!"* It became the rage to have hourglass figures, feather boas, and all that stuff. This was an amusing, gay, camp kind of thing, and Paris was amused by it. But it was definitely not fashion.

Mae West was 5'5" and weighed 130 pounds, according to studio publicity. For Diamond Lil, her role in *She Done Him Wrong*, West became 5'9" and 160 pounds through the use of specially boned corsets which brought out the hips, nipped in the waist, and pushed up the breasts.

The gowns worn by Mae West were in a category all to themselves. As Head further commented:

> Mae West always knew what she wanted. She has a certain look. She knows what colors, what beads. In other words, Mae West is a type. . . . The thing is that it is very hard to wear all the fur and beads, but she handles clothes very well. Don't forget she has been on the stage and handles her body magnificently. She can take a dress with fur on the bottom and walk across the room when a lot of people would break their necks.

When asked about the famous hourglass figure and if corsets were worn, Head replied, "In the period pictures she did. Not in the contemporary ones. All stars wore corsets in the period pictures."

George Cukor, speaking as an astute observer of the Hollywood scene, added:

> The Hollywood designer knew what was practical. For example, Travis Banton dressed Mae West in the most wonderful way and so did Edith Head because they were exaggerated clothes. West talked to the jury in long clothes, in long dresses. She wanted a big splash. That wasn't really what was fashion, it was what Mae West wanted and looked best in.

Mae West always wore what suited her special, unconventional image, on screen and off, and she supervised every detail of her wardrobe to maintain and cultivate the Mae West look. It may not have been glamour in the elegant Thirties mode, but the West style was Hollywood glamour in the classic sense.

Mae West in Every Day's a Holiday *by Paramount, 1937. Designer: Schiaparelli*

Loretta Young in Suez by 20th Century-Fox,
1938. Designer: Royer

Suez was not an extravagant picture on the order of *Marie Antoinette* or *The Scarlet Empress*, but the simoon scene was staged on an artificial, two-acre desert with twenty-eight wind machines creating 40 mph winds, and 20th Century-Fox did spend $38,000 on eighteen gowns for Loretta Young, two of which were replicas of those worn by Empress Eugénie. Included was a gold inlaid crown with paste rubies and pearls also modeled on one of Eugénie's actual crowns. Each stunning gown appeared only briefly on the screen but implied the mood and maturity of the on-screen character. Eugénie is first seen in a frothy, light chiffon sport dress with flowers for accent in her enormous filmy hat. The character at this point is young, carefree, and in love. The dress fits this attitude exactly. Her party gown for the same period follows the gay, youthful air. As the story progresses, Eugénie marries Napoleon despite her love for the Tyrone Power character, and civil revolution and dramatic world crisis now overtake and permeate the mood of the costumes. Heavy satins, darker colors, more mature lines emerge. One of the most dramatic scenes shows Young in black velvet, elegant but not distracting. The final gown is one Empress Eugénie wears to honor her former lover for building the Suez Canal. The color is light, but the style is very serious and formal. In the movie she is also heavily weighted down with large, ostentatious jewelry symbolic of the heavy responsibilities she must carry.

In *Suez*, Young's skirts were always bigger, wider, more enormous than anyone else's. Regarding Loretta Young's mastery of her costumes, Gwen Wakeling commented:

> Nothing caused problems for that girl. She could handle anything. She knew exactly how to handle the big hoop skirts in *Suez*. First of all she wore bedroom slippers when she was sure her feet wouldn't show because it was more like being barefoot and gives a graceful action. If you walk barefoot you can really control your body. And as long as it is a long, long skirt, no one can see your feet anyway. This was for evening gowns as well as costumes. The thing with hoop skirts is to watch out when you sit down. They can fly up, but she knew exactly how to do it. In going through a doorway she would take her skirt and go through semi-sideways. She knew how to handle clothes exactly. She was exceptional. She knew she was a clotheshorse and she collaborated with the designers. We did things together and it was fun. We would make rough sketches together, talk things over, look over materials, and talk about the effect we wanted.

When asked if there was anything Young could not wear or handle, Wakeling replied, "Well, I don't know. There was nothing that we tried that we were not able to do."

After filming costume epics like *Suez*, the gorgeous gowns were put away for possible use later. This included accessories, jewelry, and even slips. However, as Wakeling revealed, there were exceptions:

> Loretta used to get the petticoats—without paying for them—from period dresses, and she gave them to her mother, who was a decorator who used to make lamp shades out of them.

Period movies started many fashion trends, directly and sometimes indirectly. *Gone with the Wind* or Hedy Lamarr is most popularly credited with starting the snood on the way to fashion success, but Young wore one first, shown here with the white evening ball gown, in *Suez* in 1938.

Loretta Young in Suez *by 20th Century-Fox, 1938. Designer: Royer*

Loretta Young in The House of Rothschild
by United Artists, 1934. Designer: Wakeling

Loretta Young in The Crusades *by Paramount,
1935. Designer: Banton*

Making an epic movie was no simple task, and making a Cecil B. De Mille epic was even more formidable. For *The Crusades*, for example, there were 300,000 feet of film exposed and 1,500 people and 800 horses in daily employment. One set covered four acres, and the movie used 3,800 pounds of nails for props, forty-six tons of lumber and metal for one seige tower, 2,500 pounds of crepe hair for mustachios, 18,000 yards of cloth, several thousand wigs, fifty gallons of imitation blood, and a few tons of chain mail. The De Mille coat of arms appeared in the picture, and Katherine De Mille received her role as a Christmas present from Papa. Twenty falcons were trained for the film with hoods and bells, all captured by De Mille's assistants from cliffs around Hollywood since few falcons were in captivity at that time. Two falcons, Ethel and George, had offspring on the set. The cast and crew named them Henry, Cecil, Loretta, and Saladin.

Regarding the problem of casting the key role of Berengaria, De Mille said the actress must "act like Helen Hayes, have the vivacity of Miriam Hopkins, the wistfulness of Helen Mack, and the charm of Marion Davies. And as for looks, she must be a combination of all four of these actresses." He first considered Merle Oberon, then selected Loretta Young.

Gwen Wakeling, who started her career with Cecil B. De Mille, recalled he "wanted people to resist him. He also had a need to dominate, so you had to fight him or he would tear you apart bit by bit." One of the few people who could manage De Mille, according to Wakeling, was Mitchell Leisen. Only he could get away with saying, "Sir, do you want it now or do you want it right?"

The House of Rothchild was set in Napoleonic times, when styles attempted a Greek revival. Many fashionable ladies then wore flesh-colored tights underneath very sheer garments, like the costume on Loretta Young. Young is completely covered with long sleeves and high neck, but the gown is very provocative. Walter Plunkett also used this style for one of Katharine Hepburn's costume from *Quality Street*, shown previously. Everything about costumes, period or contemporary, had to be coordinated. Wakeling recalled that "we'd all work together. We were like teams. When you had a lot of people in a scene, you had to make sure of proper composition colorwise, for example." All costumes were screen-tested.

Although the glamour of the Golden Era of the Thirties is gone, Wakeling feels eventually some of it may return to the screen. She said, "Human life is very short and everything goes in cycles; it doesn't come back to exactly the same thing, but it is in cycles."

Loretta Young in The Crusades *by Paramount,*
1935. Designer: Banton

Chorus Girls in Murder at the Vanities
by Paramount, 1934.

Chorus Girls in International House *by Paramount, 1933. Designer: Banton*

In November 1934, 17,541 people were registered with Central Casting in Hollywood, and every year thousands more starry-eyed men and women flocked to Tinseltown in quest of a dream. A few hundred were hired by each studio for chorus lines, bit parts, or just background. Epics produced by De Mille and other spectacular, big-budget productions could employ a few thousand extras for several weeks. *Captain Blood* paid $5 a day for extras in mob scenes, $15 a day for dress extras, and $25 and up a day for stunt men. The movie used 400 extras daily, one-fourth of whom were injured in the battle scenes. Von Sternberg claimed a cast of over a thousand players for *The Scarlet Empress,* but he saved money by using large crowd scenes from Lubitsch's silent epic, *The Patriot,* made in 1928.

In between movies, or while waiting for a big break or even little crack that never came, these people melted into the faceless scenery of the real world. Most were never seen by movie audiences. Only a handful attained any recognition, and only a small fraction of that handful achieved real and lasting success. The odds were incredible, but the flood continues even today. The magic that is Hollywood still draws the dreamers.

Many of the costumes worn by chorus girls or extras were not specially designed for them, depending on the studio, budget, and designer. Adrian in the early and mid-Thirties designed for everyone on the set, later for only the cream of the stars. Orry-Kelly designed for stars in early Warner Brothers musicals, and Milo Anderson handled the chorus. Some movies were completely designed by Kelly, some by Anderson. Many times the chorus wore reworked costumes from previous blockbusters. Later, outfits were rented from large companies like the Western Costume Company.

In the early Thirties, as the era of sound took hold, the studios produced large musical extravaganzas. Then the Depression hit the studios hard, and budgets for extras dwindled. By the mid-Thirties a new cycle had begun, and extras were once again being hired in significant numbers. There were 1, 864 applicants for the chorus line in the ball sequence in *Artists and Models.* Those chosen were dressed by Travis Banton completely in cellophane.

You might note that the chipmunk-fur trim seen earlier on Kay Francis on a daytime coat now appears as the costume for a chorus girl in *Murder at the Vanities,* and the exotic Chinese-inspired ensemble on a lady in *International House* also adorns Anna May Wong in a later section on Chinese costumes.

Chorus Girls in Fashions of 1934 *by Warner Brothers, 1934. Designer: Orry-Kelly*

Chorus Girls in The Great Ziegfeld *by MGM, 1936. Designer: Adrian*

Mary Ellis in Paris in Spring *by Paramount, 1935. Designer: Banton*

Ever since sound stirred the nation's screens and studios scoured the stage for singing stars, the musical has been a cyclically popular type of moneymaker. The first forays into music were generally loud and gaudy affairs that did not rely on technical excellence or pluperfect tones to entertain. There were singers to be sure, and good ones, but mating sound with action was primitive for the first couple of years, and glaring tonal distortions, fluctuating volumes, and severe technical limitations daunted all but the hardiest. Operatic singers in particular, with the obvious and unique exception of Jeanette MacDonald, suffered disastrous failures that discouraged further attempts for years. There were scores of musicals, so-called popular musicals, but the true operatic voice was not heard until the mid-Thirties, when technical achievements had not only conquered earlier deficiences, but in fact could significantly augment and enhance the sounds made by a vocalist. It was this technical excellence that became the salvation and the bane of operatic singers.

Lily Pons in That Girl from Paris *by RKO, 1936. Designer: Stevenson*

In producing a singing picture, the story was first acted out with the artist singing, but only strongly enough to shape the words with her lips. Producers and directors felt full-throated renditions would be terribly unsightly in close-ups. Audiences would be offended by ten-foot-tall tongues, tonsils, or teeth, and straining neck cords and sweat were grossly unphotogenic. The mouth should therefore never be fully opened, and grimaces were not allowed. After the movie was filmed, the singer was imprisoned in a projection room where she watched herself perform each song, which was split into segments of eight to sixteen bars and run over and over until every nuance was rehearsed and perfected. Finally, the singer entered the acoustical studio, where physical and technical conditions allowed for no less than a flawless singing environment. By this time the original sound had been deleted from the movie, and the silent version was run while the vocalist sang into the microphone, applying the long hours of intense practice done previously. Not just one but several tracks were recorded of the same song. After the singer had done her part, technicians in the studio's sound department went to work amplifying the volume where necessary, increasing the resonance and body of the voice for effect, and deleting the mistakes of imperfections from each track until only one spliced and perfect version was mated with the film to produce an aria of unsurpassing brilliance and technical impeccability. Thus an inexperienced, relatively weak singer could be made to sound like a peerless prima donna.

The movie industry sought to enhance its prestige by showcasing its contributions to the fine arts, and ballet and opera had long been esteemed as socially productive and worthwhile projects. The finest costumes, the best sets, and the most detailed attention were utilized to present real art to the public. Cinema operettas were designed to allow no controllable imperfection to mar the production. Therefore, petite Lily Pons, called "Spooks" first by Jack Oakie and then by everyone, sang on the screen with the full, strong voice of a 250-pound German Valkyrie prima donna. Grace Moore, who was extremely popular and successful on screen but prone to disturbing weight gains, thrilled audiences with pluperfectly performed arias. Mary Ellis, whose loveliness and excellent figure made overtures from Hollywood almost mandatory, sounded relaxed and unstrained as she bustled about the set in a blur of motion. Audiences, however, tended to be disappointed with the cracking voices, glaring faults, inaudible passages, and poor fidelity inherent in live performances. It was impossible to duplicate on the stage the utter perfection a vast audience had come to expect from the artist's cinema exhibitions. Yet, despite the disappointments, these opera starlets had become cinema stars, and their well-known names could command large salaries and fill vast halls. The glamorous images they now exuded helped bridge the gap created by immature, inexperienced, or simply human voices.

Grace Moore in When You're in Love *by Columbia, 1937. Designer: Newman*

Frances Dee and Ronald Colman in If I Were
King *by Paramount, 1938. Designer: Head*

High Renaissance and medieval days provided the opportunity for splendidly elaborate, ornate costumes. Less ostentatious than the billowing hoops of later periods, the twelfth to sixteenth centuries relied on brocades, veils, and rich materials to awe the public. Ornate costumes such as these took weeks to make because most were done by hand and required three or four fittings. Sufficient lead time for research as well as actual construction of the garments was very important.

After filming, lavish, heavy costumes were most often hung on hangers to await their next use, which often did not come before the weight of the encrusted jewels and fabric combined with gravity to tear the gown from the hanger and ruin it. Time, wooden and wire hangers, and neglect have destroyed thousands of dollars' worth of valuable, irreplaceable costumes. Gwen Wakeling remembered that people used to write letters and ask, "Do you just put them together with chewing gum and pins?" and she would reply, "No!" The costumes had to be properly made and put together beautifully, or they would not stand up for the duration of the movie: "The clothes were built to last."

Wakeling's sketches for *Affairs of Cellini* detailed the ornate designs evident on every costume, but not every bead. Often the material itself formed a pattern, which was then hand-encrusted with stones and sparkles. Jewelry accessories were a different matter. Wakeling recalled:

> We were very rich in those days. We had jewelry made to order. Sometimes you could find it but sometimes you couldn't. There was a jewelry firm called Sunset Jewelry Manufacturers and they went around to all the studios and worked with the designers.

Affairs of Cellini was a costume high point, and the designer, reviewing her work forty-six years later, commented:

> It was sort of Renaissance; I wouldn't say it was the most perfect, literal translation by any means. We did modify history to fit the actress from time to time, although none of this is too far off. It's not bad. Maybe that hat is a little bit bigger, or she didn't wear it quite properly, but it was a very interesting period.

Bennett's black velvet dress featured gold braid and embroidery. Wakeling elaborated:

> This was what they call bullion embroidery. It was gold wire, maybe not pure gold, tiny; it was a time-consuming job. You could not just stitch, you had to push the needle through the outline so you could see what the pattern was, and then cut this stuff and put the needle through again, one line at a time. One little spiral at a time. It was not a continuous spiral. It was very beautiful, it had a height, a texture, a thickness to it.

Myrna Loy in A Connecticut Yankee *by Fox, 1931. Designer: Wachner*

Constance Bennett in Affairs of Cellini
by United Artists, 1934. Designer: Wakeling

Constance Bennett made a very elegant lady, despite the very uncomfortable costumes, but Wakeling reminded her, "Well, if you want to be authentic and wear the proper clothes of the period and look good, you've just got to be uncomfortable sometimes."

One detail not noticed for decades was the fact that Bennett was wearing dark red nail polish throughout the movie. Hardly appropriate for the period but overlooked by the wardrobe lady in charge of the picture, by the director, and probably unconsciously by Bennett herself. A small footnote: Sam Goldwyn brought one of New York's famous models to Hollywood to carry Constance Bennett's train in *Cellini*. The beautiful train bearer was Lucille Ball.

Although significant time was spent researching medieval and Renaissance styles, a designer could only go so far. The body could not be remodeled to conform to authentic physical vogues, and hair fashion was severely limited by accepted conventions of chic. Just as eighteenth-century actresses enacted Greek tragedies with a few swatches of material draped to their hooped skirts and a leaf or two stuck into their high, white powdered wigs, so Bennett's hair in *Cellini* looked smart to Thirties audiences and Myrna Loy's make-up was the very latest in *A Connecticut Yankee*. Historical accuracy for cinema costumes was a fine line trod by the designer who attempted authenticity as much as possible, but who still was directed by studio executives as well as the public to make the star look as glamorous as possible according to the prevailing standards of beauty.

Period day wear ran the gauntlet from exquisite brocades and velvets to simple little taffetas. Even if the period were rather drab, designers sought to insure that the cinema wardrobes worn by starring characters, especially rich starring characters, would be one of the greatest satisfactions of moviegoing. Cinema costumes, contemporary or period, fed the public's treasured fantasies of elegance. The clothing designed for a star was never meant to be worn by anyone but that star—or copied very generally by the public in fan magazines. Created to make the character real and believable, costumes in essence taught unreality. Stars emerged on the screen in looks tailored for movies.

The Gorgeous Hussy was Joan Crawford's only Thirties period movie. Stunning as the 1830s costumes were, they failed to hide the thoroughly modern woman everyone knew Crawford to be. Crawford's dresses and hats were exaggerated on screen to denote her as the star and to subdue or at least match her strong screen personality. Clarence Brown directed Crawford in *Hussy* and four other films. In *The Velvet Light Trap,* volume 18, he said:

> Contrary to her popular image, she's extremely vulnerable. The start of every scene was always the same: we'd stand off by ourselves, not saying anything. She'd hold my arm tightly for a minute or two and then she'd say, "All right, I think I'm ready now," and do the scene. She needed the security of knowing somebody was in sympathy with what she was trying to do.

Props of all kinds caused problems of all kinds in any film. For *Hussy* the property man had to feed the chickens on the set every five minutes to keep them quiet during Crawford's speeches.

The Black Box was a period movie set in the heart of Austria-Hungary. Marian Marsh's exquisite gown was complete even to the fine handmade net gloves. The low off-shoulder effect was a dash of Hollywood. Sumptuous day dresses like those on Marsh and Elsa Lanchester were often more ornate than some evening ensembles.

David Copperfield had sixty-four speaking parts, of which twenty-six were cast players. The movie took place in early Victorian times and covered about twenty-five years; the costumes were dated from 1835 to 1845. Ten researchers worked in England collecting all bits of Dickens-era memorabilia. A moving van full of collected English material—old books, photographs, sketches, costumes, etc.—was shipped from England to California and catalogued for reference. The original green-backed paper pamphlet edition of *David Copperfield* with its original drawings by "Phiz" (H. K. Browne) was consulted for costume details. Despite the costs lavished on this production, costumes for *Copperfield* were far less opulent and far more subdued and simple than for most period movies because there were no real glamorous characters and the story was considered a classic not to be fussed with. The movie was a critical, artistic, and financial success.

Movie designers took their ideas from cartoons, line drawings, paintings, magazine reproductions, books, and originals. Many old English costumes could still be found in old clothing stores from Paris to San Francisco in the early Thirties. Of course, not everyone on the set wore authentic dresses and suits that cost large sums to reproduce. Only those near the camera wore "authentic" silks and woolens. Those sufficiently out of focus cheated on materials but were still correct in pattern.

Joan Crawford in Gorgeous Hussy *by MGM. 1936. Designer: Adrian*

Maureen O'Sullivan in David Copperfield *by MGM, 1935. Designer: Tree*

Marian Marsh in The Black Room *by Columbia,
1935. Designer: Kalloch*

Elsa Lanchester in Naughty Marietta *by MGM,*
1934. Designer: Adrian

Phyllis Brooks in In Old Chicago *by 20th Century-Fox, 1937. Designer: Royer*

Franciska Gaal in The Buccaneer *by Paramount, 1938. Designer: Head*

Evening gowns for period pictures displayed some of the finest taste of the decade without gaudiness. Because a moviegoer could usually detect true silks and brocades from substitutes, even when seen as lights and shadows, evening gowns appearing in a historical picture cost at least $1,000 to make in the early Thirties.

The designers began with authenticity down to the construction of petticoats and corsets. According to *Scientific American* for February 1933, designer Earl Luick was hired for a movie to reproduce eighty dresses and suits worn in England at the turn of the century. He started by procuring originals wherever possible, and these he took into his workshop and ripped each into all its parts. From the parts he made patterns, and from the patterns he built new costumes to fit the various people. He said:

> Cloths repeat every seven years. For 1900, there's something made today which we can use to look like the silk, satin, or silk muslin then in vogue. When we go back to, say, 1730, we find cloths very stiff, but drapery fabric usually serves to reproduce them. Whatever the cloth, however, we must use the best we can get; otherwise it would not tailor correctly.

After authenticity was established, and depending on the studio, star, director, producer, and designer, the gown was created to best display its wearer. Virginia Bruce's lovely chest was amply emphasized before the Hays Office could take offense.

Although Greek at first impression, Rosalind Russell's unique satin gown was very eye-catching on the screen. With it she wore a full-length circular-cut dark cape with a full hood and face veil. The story for *Under Two Flags* concerned the French Foreign Legion before World War I and took place in North Africa. For filming this movie, the Fox studio rounded up and hired twenty of the twenty-three camels in California and shipped them and 3,000 persons to the shooting location in an Arizona desert.

Rosalind Russell in Under Two Flags *by 20th Century-Fox, 1936. Designer: Wakeling*

Virginia Bruce in The Mighty Barnum *by United Artists, 1934. Designer: Kiam*

Helen Gilbert in The Secret of Dr. Kildare
by MGM, 1939. Designer: Tree

Every little girl and woman who dreams of being a Hollywood star looks forward to sweeping across the screen in a wide, lovely hooped wonder like the gowns on these pages. The height of femininity, the ante-bellum frock of the Old South, competes with the slinky glamour gowns of the mid-Thirties as the most elegant and desirable of cinema costumes. The ultrawide hoop styles of the 1800s were incredibly eye-catching and inevitably flattering when created by Hollywood designers. The enormous width of the skirt accentuated a small waist and covered all posterior sins. In the actress were graceful, each movement would be prettily accentuated by a dainty swirl of the skirt.

Each dress required layers of ruffles and laces and took weeks to make. Most embroidery was hand-done, all flowers were hand-sewn. It is amazing how similar the styles were; all these stunning dresses were off-shoulder, all had flower detailing, all had varying degrees of ruffles, and most were accompanied by sausage-curl hair-dos—the exception being Helen Gilbert sporting the very latest in an up-piled coiffure. Gilbert's sleeves are three-quarter-length, the rest are short.

It has been said that some stars would look fantastic in potato sacks, but would they still be "stars"? A glamorous image depended on the clothes an actress wore, and because of the camera's all-seeing eye and those terribly cruel close-ups, the costumes had to be perfectly becoming and correct for her role. During the Thirties motion pictures grew from an amusing form of entertainment to *the* entertainment for millions. Women once content to wear the best their local store offered were suddenly assaulted by beautiful, elegant attire worn by the most dazzling clotheshorses of the era. As important, audiences saw clothing in action. Actresses stooped, walked, sat, and stretched in their cinema costumes, and movement became an important element of design. Historical gowns such as these were factors in the trend from the mid-Thirties' slinky ensembles to the fuller, Romantic-era silhouette for evening. Publicity was another factor that whetted the public's fashion appetite. Long before *Gone with the Wind* was released, an avalanche of publicity about the search for Scarlett, the production problems, the scope of the picture, and so on, caused manufacturers to produce bonnet hats, wider skirts, lovely capes, and the like in anticipation of the expected popularity of the ante-bellum styles. The success of *Jezebel* should also be noted.

Although it is a fact that cinema costumes help make a star, Edith Head prefers to emphasize the other half of the glamour relationship. In January 1957 in *Western Family* she said:

> We're one-shot artists who stick to the script, dressing a certain star for a certain role at a certain year and season. What influence we have on world styles is not from the fashion but from the star who wears it and from the audiences that may idealize her.

Luise Rainer in The Toy Wife *by MGM, 1938. Designer: Adrian*

Claire Trevor and Andy Devine in Stagecoach *by United Artists, 1939. Designer: Plunkett*

Loretta Young in Ramona *by 20th Century-Fox, 1936. Designer: Wakeling*

Nineteenth-century western America, especially during the middle and late years, was not particularly fertile ground for cinema fashions. The West and westerns, with few exceptions, extolled the hard-working pioneer wife—not very fashionable; the cowgirl—definitely not chic; the dance-hall devotee—typically gaudy; or some other, less exciting type. While the country swooned over Civil War hoops from Dixie, few western films caused a ripple in the fashion mainstream.

Occasionally a female star would balk at wearing authentic period underwear, especially if her legs and petticoats would remain unseen. Such was not the case with Claire Trevor, whose ugly shoes and practical stockings were authentic. *Stagecoach* has been proclaimed *the* classic western motion picture. Unfortunately, it competed for awards in 1939, a year which produced an unusual number of fine and memorable motion picture masterpieces.

Early California history provided both Spanish and western influences on cinema fashions. Loretta Young's exquisite gown from *Ramona* was basically very simple, but the handmade ruching and lace made a very elegant everyday costume. One trick to age cinema western wardrobes to give them that well-worn look was to spray them with oil paint and gasoline. Despite dusty roads and no vacuum cleaners, however, western heroines usually had clean and well-pressed dresses.

Western history encompassed many periods, yet styles were relatively uniform. Early California, pioneer days, the gold rush, cowboys and cattle from Texas to California, Dodge City, post–Civil War days, Indian raids and reservations—whatever the situation, the ladies appeared in full skirts natural waists, and bonnets. *Barbary Coast* depicted the San Francisco waterfront in its early heyday, around the 1850s. Sam Goldwyn bought the novel *Barbary Coast* by Herbert Asbury without reading it because he wanted a western story about early San Francisco. The book turned out to be a record of the city's underworld, and critics called it "one of the filthiest, vilest, most degrading books that ever had been chosen for the screen." Goldwyn discarded the story and retained the title. Research discovered that a "blue blazer" was a favorite drink in the 1850s; the recipe was to set fire to a glass of whiskey and down it as an appetizer.

Miriam Hopkins was characterized as having an insatiable thirst for knowledge. Her dressing room was cluttered with an imposing variety of books—philosophy, biographies, science, and fiction—and she read them all. She wanted to learn painting and the violin but refused to touch a piano because of her daily lessons when she was young. She once said, "That metronome clicking away on top of the piano used to drive me frantic. So now I have a player [piano]. It makes better music than I can and does it with a lot less effort."

Miriam Hopkins and Joel McCrea in Barbary
Coast *by United Artists, 1935. Designer: Kiam*

Gail Patrick and Buster Crabbe in Wanderer of the Wasteland *by Paramount, 1935. Designer: Head*

The first commercial motion picture was a western, *The Great Train Robbery,* made in 1903. The typical western was pure escapism, easy to understand, full of action, and featuring great outdoor scenery. In the Teens a $9,000 investment in a western made it a major production; in the Twenties real cowboys would fall off horses for $1 a throw; and in the Thirties the average western cost $15,000 to $35,000 and returned a minimum fifty-percent profit. Westerns became family staples and have always remained popular. Audiences wanted escapism, and in westerns the hero was seen actually doing something about the bad guys. There was a strong tradition in a western: no cussing ("shucks" was pretty strong), no drinking, no smoking, the villains always picked on little fellows, and the hero always won. Although westerns generally played in smaller, less prestigious theaters, a few, like Hopalong Cassidy movies, were released through Paramount and played in better theaters.

In class "B" oaters, most heroines were fairly wooden, lovely props. A few had relatively meaty roles, but most often they played second fiddle to the horse and were subjected to lots of real danger while filming, in addition to low pay, low prestige, long hours, exposure to raw elements in the outdoor locations, and hand-me-down wardrobes. Even in the Forties Trigger was always billed above the female lead in a Roy Rogers picture, and Trigger's contract even called for a minimum of three close-ups in every movie. There were six Triggers for every picture: three chief Triggers (a principal for closeups, one trick, one running), and three stand-ins or assistant Triggers. The female was usually an object to be saved, although some of the better heroines, like Dale Evans, competed successfully with the scenery and were able to wave good-bye to the hero as he rode off into the sunset.

A significant break with this stereotyped female in the West was seen in *Destry Rides Again,* starring James Stewart and Marlene Dietrich. *Destry* was a western spoof in which Dietrich played a brawling beerhall hostess named Frenchie (because before filming she had been staying in France), a hussy with a heart of gold. Dietrich's traditional glamorous image was relatively well preserved, but a new element was added, humor, which endeared her once again to the American public. Before *Destry* Dietrich was considered box-office poison. Joe Pasternak pushed for Dietrich, but Universal executives didn't think she would draw flies. The story changed from a typical western with a strong, gun-slinging hero and frail heroine to a frail hero who didn't like guns and a strong, tough heroine. James Stewart loved to read Flash Gordon comics, so Dietrich had the art department make him a life-size doll of Flash while filming. He loved it. According to the book *Marlene* by Charles Higham, for the big fight scene with Una Merkel, the director told Dietrich and Merkel to make it in one take; stunt women were around if the action lagged. They were not used. The fight was spontaneous even though neither Dietrich nor Merkel had ever laid a hand on anyone before. Merkel was bruised from head to foot, Dietrich relatively untouched. In the end, Stewart had to drop water on both to end the scene, and it had to be done in long shot as well as close-up for the cameras, also for publicity shots. The dowsing took hours. Merkel went to the hospital for two days' observation to insure that there were no internal injuries. Dietrich was thirty-eight years old when she made *Destry.*

Marlene Dietrich in Destry Rides Again *by Universal, 1939. Designer: Vera West*

Marlene Dietrich in Destry Rides Again
by Universal, 1939. Designer: Vera West

Jean Arthur in Diamond Jim *by Universal, 1935.*
Designer: Vera West

Binnie Barnes in Diamond Jim *by Universal,*
1935. Designer: Vera West

350

Fay Wray in One Sunday Afternoon *by Paramount, 1933.*
Designer: Banton

Although several "A"-class westerns, like *Union Pacific*, generated a few fashion notes, for the most part the average western dress did not excite style circles. Homespun materials and plain styles could not compete with the more glamorous design details produced by contemporary movies.

The late eighteen hundreds did manage spin off fashions in millinery. The sweet western bonnet framed the face nicely or added a profusion of femininity with flowers, ribbons, and straw. Grandmother's hat became acceptable chapeau chic. *One Sunday Afternoon* was set in the 1880s era, and a publicity still from the movie demonstrates how cinema period costumes evolved into contemporary fashion. The wide-brimmed straw hat became required headgear for summer teas and garden parties. Angles could be adjusted, the tilt exaggerated for extra flair. Sweet, small chapeaus modified readily into the close-fitting tiny hats of the early Thirties.

It is difficult to say which came first, the cinema hat or contemporary styles. The modified hat seen on the screen, worn by a popular personality like Fay Wray, itself generated an interest in the historical vogue, which in turn slightly changed the current style. It was a lovely, creative circle. The two hats from *Diamond Jim* amply demonstrate how modern a historical accessory could look. Binnie Barnes's hat is tilted at the popular mid-Thirties angle over the right eye; fewer plumes on top would make it completely elegant for daytime wear. A classic style, becoming in any era, is the softly feminine mass of cloth violets on Jean Arthur, stylishly tipped forward and featuring a nose-length veil. Arthur could have worn this creation anywhere. *Diamond Jim* was a big production for Universal, and much care was taken to insure authentic and appealing sets and costumes. One set alone cost $103,000.

Filming a late 1800s period movie required creating the illusion of authentic settings as well as costumes. One company needed a wood-burning railroad engine, so they made one of papier-mâché. Carpenters pushed it across a set as "smoke"—actually liquid fog—poured from the funnel. Another time a director wanted to film a ship sailing from a great port, but the only ship that fit the era was a permanent structure, built on land and weighing many tons. An ingenious property man suggested that since the ship could not steam away, the dock should. Accordingly, the dock was built on rollers, and when the time came for the ship to depart, the dock slowly rolled 200 feet down a slight incline.

Rosalind Russell in Rendezvous *by MGM, 1935.*
Designer: Adrian

World War I does not seem to be a very popular period for movie scenarios—unlike World War II, which continues to reappear on television as well as in theaters. Perhaps World War I was too much a shock for the world, the carnage and poor military tactics too senseless to be exalted on the screen. Whatever the reason, this period of history has not been overworked.

Cinema clothing for the Teens follows authentic vogues of the time, but interpretation by the cinema designer and the personality of the actress combine to create some memorable costumes.

Kay Francis stole the show in *Virtuous Sin* in her stunning dinner dress of lamé, sable, beads, jewels, and lace. Despite the extreme lavishness of the ensemble, Francis's face and screen character are not overpowered and in fact are enhanced. Few women have this magnetic power.

A fashion leader for all the many years she was a Hollywood star, Rosalind Russell wore this lovely day dress by Adrian to fit a World War I time period. The unusual draping of the skirt and tunic top and the subtle dolman sleeve treatment were Thirties cinematic style points, but the dress conformed nicely to the standards of the movie setting.

Ginger Rogers's gay ruffled dinner dress from *The Story of Vernon and Irene Castle* was designed for a highly dramatic scene. Unlike the normal practice of subduing the costume so as not to detract from the histrionics, Plunkett dressed Rogers in a frilly, ruffled style to play up her surprise and emphasize to the audience the loss of all things young and gay. Regarding the costumes for the movie, Plunkett recalled:

> I did Ginger's things. Mrs. Castle arrived and they had already signed me to do the costumes. In fairness to her, I used stills of her and the clothes she had worn as my research because Ginger had to look like Mrs. Castle. But I designed them for Ginger with Castle research in the background. Castle arrived and there was something in her contract that said she would have the credit and make the designs for Ginger. So it immediately started a battle because Ginger said that I would do them and the director and producer said that I was going to do them. Mrs. Castle was very adamant. It was battle after battle throughout the thing, and she tried to change the sketches of the costumes I had made to make them look exactly like the costumes she had worn instead of the things that were becoming to Ginger. When I had finished that movie and left RKO to do another picture somewhere else, Vanderberman called me and said, "Walter, I'm in an awful bind, we want to release the film, and Mrs. Castle has shown us her contract and the film cannot be released unless it says she designed Ginger's clothes. So would you, would you please, sign a thing saying you did not design Ginger's clothes and Mrs. Castle did." So that is why the credits on the screen read as they do.

Even hose designer de Mond had his problems with this film. It was his most expensive job to date. He made a special trip to New York for specific laces to reproduce the stockings Irene Castle wore just before World War I; dozens of workers labored for weeks to produce them. The cost was $25,000.

Ginger Rogers and Fred Astaire in The Story of
Vernon and Irene Castle *by RKO, 1939.*
Designer: Plunkett

Kay Francis in Virtuous Sin *by Paramount,*
1930. Designer: Banton

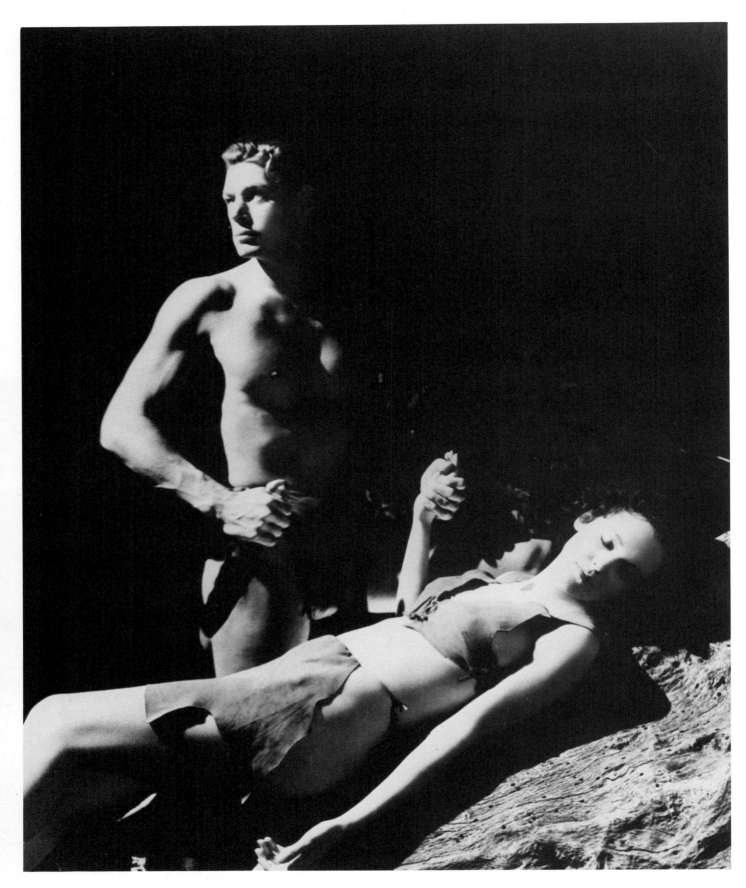

*Maureen O'Sullivan and Johnny Weissmuller
in* Tarzan and His Mate *by MGM, 1934.
Designer: Tree*

Dorothy Lamour in The Jungle Princess
by Paramount, 1936. Designer: Head

Let's Go Native is not only the name of an early Thirties jungle
teaser, but also an invitation periodically offered by studios to
frustrated urban dwellers. The theme of leaving the facade of
civilization and finding true peace and contentment by being ship-
wrecked on some paradise island is constantly repeated throughout
cinema history and was particularly appealing in the Thirties.
Movies which depicted jungles in Africa or the South Pacific inevitably also depicted happy, satisfied natives thrown into upheaval
and distress by the absurdities demanded by an influx of nasty,
civilized intruders.

Native costumes as envisioned by studio designers combined
authenticity, imagination, existing stereotype images, the Hays Code
(or lack thereof), an actress's physical attributes, and the mood of
the movie.

Dorothy Lamour established herself as the "Sarong Girl"
thanks to Edith Head's invention for *The Jungle Princess,* and the
studio managed to slip her into that or similar ensembles at every
opportunity. She and Jon Hall were native lovers in the classic
movie, *The Hurricane.* Making a simple tropical paradise and then
destroying it was no easy task in 1937. The twenty-minute hurricane
sequence alone cost $400,000. The biggest pool ever constructed
represented a lagoon in the South Seas; it held 981,250 gallons of
water and covered an acre of land.

To get her native skin, Dorothy Lamour set herself a nine P.M.
curfew to arise by six A.M. and allow two hours for body make-up.
Jon Hall was nervous about filming a scene where he had to swim
while bullets splashed near him. Director Ford hired three expert
sharpshooters for the scene, but as a gag had them show up on the
set apparently roaring drunk. In practice shots they hit the dummies
they were supposed to miss. Hall nearly fainted.

Deepest, darkest Africa also required the proper outfit, but
Maureen O'Sullivan's Jane togs did not set too many fashion trends.
Her costume for *Tarzan and His Mate,* filmed before Hays Code enforcement, was four pieces of leather. The first productions of Tarzan movies were quick and inexpensive, but cast and crew gave
their best. Some were filmed three at a time but took a year to complete.

Jeanette MacDonald in Let's Go Native
by Paramount, 1930. Designer: Banton

Hedy Lamarr in Lady of the Tropics *by MGM, 1939. Designer: Adrian*

Exotic locations called for exotic costumes, and designers could eliminate or exaggerate style details for less well known times or countries. Some countries' native clothing, like those of Thailand, lent themselves to cinema spectacle. Hedy Lamarr's magnificently impressive classical Thai dancer's costume continued the basic Thai concepts, but the studio added plenty of extravagance to take any audience's breath away. Exaggerating the shoulders and ears into elaborate wings, Adrian obviously borrowed from a temple "kinnari" figure, part woman, part bird. The cluttered headdress was strictly Hollywood, but combining the real with the fantastic was a motion picture speciality. Since surface truth in visual detail usually satisfied an audience's sense of realism, and deeper efforts were expensive, unflattering, or unnecessary, the sense of specified periods or locales could be perfectly well conveyed by general signals, not details, and the details could even be wrong (hair, make-up, shoes, etc.). Rochelle Hudson's ornate native costume included a fashionable hair-do, modern shoes, and contemporary make-up, all to soften the foreignness of the outfit.

If the story concerned a partial or total fantasy, or if the character was a dancer or entertainer type, then imagination was allowed even greater freedom. *Ali Baba Goes to Town* had magic words, magic carpets, and magically fantastic costumes. A key prop, for example, was a magic carpet that rose when the magic word "inflation" was said and dropped when "deflation" was uttered. Gypsy Rose Lee's lavish ensemble not only contributed to the fantasy element of the movie, but the long, pointed wrist cuffs, padded shoulders, and modified turban were also high style points that made the whole thing acceptable to audiences. Lynn Bari's Ali Baba–type outfit emphasized the body more than Lee's, with the standard vamp draping at the hips and bodice.

When Gwen Wakeling was asked how she created such incredible designs for *Ali Baba*, she replied, "Not really incredible; you sit down and begin sketching and look at a few things and think about it a bit and things begin to come out." Her sketches, and those of most designers, visualized the character in a scene, complete with a probable pose or movement, and then the designer sketched the costume to fit that image. The arm resting against a column or reaching up toward someone could inspire unusual shoulder details or eye-catching sleeves. A languorous, sexy exit could be heightened by a backless design or a train. Unfortunately, the pose or movement that best showed off the gown did not always appear in the movie.

Gypsy Rose Lee in Ali Baba Goes to Town *by 20th Century-Fox, 1937. Designer: Wakeling*

Ever since Mary Pickford played Cho Cho San in *Madame Butterfly* in 1915, it was a Hollywood tradition to have Caucasian women star in Oriental roles. It was also tradition that the Oriental female be depicted as either a sweet and shy geisha girl or a sly and sensual dragon lady. There were no in-betweens. All Oriental women, of course, were inherently exotic and mysterious, and costumes and sets were specifically made to enhance these elements.

True Orientals were relegated to extra and bit parts, with the great exception of Anna May Wong. Born Wong Liu Tsong in Los Angeles between 1902 and 1907 (researchers can't agree), she was a full-blooded Chinese. Only Wong seemed able to win public acceptance in roles portraying both extreme types of Orientals. Her beauty and talent made her believable as a dragon lady and a geisha, and she became Hollywood's first authentic Asian sex symbol and long-enduring star. Easily making the transition from silents to talkies, Wong finally escaped the incredible restrictions placed on Orientals when she went to work for the Free China Drive and toured with the USO in 1942. As a top Hollywood star who dazzled audiences countless times with her desirable Asian beauty, she was never kissed on the screen. Nor was a female Oriental allowed happiness in the last reel if she loved a white man or was his mistress. If the Caucasian actress who played an Oriental could prove her blue eyes came from her missionary parents or long-lost wealthy family, she was not killed or abandoned. Most Oriental females simply provided a showcase for exquisite costumes and were expendable in the end.

A switch on the usual theme was *Bitter Tea of General Yen*, in which Barbara Stanwyck played an American missionary attracted to a Chinese general. In the end *he* drinks the poison. The film was one of Frank Capra's favorites and Barbara Stanwyck's only truly "arty" film, but the subject was too sensitive for the 1930s moviegoer. *Bitter Tea* was banned in the whole British Empire for miscegenation, and American audiences questioned how Stanwyck could fall in love with a Chinaman—even if the Chinaman was the handsome and sexy Swedish actor Nils Asther.

Tilly Losch's costume from *The Good Earth,* which was filmed in Chatsworth, California, first appeared in *The Great Ziegfeld.* The ornate lamé jacket and headdress were added to Adrian's original design.

It should be noted that most Chinese costumes, far more than any other type, were definitely authentic, except when called upon to be showy. Wong's attire from *Daughter of Shanghai* was a complete and accurate Chinese dress; the handwork was incredible. This is not the case with the outfit from *Daughter of the Dragon*, which also appeared in advertising for *International House* in 1933.

Tilly Losch in The Good Earth *by MGM, 1937.*
Designer: Adrian/Tree

Martha Raye in Tropic Holiday *by Paramount, 1938. Designer: Head*

Barbara Stanwyck in Bitter Tea of General Yen *by Columbia, 1933. Designer: Stevenson*

Anna May Wong in Daughter of Shanghai *by Paramount, 1937.*

Ruby Keeler in Go into Your Dance *by Warner Brothers, 1935. Designer: Orry-Kelly*

If audiences learned to identify Chinese costumes as exotic, intriguing, and fascinating, Spanish and Mexican outfits promoted a flair for excitement, wild dancing, and an enjoyment of life. The Spanish costume was easily identifiable by the tight, slinky, and wonderfully ruffled-bottom flamenco style or the gorgeous, lacy, ornate, and wonderfully full and ruffled señorita style. Large flowers, bright colors, and ruffles captivated audiences, as did the stereotype poses and pulsating music. Although relatively few historical movies dealt with Spanish or Mexican history, Spanish costumes and influence were often seen in musicals. Walking in dresses with hundreds of yards of ruffles was not easy, and dancing in them took skill, yet the visual impact of the ruffles and materials was striking and sought after.

Another costume of Spanish origin, but one rarely appearing on a female star, was the famous suit of lights worn by bullfighters. Martha Raye's elegant suit was designed by Edith Head to copy exactly Rudolph Valentino's costume in *Blood and Sand.* Completing this outfit was a wide and ornate red satin cape, a traditional touch. The workmanship of Raye's suit is flawless, complex, costly, and probably not attainable today in Hollywood.

Martha Raye could have become one of this country's great jazz singers if she had not succeeded so well as a comedienne. Her mother and father were the vaudeville team of Reed and Hooper, and Raye was born on the road in Butte, Montana. She was a trooper at age three and speaks Italian and Spanish.

Gladys Swarthout and John Boles in Rose of the Rancho *by Paramount, 1936. Designer: Banton*

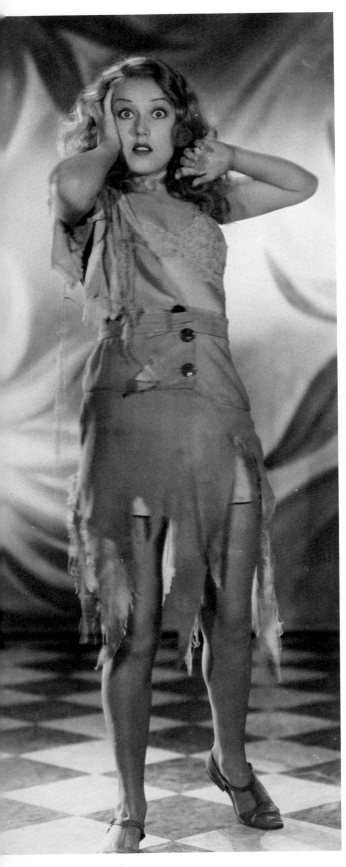

Fay Wray in King Kong *by RKO, 1933.*
Designer: Plunkett

When horror movies first burst upon audiences as early as the silent Twenties, they were not the "B" productions most often seen since the Fifties. Class "A" actors and actresses toiled to show fear and dread of bestial things and unnamed horrors. As bizarre as horror films could be, they still had to fulfill the audience's preconceived notions of what was weird and scary. Ape-men, mechanical monsters, and even mummies had to appear "correct." Boris Karloff as *The Mummy* had rotting cloth covering his body, yellowed and dusty hair, and dead-looking eyes. The make-up artist developed various colors, which, combined with fuller's earth and applied to Karloff's face, gave him the ghastly, dried façade of one dead 4,000 years. Karloff's body was encased in 1,500 feet of cheesecloth, "rotted" over a gas flame.

Before 1930, the Lon Chaney and Browning films were called *cinéma de grotesque.* During the Thirties, horror films separated into their own genre. The culmination of the first popular horror-film cycle of the Thirties was *The Bride of Frankenstein,* a movie that surprised audiences by combining the bizarre with humor. *Bride of Frankenstein* continued the character of Frankenstein's monster played unforgettably by Boris Karloff. Karloff required three and a half hours to make up as the monster and one and a half hours to return to normal. Universal copyrighted the make-up invented by Frank Pierce. Karloff was forty-eight years old when he did *Bride of Frankenstein,* and he endured a costume that had a five-pound steel spine, asphalt spreader's boots weighing eighteen pounds, steel struts to stiffen his legs, and a shabby suit that weighed fourteen pounds. Karloff broke his hip on the first day of shooting *Bride.* Elsa Lanchester was rolled into two miles of linen; she had to be carried around the studio and fed through a tube. Her 5'4" height was built up to 7'. She was designed to look like Queen Nefertiti, but actually appeared like "a creature born of a thunderstorm, a wild jungle animal in captivity, with a suggestion of pride and dignity." *The Bride of Frankenstein* cost Universal $250,000; because of its offbeat and humorous traits, studio executives thought director Whalen had gone too far, so it was Whalen's last horror movie. It is a classic.

The movie that boosted the horror genre to incredible new heights and direction was the memorable *King Kong;* it also rescued RKO from financial oblivion. Walter Plunkett not only designed Fay Wray's costumes but also dressed the natives of Skull Island.

The intricacies of filming a movie as complex as *Kong* and the time it took to master new photographic techniques made life very difficult for the cast and crew. One marathon shooting session went nonstop for twenty-two hours. Fay Wray was hardly glamorized as the beauty that kills the beast; the public today still remembers her as a blonde, although in most movies she appeared with her own natural brunette color. Just as many people think of Karloff only as Frankenstein's monster, after the phenomenal success of *Kong* Wray was also typecast for many years as a horror ingenue.

King Kong failed to be nominated for any Academy Awards and won no film festival medals.

Frances Drake and Peter Lorre in Mad Love
by MGM, 1935. Designer: Dolly Tree

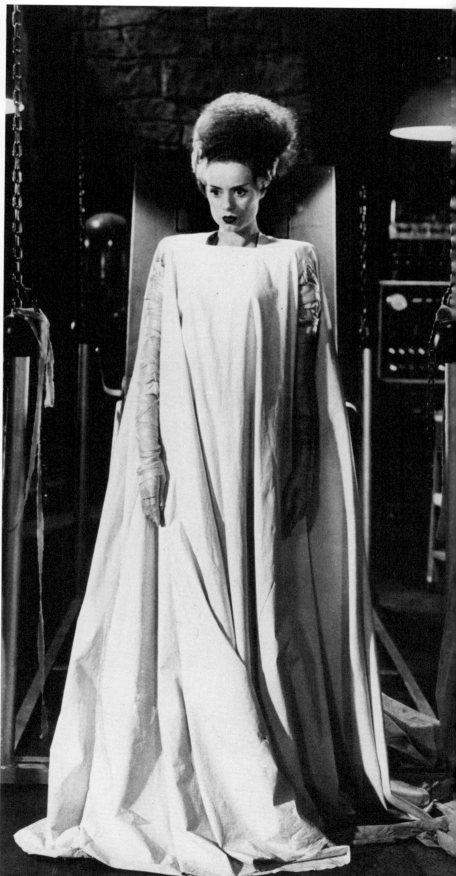

Elsa Lanchester in Bride of Frankenstein
by Universal, 1935. Designers: West and Pierce

Katharine Hepburn in Christopher Strong *by RKO, 1933. Designer: Plunkett*

Costume balls were great fun on the screen because anything was possible and most likely probable. One of the most fantastic costume balls seen in a movie was the extravagant climax in *Madame Satan*. Lillian Roth's spectacular feathered outfit and the imaginative costumes worn by the extras were notable excursions into the bizarre for designer Adrian. Far more elegant and sensational was the black, slinky costume worn by Kay Johnson. The wrap for this outfit was simply done and very dramatic—a long slither of black with a glittering serpent. Thrown back at the most exciting moment, the wrap is used as background to reveal and heighten the impressive, stunning gown beneath. Cecil B. De Mille preserved only two costumes from his movies as part of his estate: the peacock-feather gown from *Samson and Delilah* and this black and sparkling Adrian creation from *Madame Satan*.

Christopher Strong also included a costume ball, and Walter Plunkett recalled his involvement with it:

> I was head of the wardrobe department. Howard Greer, through friendships and what-not, and because he rightly was a very good couturier and had a shop on Sunset Boulevard and dressed many of the people, he did many of the RKO pictures in the early Thirties. He was assigned to it [*Christopher Strong*], but he had no facilities or interest in making up a costume; it was only fashion for him. So this was left for me to do. The difficulty was that all these little metal squares had little prongs on the back of them holding them together. It was all fine for fitting and everything until she [Hepburn] got on the set and spent a few hours in it and discovered that these little prongs were scratching and irritating her body. So I got in a crew and put in a lining of very, very thin chiffon velvet throughout the thing to keep it from digging into her.

The weight of the metal outlined every inch of Hepburn's figure, and the costume seems as remarkable and undated now as then.

Kay Johnson in Madame Satan *by MGM, 1930.*
Designer: Adrian

Lillian Roth, Reginald Denny, and Roland
Young in Madame Satan *by MGM, 1930.*
Designer: Adrian

Ilona Massey in Balalaika *by MGM, 1939.*
Designer: Adrian

One aspect of clothing most commercial fashion designers overlook is the fact that humans move about. Actresses on the screen do not merely strike graceful poses, they also run, dance, jump, roll and cavort in their cinema wardrobes, and designers had to insure that clothing would not restrict any action required by the script. All the costumes on these pages were required to move with the wearer and permit as much freedom as possible.

Harriet Hoctor was more contortionist than prima ballerina. Her specialty was an extreme back bend on point; she first appeared in *The Great Ziegfeld*. Her screen costume took advantage of the eye's fascination with plumes and wispy feathers to garner center-stage attention and enhance and exaggerate her movements.

Adrian envisioned Ilona Massey as a beautiful, fantastic Russian doll in this still from *Balalaika*. The ultrawide hoops and prodigious use of material were very hard to handle while singing. Less demanding was the uniform on Eleanor Powell.

Split seams on costumes caused delays on the set, and delays meant money, so everyone had to have well-fitting costumes. Poor fit also was unphotogenic. For a musical sequence in *Rosalie*, 500 dancers high-stepped, kicked, tapped, and twirled, and a poorly designed chorus outfit would have been disastrous. For Powell in particular, cinema costumes had to be comfortable for long and strenuous dance sequences. Eleanor Powell, who at twelve danced in a night club for $75 a week, was 5'6½" tall and weighed 120 pounds. She made a very favorable impression in her first movie, *George White's Scandals of 1935*, and was immediately snatched by MGM to become one of Hollywood's most popular musical stars.

Uniforms could quite literally be a pain. Most had high necks which chafed, or a tight fit across the chest. Some had color problems. Although not a Thirties incident, a memorable experience of Cary Grant's demonstrates what could go wrong when a costume uniform is created to fit the camera's requirements and not reality's:

In one film, *I Was a Male War Bride*, I wore a pink shirt with my French Army uniform because it was very glary sunlight. As a matter of fact, I was sitting in a car outside of a square in Heidelberg, waiting to come in (I was about two blocks away) to photograph the car entering with me sitting in the back. While I was sitting there waiting for the camera to set up, someone came over and told me, as best I could understand, that I had no right to be sitting there in that uniform. I didn't know what he was talking about, but he called for some police and they came and got me and took me away becaue I was impersonating a French officer.

The light pink shirt had caught the man's attention; Grant was obviously out of uniform.

Eleanor Powell in Rosalie *by MGM, 1937. Designer: Tree*

Harriet Hoctor in Shall We Dance *by RKO, 1937. Designer: Irene*

Ginger Rogers in Professional Sweethea
by RKO, 1933. Designer: Plunkett

Studios spent over $500 million in new capital to change from silent to sound pictures, and most studios made the complete transition in one year. *The Jazz Singer* was not only the first talkie, but also the first motion picture to interpolate songs into the dramatic plot—the first "musical" was born. Musicals became the most successful means of selling sound, but the public soon became surfeited with the flood of quick, gaudy ones first made. By 1931 the first cycle had sputtered to an end. In 1933 *Flying Down to Rio* gave musicals another spurt, as did the elegant new dancing team of Fred Astaire and Ginger Rogers. *Rio* broke with the old form of song after song, according to theatrical tradition, and sprinkled musical gems throughout a real plot. This formula was invented strictly by motion pictures and owed no allegiance to opera or theater rules. The mid-Thirties saw a musical renaissance, a new genre with new personalities and new story, song, and dance treatments. Gone forever were the limitations which producers had felt obliged to copy from the theater. However, to be successful, musicals must always be in current taste and style, so there must always be adjustments in type of story, song, or dance. In the Thirties the studios tried constantly to anticipate the public's next whim or desire. MacDonald operettas were very popular, for a time; Fox musicals were very popular, for a time; *Big Broadcasts* and *Broadway Melodies* were popular, for a time. One criterion for judging worth is the size of budget and time devoted to a production. In 1933 Warner Brothers spend an average of $211,825 per picture. *Gold Diggers of 1933* was shot in forty-five days at a cost of $300,000; *42nd Street* took twenty-eight days and $340,000. In comparison, that same year Warners filmed *Keyhole*, with Kay Francis, in twenty-five days and for $169,000; *Ex-Lady*, with Bette Davis, in eighteen days and for $115,000; *Silver Dollar*, with Bebe Daniels, in thirty-three days and for $269,000, and *She Had to Say Yes*, with newcomer Joan Bennett and Billie Burke, in seventeen days and for $111,000. In 1938 MGM spent $1.8 million to make *The Big Broadcast of 1938*.

Costumes for musicals were normally lavish and glittering creations made for movement or display with little regard to "fashion." Joan Crawford's extravagant costume from *Dancing Lady* was seen very briefly as part of a musical number. It reportedly cost the studio over $10,000 to make this one gown. Imagination spanned the ages and locales, and the outfits looked like great fun to design, wear, and view. Walter Plunkett has designed for many movies, of all types, but when asked which was his favorite, he replied:

> My favorite costumes are for a thing called *Diane*, which I am
> sure you never saw because no one ever saw it. It was badly
> cast and badly made, . . . but they were the best clothes I ever
> did. They made *Mary of Scotland* look like nothing. My
> favorite in the Thirties . . . There were several Ginger [Rogers]
> things I did. The very first thing I did with Ginger was a little
> nothing thing called *Professional Sweetheart*, which was just
> great fun, just camp clothes, crazy clothes. Absurd, crazy, com-
> ic stuff. A fun movie to do.

Professional Sweetheart was not strictly a musical, but can anyone say Roger's extravagantly ruffled circular frock was made for anything except dancing? And Plunkett's goal when he designed it? "I dressed her as a little doll in this scene." He succeeded.

Joan Crawford in Dancing Lady *by MGM, 1933. Designer: Adrian*

Shirley Ross in The Big Broadcast of 1938 *by Paramount, 1938. Designer: Head*

Dorothy Lamour *in* Swing High, Swing Low *by Paramount, 1936. Designer: Banton*

Claire Trevor *in* Star for a Night *by 20th Century-Fox, 1936. Designer: Herschel*

370

According to figures compiled by Bob Hill, a Hollywood director, star-struck girls had one chance in 137,417 to become a star in 1932. If they did become a Dorothy Lamour, Claire Trevor, or Ginger Rogers, they too could have worn glamorous, showy costumes such as these.

Claire Trevor's flashy musical costume is a timeless style that would be stunning in discos today. Plunkett thought Trevor "had a nice little figure. She's tiny. Cooperative and fun." Although not known as a musical star, Trevor and all the top names had to do their song-and-dance thing for a musical at some point. Even Clark Gable was ordered to hoof a singing number, and that caused no end to the crisis on the set of *Idiot's Delight*. For two days Gable practiced his routine on a set guarded by police. The worst blow to his sensitivity came when Carole Lombard sent him a present—a man-sized ballet skirt with "C.G." lovingly embroidered on it. Most stars, however, enjoyed their musical requirements, and their enthusiasm was a most necesary element. Dorothy Lamour was enthusiastic, but she was also very frightened when assigned to *Swing High Swing Low*. It was Lamour's second movie; Carole Lombard, the star of the film, was a big help to her. Lombard fixed Lamour's eyebrows and also muffed scenes deliberately to put the new star at ease. Lamour and Lombard also worked closely with Popsey, the director, also known as Mitchell Leisen.

In the early Thirties, before Hays, baring legs was not the only thing normally required in musicals. Chorus girls often bared a lot more. This screen nudity sparked a lot of discussion about morals, but costume designers viewed it differently. Kalloch, at Columbia, designed for Ziegfeld before his cinema work, and he analyzed the situation in February 1934 for *Photoplay* this way:

> We are experiencing a great relaxation from worry—the same thing that occurred immediately after the war, when people said, "Let's be gay, let's be naughty, in spite of everything. Look what we have been through!" The *instant* response in pictures was the cycle of bright, happy musicals, with the laughing, half-naked chorus girls.

However, like most designers, he felt there was a difference between "happy, half-naked chorus girls" and real allure for the star.

> The idea of suggesting undress has always been more seductive than stark nakedness. The naughtiest lady in pictures or any place else is more sex-alluring when slightly covered and *suggesting* her possibilities, than enticing sans raiment. There is always that piquing idea of wondering "What has she?" Much more intriguing than "That's all there is—there isn't any more."

After Hays, musical and costume pictures continued to lavish the public with spangles and sparkles, and the stars continued to look fantastic. Cinema designers were professionals, and their talent could create fantasy or truth, elegance or gaudiness; whatever was real or imaginable, they could duplicate or modify. They were a remarkable, fantastic breed of artist.

Ethel Merman in Alexander's Ragtime Band *by 20th Century-Fox, 1938. Designer: Wakeling*

Jane Wyman for publicity for Warner Brothers, 1939. Designer: Orry-Kelly

In 1938 the American public supported sixty trade and fan publications dealing with the motion picture industry; 1,600 ads were placed *daily* in other media channels like newspapers. The U.S. film industry spent $110 million just on paid advertisements in the world in 1938, and $78 million of that was spent in the U.S. ($64 million in newspapers and magazines, $8 million for outdoor advertising, and $6 million for accessories and direct mail). All this expense did not include the so-called "free" publicity given to a movie or star in the form of gossip columns, interviews, and general notoriety. The studios produced hundreds of thousands of stills which were disseminated and usually earned many times their cost in "free" publicity.

Much satire has been created regarding the Hollywood publicity machine, and most of it reflects the truth. There were great exaggerations, downright fibs, lots of fantasy and imagination, and a lot of time and hard work to hype a product, be it movie or star. The publicity still was an important tool to gain attention, and most stars could not escape publicity department demands. Very often starlets were posed in eye-catching ensembles with interesting backgrounds not related or only indirectly related to a current or proposed movie. Jane Wyman was almost unrecognizable in her publicity shot for Warner Brothers in the very late Thirties. Wyman's costume is one dredged up from storage and was first worn by Ginger Rogers singing on a white piano in *Gold Diggers of 1933*. The number was cut. For Wyman, the pants legs were ruffled and modified into more exotic fare, and mounds of unneeded jewelry were added.

It was far better, however, to pose a star in her cinema wardrobe, usually in the most stunning outfits, so movie and star could be linked in the public's mind as they rushed to see both. Perhaps the most famous still taken of Clara Bow is the one from her last picture, *Hoopla*. This costume appears in most stories and books about Bow and depicts her "It" quality, Thirties-style. Another favorite still is of Ginger Rogers in her *Gold Diggers of 1933* coin outfit. Used extensively in publicity for this movie, it is another classic. When *Gold Diggers of 1935* was released, publicity for it drew on the popularity of the earlier version. *Photoplay* in September 1935 ran a feature, "What Happened to the Gold Diggers of 1933?" The article stated that thirty-one were still film chorines, twenty-four had gotten too fat, twenty had given up Hollywood and gone home, eighteen had married, eleven had studio acting contracts, three were in eastern stage shows, two were schoolteachers, and two were public librarians. The ideal chorus girl in 1935 was 5'4", 120 pounds, and 34–26–35.

Loretta Young's publicity still from *Eternally Yours* was a publicity still within a publicity still. The outfit was used for advertising posters for a club act in the film.

Marian Marsh in The Black Room *by Columbia, 1935. Designer: Kalloch*

Chapter Seven

Wedding Glamour

Any fashion show traditionally ends with the *piéce de résistance*, a lovely bridal ensemble. This book shall be no different, for it is a fashion show of some of the finest designs created for the Thirties cinema. Most of the virginal white wedding gowns seen on the screen, however, were in fact off-white or a pastel blue or pink. Because of the cameras and films then in use, dead white created far too much glare and trouble. Underexposing the scene to reduce the glare and reflection from the gown would make dark objects photograph much darker; correctly exposing the scene would make the gown stand out like a neon light. Wedding scenes, therefore, could be very tricky to film, and the simple gray and whites that appeared on the screen usually required a rainbow of colors on the set.

Historical and period wedding gowns were usually very romantic, feminine, and traditional. Marian Marsh was a vision of beauty as a Viennese bride. Kalloch caught the spell of romance and beauty in her graceful pink satin gown with its floral appliqué motif accented by delicate lace and tiny seed pearls. Fresh gardenias were strewn down the front of the huge hooped skirt. Gardenias and fresh orange blossoms created the tiara-crown that held an enveloping veil. The off-the-shoulder bodice and pearl necklace were stylish for Viennese princesses of the time. The exquisite photography by Ray Jones accentuated the totally enchanting mood of this stunning still.

Historical accuracy in wedding gowns was often not recognized by audiences. Walter Plunkett paid strict attention to Margaret Mitchell's book when he designed Scarlett's bridal dress, but only those who read the book can appreciate his efforts. He recalled:

There wasn't enough time in the film to tell the full story of the dress. If you read the book, Scarlett was married almost overnight and she used her mother's wedding dress, so it was made on her mother's figure, and you can see it is too long for her [Leigh], because her mother is that much taller. It is made of a period about twenty to twenty-five years earlier than the *GWTW* period, when they were wearing big sleeves. In *GWTW* they were not. The mother had come from a very wealthy family, so it had to be an extremely costly looking wedding dress, of the wrong period and the wrong size.

The wedding gown from *The Old Maid* is a lovely example of what Scarlett should have been wearing to be in style in 1861. The wealth of detail is particularly evident on Hopkins's gown. Filming *The Old Maid* was not all sweetness on the set. The alleged arguments between co-stars Bette Davis and Hopkins over who got the best designs was widely publicized. The dislike between the two stars sparked excellent performances. Davis was thirty-one years old when cast for *The Old Maid*, and she was often spotted in her long, full-skirted costumes flying around the Warner lot on a scooter bike.

Miriam Hopkins in The Old Maid *by Warner Brothers, 1939. Designer: Orry-Kelly*

Vivien Leigh in Gone with the Wind *by MGM,*
1939. Designer: Plunkett

Frances Dee in Strange Case of Clara Deane
by Paramount, 1932. Designer: Banton

Modern wedding dresses did not always follow the traditional styles or detailing. Rosalind Russell's medieval headdress appeared in a modern movie. Frieda Inscort's white silk broadcloth gown emphasized the monkish motif with a long, white silk cord and standing collar caught at the throat with a pearl clip. Ancient Greece inspired Frances Dee's cinema wedding gown of ivory satin and white tulle, both edged with pearls and brilliants. Dee's bouquet was four perfect calla lilies. The gown was so beautiful, Juliette Compton wore it for publicity purposes that same year. Frances Dee's Hollywood discovery sounded like a press agent's dream. According to fan magazines, she came from Chicago to visit friends and toured a movie studio. Spotted by a studio executive, Dee signed a contract before leaving.

Loretta Young was too poor in *A Man's Castle* to afford a proper new wedding dress, so she wore a family heirloom instead. When Gwen Wakeling was asked if she designed private wardrobes, she replied:

> Occasionally. The only thing I can remember doing very successfully was a thing I did for Loretta Young for a costume party. The theme was brides. I got most of it out of stock. I made her the bride from hell. Satan's bride. She had a black velvet gown and a tight skullcap with two little horns made out of sequins, all the hair concealed, a black veil hanging from it, and one red sequin between the eyes. She took first prize. The prize was a magnificent nightgown, and since she didn't wear those things she gave it to me, and I still have it.

Frieda Inescort in If You Could Only Cook *by Columbia, 1935. Designer: Lange*

Rosalind Russell, Myrna Loy, and Walter Pidgeon in Man Proof *by MGM, 1937. Designer: Tree*

Loretta Young in Man's Castle *by Columbia, 1933. Designer: Kalloch*

Constance Bennett and Anita Louise in Our Betters *by RKO, 1933. Designer: Hattie Carnegie*

Claudette Colbert in It Happened One Night *by Columbia, 1934. Designer: Kalloch*

One of the most impressive and photogenic aspects of a wedding dress is its veil. It can envelop the bride in a blur of white or trail after her like a lovely white wave. Veils were often more spectacular than the gown itself, especially if designed for long shots. Claudette Colbert's wedding ensemble from *It Happened One Night* is a perfect example of designing to fit the screen and script. The dress itself was very plain except for the low, flowered neckline. The neckline had to be interesting because that is all the camera saw as Colbert walked slowly up the aisle with her screen father. The high point of the wedding scene is Colbert's saying no to the minister and running across a wide expanse of lawn to reach a waiting car and life with Clark Gable. While she ran in a long shot, nicely backlit, the veil flowed straight out and created a dramatic emphasis to Colbert's exit. The veil could not be too heavy or lacy because it would not fly properly or reach a good height and would pull to much on Colbert's head and neck. The veil could not be too short or the effect would be lost, and it could not be too long or it would drag on the ground or get tangled in something. The veil was simple, light chiffon net, just long enough and light enough for its purposes.

Most veils were not required to fly, just cause gasps of envy from the audience and gracefuly contribute to nice long shots of the scene.

Constance Bennett's brand of glamour was superb and special, but more down-to-earth and attainable than Dietrich's, for example. Bennett was *the* clotheshorse for the mid-Thirties and once cautioned her fans, "*Never* follow fads. There is a difference between novelty and originality. The former is for women who allow others to think for them. The latter for those who think for themselves."

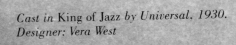

Brief Biographies

ADRIAN

Born Gilbert Adrian in Naugatuck, Connecticut, 1903. Died 1960.

A child prodigy, he was sketching beautiful pictures at the age of three.

Studied at the School of Fine and Applied Arts.

Designed for several New York stage productions including George White's *Scandals* and *The Music Box Revue*. Discovered for Hollywood by Natasha Rambova (Mrs. Rudolph Valentino). Worked for Cecil B. De Mille in 1926; when De Mille went to MGM in 1928, Adrian also went, but when De Mille left MGM in 1930, Adrian stayed and became MGM's chief designer until 1942. When the studios felt the economic pinch of World War II, the budget for glamour was downgraded. Adrian was asked to design a "more plebian" wardrobe for Greta Garbo in *Two Faced Woman*, to humanize her. Adrian left MGM stating, "When the glamour ends for Hollywood, it ends for me."

Opened a highly successful couture salon in Beverly Hills, but occasionally did freelance work for special motion pictures.

Adrian was well known for his imaginative skill which expressed itself in exotic and dramatic notes in his designs. He dressed such stars as Norma Shearer, Joan Crawford, Greta Garbo, Jeanette MacDonald, and Jean Harlow with a flair and yet with enormous good taste. His favorite movies were *The Great Ziegfeld*, *Idiot's Delight*, and *Marie Antoinette*. Adrian designed all the costumes for the top MGM pictures, sometimes numbering in the thousands per picture. He could make 50–75 sketches per day, and did not have a sketch artist assistant. Some of his best known designs are found in *Letty Lynton*, *Madam Satan*, *Let Us Be Gay*, *The Mask of Fu Manchu*, *Dinner at Eight*, *Queen Christina*, *Secrets*, *The Painted Veil*, *No More Ladies*. *Anna Karenina*, *Naughty Marietta*, *San Francisco*, *Romeo and Juliet*, *Born to Dance*, *The Firefly*, *The Bride Wore Red*, *The Wizard of Oz*, *Ninotchka*, *The Women*, *Ziegfeld Girl*, and *Dr. Jekyll and Mr. Hyde*.

Adrian was the chief designer at the top studio in the Thirties and was the lead in the costume-designing triumvirate of Adrian-Banton-Orry-Kelly.

MILO ANDERSON

Born 1912 in Chicago, educated in Los Angeles.

At the age of seventeen, Anderson went to work for Sam Goldwyn. His first job was to design Eddie Cantor's costumes for *The Kid From Spain*. The success of these designs led to a two-year contract offer. He worked at Warner Bros.-First National Studios from 1933 to 1952.

After leaving Warners, Anderson continued a very successful interior decoration studio and also worked for a bathing suit company. Anderson is currently living in West Hollywood.

Anderson was generally relegated to designing for the "B" class of pictures at Warners, where Orry-Kelly was chief designer. However, he was the favorite of several important stars, including Olivia de Havilland. He also designed the famous "red" dress in *Jezebel* although Kelly did the rest of the picture. Some of Anderson's better known pictures are *A Midsummer Night's Dream*, *Anthony Adverse*, *Captain Blood*, *The Adventures of Robin Hood*, *Manpower*, *Mildred Pierce*, *Night and Day*, *Lullaby of Broadway*, and *On Moonlight Bay*.

Anderson became a recognized authority on period costumes.

TRAVIS BANTON

Born 1894 in Waco, Texas. Died 1958.

Studied at Columbia University and the Art Students League of Fine and Applied Arts in New York.

Served in World War I aboard a Navy submarine chaser.

While he was working at the famous couture house in New York called Madame Frances, Mary Pickford chose one of his designs to be her wedding dress when she married Douglas Fairbanks.

Went to Hollywood in 1924 and achieved instant success in his first movie, *The Dressmaker From Paris*.

Took over as head of the Paramount design department in 1929 from Howard Greer; stayed at Paramount until 1938. Worked for Fox from 1939–1941; was head stylist at Universal from 1945–1948.

Opened his own couture shop after leaving Paramount, but continued work with studios. In 1956 he opened a custom shop in Hollywood with Marusia.

Was best known for creations of good taste, simplicity of line, and refined concepts of classic style. With Paramount he dressed glamourous stars such as Carole Lombard, Marlene Dietrich, Kay Francis, Lilyan Tashman, Claudette Colbert, Mae West, and Clara Bow. Later he designed for Alice Faye, Rita Hayworth, and Linda Darnell. His most famous movie designs include *Blonde Venus, Shanghai Express, Belle of the Nineties, The Scarlet Empress, Cleopatra, The Devil Is a Woman, Goin' to Town, The Princess Comes Across, Angel, Bluebeard's Eighth Wife, Love Before Breakfast, Swing High, Swing Low, Eternally Yours, Lillian Russell, Blood and Sand, Charley's Aunt*, and *That Night in Rio*.

Banton was one of the great three in the well recognized triumvirate of top designers for the Thirties. Adrian and Orry-Kelly were the other two.

HOWARD GREER

Born 1886 in Nebraska. Died 1974.

Started his fashion career in the Chicago fashion house of Lucille, Ltd., in 1916.

During World War I he worked for eleven months as a machine gun corporal in the front lines.

After the war he stayed in Europe, where he designed costumes for London and Paris stages. In 1923 became the chief designer for the West Coast studios of Famous Players–Lasky which later became Paramount Pictures. Left Paramount in 1927. Worked on and off for RKO between 1932 and 1954.

Was the first big name costume designer to open a custom clothing shop in Hollywood (27 December 1927), and one of the first West Coast designers to establish his own wholesale business. Retired from his business in 1962.

Published his autobiography, called *Designing Male*.

While at Lasky and Paramount, he gained a lot of publicity by dressing such famous actresses as Pola Negri, Agnes Ayres, Bebe Daniels, and Nita Naldi. Many of his customers at his couture shop demanded his services for their motion pictures. His most famous pictures include *The Ten Commandments* (silent version), *Hell's Angels, Call Her Savage, Bringing Up Baby, Carefree, Holiday, Spellbound, His Kind of Woman*, and *The French Line*.

Greer also designed wedding gowns for Shirley Temple and Gloria Vanderbilt.

EDITH HEAD

Born 1907 and raised in mining camp called Searchlight, Nevada, where they had more saloons per capita than any other city in the U.S.

Studied art at the Otis Art Institute and Chouinard School of Art.

Started at Paramount in 1923 as sketch artist for Howard Greer. Became head of Paramount costume design department in 1938 after Travis Banton left. Worked with Paramount until 1967. Currently with Universal; still active in the business.

Has written three books.

Thirty-five academy nominations, eight awards.

Has designed for elephants and snakes. One early assignment was to outfit an elephant for Cecil B. De Mille. The costume was jewelled anklets and a gold cloth belly band. Also made an elaborate fruit headdress for an elephant. The elephant ate the whole thing.

Head's two favorite actresses are Carole Lombard and Grace Kelly. She has dressed the best of Hollywood. Some of her finest known designs have been from the movies *The Sting, Samson and Delilah, Roman Holiday, To Catch a Thief, She Done Him Wrong, The Jungle Princess, What a Way to Go, A Place in the Sun, Lady in the Dark, Sunset Boulevard, Love Me Tonight, Mississippi, Artists and Models Abroad, I Married a Witch, Holiday Inn, Elephant Walk, Sabrina, Anything Goes, The Rainmaker, Gunfight at OK Corral, Houseboat, Vertigo, The Five Pennies, Hud, The Oscar, Airport, Sweet Charity*, and *Gable and Lombard*.

Has the longest, most extensive record of any designer. Has avoided involvement with couture shops and wholesale work except for Vogue patterns.

Very active in volunteer and charitable organizations. Many awards for civic, business, and educational work including *Time's* Woman of the Year.

Miss Head died on October 26, 1981.

RENE HUBERT

Born 1899 in St. Gall, Switzerland.

Studied painting at l'Ecole des Beaux Arts and Academie Calorossi in Paris.

Was brought from Europe by Gloria Swanson. Worked at Paramount from 1925–36, MGM 1927–31, Fox 1931–35 and 1943–64, and United Artists/Korda in London 1936–41. Designed for Gloria Swanson at the height of her career, when she was the clotheshorse of Hollywood. Some of his most interesting costumes were in the movie *Things to Come*, a futuristic setting in which all the men and women were dressed in fine, thin white rubber sheeting.

Some of his more famous movies include *Monsieur Beaucaire* (with Valentino), *Body and Soul* (silent), *Music in the Air, Curly Top, The Farmer Takes a Wife, Knight Without Armour, That Hamilton Woman, Heaven Can Wait, Jane Eyre, State Fair* (1945), *Forever Amber, The Beautiful Blonde from Bashful Bend, Ticket to Tomahawk, Desiree, Anastasia*, and *The Visit*.

Hubert was known for his flair for color and lines. His modern clothing often had a "Hubert split" on the skirt.

IRENE

Born 1901 in Brookings, South Dakota. Died 1962.

Known as Irene Lentz Gibbons.

Studied at the Wolf School of Design.

Opened her first dress shop across the street from the University of Southern California campus administration building, where an Irene original could be purchased from $16 to $29.50. After the death of her first husband she toured Europe for two years, concentrating on Paris. When she returned, she opened a second shop and was hired by Bullocks-Wilshire as head of their designing salon. While there, she freelanced as a costume designer for several studios. In 1942 she replaced Adrian as head of the MGM Costume Department. Although with MGM until 1949, in 1947 she opened her own couture shop. She continued to freelance costume design after she left MGM and was extremely successful with her salon. She was also associated with Universal Studios from 1960 to 1963.

Irene became known for her beautifully designed suits and evening gowns. She was considered a top designer in her profession.

Irene's favorite stars were Barbara Stanwyck, Loretta Young, Katharine Hepburn, and Joan Crawford. Her most outstanding movies include *Weekend at the Waldorf, Midnight Lace, A Gathering of Eagles, The Great Morgan, Flying Down to Rio, Vogues of 1938, Algiers, Vivacious Lady, Eternally Yours, Intermezzo, Topper Takes a Trip, Midnight, The Housekeeper's Daughter, Thousands Cheer, The Postman Always Rings Twice, 10th Avenue Angel, The Barkleys of Broadway, In the Good Old Summertime, Neptune's Daughter,* and *Lover Come Back.*

ROBERT KALLOCH

Born in 1893 in New York City. Died 1943.

Studied at the New York School of Fine and Applied Art. Rather than go to college, he became associated with Lucille Ltd, a famous couture shop. Worked in New York, Paris, and London. Designed many dresses for Irene Castle, Grace Moore, and Anna Pavlova. At the age of eighteen, interested Pavlova in his designs by taking his drawings to her stage door entrance.

Went to work as chief designer at Columbia Pictures in 1933 and stayed until 1942. Worked at MGM for two years and then freelanced for studios.

At Columbia he dressed Irene Dunne, Nancy Carroll, Grace Moore, Fay Wray, and even Claudette Colbert. One of his most famous movies was *The Awful Truth.* Others were *Imitation of Life, It Happened One Night, Mr. Smith Goes to Washington, The Lone Wolf Strikes, Babes on Broadway, Honky Tonk, Mr. and Mrs. North, Mrs. Miniver, White Cargo,* and *Journey for Margaret.*

Had been called to Columbia to give its stars "class and style." Succeeded.

ORRY-KELLY

Born 1897 in Kiama, Australia. Died 1964.

A painter before he was twelve.

Born John Orry Kelly. The hyphen was due to a clerical error at Warners which was kept to add "class."

Came to New York in 1923 to be an actor; painted murals and broke into movies by illustrating titles for silent pictures. Also did costumes and scenery for several stage revues and plays including costumes for several Ethel Barrymore plays, George White's *Scandals,* and Katharine Hepburn's costumes for her stage debut, *Death Takes a Holiday.* His good friend Cary Grant was instrumental in getting his drawings shown to Warner Bros., which hired him as chief designer in 1932. He stayed with Warners until 1944 and then worked for Universal from 1947 to 1950. He also freelanced for Fox, RKO, and MGM.

Kelly was noted for his simplicity, quality, and high fashion. His most famous "protegé" was Bette Davis, whose curvey figure did not fit the desired silhouette of the early and mid-Thirties. He also dressed such screen luminaries as Kay Francis, Ruth Chatterton, Ingrid Bergman, Dolores Del Rio, Marilyn Monroe, Rosalind Russell, Shirley Maclaine, and Joan Fontaine. His most famous motion pictures include *Fashions of 1934, Stolen Holiday, First Lady, The Rich Are Always With Us, Casablanca, I Found Stella Parish, I Loved a Woman, Now Voyager, The Little Foxes, Dark Victory, The Private Lives of Elizabeth and Essex, Jezebel, Mr. Skeffington, Madame DuBarry, Dangerous, Gold Diggers of 1937, Cain and Mabel, Juarez, The Maltese Falcon, The Strawberry Blonde, Arsenic and Old Lace, Mother Wore Tights, One Touch of Venus, An American in Paris, Harvey, Oklahoma!, Les Girls, Auntie Mame, Some Like It Hot, The Chapman Report, Gypsy,* and *Irma La Douce.*

Kelly's almost completed autobiography, *Women I Have Undressed,* was never published.

Kelly was the third member of the designer triumvirate composed of Adrian, Banton, and Orry-Kelly.

OMAR KIAM

Born 1894 in Mexico. Died 1954.

Educated at Poughkeepsie Military Academy in New York.

First designing job was in the baby cap department of a large Houston, Texas, department store. Went to Paris to study for several years. When he returned, he opened his own studio in New York. Designed for several Broadway plays.

Came to Hollywood in 1933 to become head designer for Sam Goldwyn Productions and United Artists. Also worked for David Selznick and Hal Roach. Left Hollywood in 1939.

Some of Kiam's more famous movies include *The Mighty Barnum, Cardinal Richelieu, The Barbary Coast, Clive of India, The Dark Angel, Folies Bergeres, One Rainy Afternoon, The Hurricane, A Star Is Born, Stella Dallas, Vogues of 1938, The Goldwyn Follies,* and *Wuthering Heights.*

WALTER PLUNKETT

Born 1902 in Oakland, California.

Studied pre-law at Berkeley, but switched to Little Theater. Came to Hollywood to be an actor.

In 1926 Plunkett became the head of costume for FBO Studios, which later became RKO. He left in 1930 to go to New York and design couture clothing. Katharine Hepburn persuaded Plunkett to return to Hollywood for just one motion picture and he stayed at RKO until 1939. He also did freelance work for other studios such as Selznick, for whom in 1939 he designed his most famous clothing for the epic, classic *Gone With the Wind.* Plunkett worked for MGM from 1947–1966 when he retired to devote his time to painting. Plunkett continues to carry on his successful painting career in Los Angeles.

Although Plunkett created many stylish and beautiful contemporary clothes, he decided in 1935 to specialize mainly in historical and ethnic costume motion pictures and thereby avoid altogether the constant "advice" and "guidance" that was offered by directors, crew, and others regarding costume design. Historical costumes have well-defined lines which preclude much discussion. Plunkett's great sense of taste in ever so slightly adapting true historical lines to fit the actress and times made him the acknowledged authority on period costumes.

Plunkett has dressed many of the most beautiful actresses ever to grace Hollywood, such as: Irene Dunne, Bebe Daniels, Ginger Rogers, Katharine Hepburn, Elizabeth Taylor, Judy Garland, Constance Bennett, and Vivian Leigh. A few of his best known films include *Flying Down to Rio, Little Women, Professional Sweetheart, The Gay Divorcee, The Little Minister, Stingaree, Alice Adams, Annie Oakley, Sylvia Scarlett, The Three Musketeers, Mary of Scotland, A Woman Rebels, Quality Street, The Story of Vernon and Irene Castle, Stagecoach, The Hunchback of Notre Dame, Duel in the Sun, Green Dolphin Street, Adam's Rib, Madame Bovary, Annie Get Your Gun, An American In Paris, Showboat, Singin' in the Rain, Kiss Me Kate, 7 Brides for 7 Brothers, Valley of Kings, Jupiter's Darling, Diane, Forbidden Planet, Lust for Life, Raintree County, The Brothers Karamazov, Some Came Running, Bells Are Ringing, Pollyanna, Pocketful of Miracles, How the West Was Won,* and *Seven Women.*

Plunkett's favorite costumes are from two movies, *Professional Sweetheart* and *Diane.*

ROYER

Born Lewis Royer Hastings in Washington, D.C., 1904.

Has been adviser and lecturer for Lord & Taylor, Columbia University, New York University, and the New York School of Fine and Applied Art.

Designer for Fox Studios from 1933 to 1939; worked at Hal Roach Studios from 1940 to 1942. Left cinema work to open his own custom salon.

Royer dressed such exquisite cinema beauties as Loretta Young, Sonia Henie, Shirley Temple, and Alice Faye. His best known films include *Baby Take a Bow, Orient Express, Dante's Inferno, Lloyds of London, Sing Baby Sing, Cafe Metropole, Love Is News, Thin Ice, Four Men and a Prayer, Happy Landing, In Old Chicago, Suez, My Lucky Star, Rose of Washington Square,* and *Daytime Wife.*

EDWARD STEVENSON

Born 1906 in Pocatello, Idaho. Died 1968.

Moved to Hollywood in 1922 and studied fashion with Andre-Ani. Worked as Andre-Ani's sketch artist at MGM in 1925. In 1927 became an assistant sketch artist at Fox but moved to First National in one year as head designer. Opened his own couture salon for two years, but returned to cinema designing at RKO in 1934 and stayed there for thirteen years. Worked at Fox from 1949–53. From 1954 to 1968 he worked with Lucille Ball on all her television series and specials.

Although rarely given the large, "A" class productions, some of his better known pictures include *The Bitter Tea of General Yen, That Girl From Paris, Maid's Night Out, Panama Lady, In Name Only, Gunga Din, No, No, Nanette, Irene, Suspicion, A Girl, a Guy, and a Gob, Citizen Kane, The Spiral Staircase, The Bachelor and the Bobby Soxer, It's a Wonderful Life, Cheaper by the Dozen, David and Bathsheba,* and *What Price Glory?*

DOLLY TREE

Born Dorothy Tree in England, 1906.

Worked in many Broadway plays and revues in the 1920s; designed Mae West's costumes in her original New York stage production of *Diamond Lil.* Became "fashion creator" at Fox Studios in 1929. In 1932 she went to MGM where she stayed until 1942.

Although greatly overshadowed by MGM's top costume designer, Adrian, Dolly Tree received an occassional plum and designed for several pictures starring Myrna Loy, Jean Harlow, and Judy Garland. A few better-known pictures include *The Gay Bride, The Thin Man, The Casino Murder Case, David Copperfield, A Night at the Opera, A Tale of Two Cities, Times Square Lady, The Bishop Misbehaves, Riffraff, After the Thin Man, Fury, Libeled Lady, Suzy, Wife Versus Secretary, The Unguarded Hour, Manproof, Rosalie, Saratoga, Babes in Arms, These Glamour Girls, Strike Up the Band, Congo Maisie,* and *The Trial of Mary Dugan.*

GWEN WAKELING

Born 1901 in Detroit, Michigan.

Studied for four years with Maurice LeLoir, curator of the Museum of Historical Costumes in Paris.

Discovered by Cecil B. De Mille in an advertising office. She worked with De Mille at Pathé and Paramount. Became head costume designer at Fox from 1933–1942; freelanced regularly afterwards with Columbia, United Artists, Republic, Warner Bros., and RKO. Has also designed for stage productions at the Los Angeles Civic Light Opera Association and NBC-TV.

Wakeling's favorite actress to dress was Loretta Young. She also designed for Ann Harding, Constance Bennett, Alice Faye, and a host of Hollywood beauties. A few of her best known films include *King of Kings, Samson and Delilah, House of Rothschild, Ladies in Love, Wife, Husband, and Friend, Weekend in Havana, Broadway Through a Keyhole, Affairs of Cellini, The Count of Monte Cristo, King of Burlesque, The Man Who Broke the Bank at Monte Carlo, Captain January, The Poor Little Rich Girl, Ramona, Under Two Flags, Ali Baba Goes to Town, Alexander's Ragtime Band, Love Under Fire, On the Avenue, Seventh Heaven, Wee Willie Winkie, Wife, Doctor, and Nurse, Kentucky, Little Miss Broadway, Rebecca of Sunnybrook Farm, Sally, Irene, and Mary, The Adventures of Sherlock Holmes, Hotel for Women, The Little Princess, Second Honeymoon, Brigham Young, The Grapes of Wrath, The High and the Mighty, Cattle Queen of Montana, Blood Alley,* and *Frankie and Johnny.*

Wakeling became known not only for her lovely contemporary designs, but also as an authority on historical and period costumes.

She is presently happily married and retired in Beverly Hills.

VERA WEST

Born 1900 in New York City. Died 1947.

Studied under Lady Duff Gordon at the Philadelphia School of Design. She spent four years as a couture stylist before going to Hollywood.

Joined Universal Studios as head designer in 1926 and stayed until 1947, when she left to open her own couture salon in Beverly Hills. At Universal she dressed Deanna Durbin, Irene Dunne, and even Marlene Dietrich. Her best known films include *Back Street, Destry Rides Again, Showboat, King of Jazz, Diamond Jim, Next Time We Love, The Rage of Paris, My Little Chickadee, Seven Sinners, Hellzapoppin, The Lady from Cheyenne, The Wolf Man, The Phantom of the Opera, Hit the Ice, This Is the Life, Ladies Courageous, Sudan, The Black Angel,* and *The Egg and I.*